Reform &
Growth

Reform & Growth

Ajay Chhibber, R. Kyle Peters, and Barbara J. Yale, editors

EVALUATING THE WORLD BANK EXPERIENCE

Transaction Publishers
New Brunswick (U.S.A.) and London (U.K.)

This book is printed on acid-free paper that meets the American National Standard for Permanence of Paper for Printed Library Materials.

Library of Congress Catalog Number: 2005054891
ISBN:0-7658-0317-8 (alk. paper); 1-4128-0523-6 (alk. paper)
Printed in the United States of America

Library of Congress Cataloging-in-Publication Data

OED Conference on Effectiveness of Policies and Reforms (2004 : Washington, D.C.)
   Reform and growth: evaluating the World Bank experience / Ajay Chhibber, R. Kyle Peters, Barbara J. Yale, editors.
       p. cm.
"This book is based on papers and presentations from the 'OED Conference on Effectiveness of Policies and Reforms," held October, 4, 2004, in Washington, DC'—Acknowledgements.
       Includes bibliographical references and index.
       ISBN 0-7658-0317-8 (alk paper) — ISBN 1-4128-0523-6 (alk paper)
   1. World Bank—Developing countries. 2. Economic stabilization—Developing countries. 3. Developing countries—Economic policy. 4. Economic development. I. Chhibber, Ajay, 1954- II. Peters, R. Kyle, 1954- III. Yale, Barbara J.

HG3881.5.W57O38   2005
339.509172'4—dc22   2005054891

Contents

Acknowledgements   vii

Foreword   ix
  Gregory K. Ingram

Overview   xi
  Ajay Chhibber

**Part 1: Policy Reforms in the Developing World:
Lessons from Bangladesh**

  Policy Reforms in the Developing World:
  Lessons from Bangladesh   3
    M. Saifur Rahman

Part 2: Effectiveness of Bank Support for Policy Reform

  The Effectiveness of World Bank Support   15
  for Policy Reform: ARDE 2003
    Robert J. Anderson

  Remarks on Effectiveness of Bank Support   25
  for Policy Reform
    François Bourguignon

Comments on Effectiveness of Bank Support for   26
Policy Reform
   Masood Ahmed

Comments on Effectiveness of Bank Support for   30
Policy Reform
   Otaviano Canuto

Comments on Effectiveness of Bank Support for   33
Policy Reform
   Tony Killick

Floor Discussion on Effectiveness of Bank Support   38
for Policy Reform

Part 3: Lessons from Country Program Evaluations

Lessons from Country Program Evaluations   45
   R. Kyle Peters

Comments on Country Program Evaluations   60
   Willem Buiter

Comments on Country Program Evaluations   64
   Ishrat Husain

Comments on Country Program Evaluations   67
   Miguel Urrutia Montoya

Observations on Country Program Evaluations   70
   James Adams

Part 4: Middle-Income Country Programs:
Lessons from Brazil, China, and Tunisia

Middle-Income Country Strategies for Development   75
   S. Ramachandran

The Role of World Bank Lending in Middle-Income Countries   87
   Johannes F. Linn

Comments on Middle- Income Country Programs, Tunisia   96
Kamel Ben Rejeb

Comments on Middle-Income Country Programs, Brazil   100
Joaquim Levy

Floor Discussion on Lessons from Middle-Income   104
Country Programs

Part 5: Lessons from Post-Conflict Countries

Lessons Learned from World Bank Experience in   109
Post-Conflict Reconstruction
Fareed M.A. Hassan

Comments on Post-Conflict Country Lessons from Rwanda   125
Donald Kaberuka

Comments on Post-Conflict Country Lessons from   128
Bosnia-Herzegovina
Ljerka Marić

Comments on Lessons from Post-Conflict Countries   131
Margaret Thomas

Floor Discussion on Post-Conflict Country Lessons   137

Part 6: Poverty Reduction Strategies

The Poverty Reduction Strategy Initiative: An Independent   143
Evaluation of the World Bank's Support through 2003
Victoria Elliott

Comments on the Poverty Reduction Strategy Initiatives   156
Pedro Couto

Comments on the Poverty Reduction Strategy Initiatives   161
Eveline Herfkens

Comments on the Poverty Reduction Strategy Initiatives 167
   Ana Quirós Víquez

Comments on the Poverty Reduction Strategy Session 170
   Danny Leipziger

Floor Discussion on Poverty Reduction Strategies 171

Part 7: Improving the International Context for Reform

Seven Deadly Sins: Reflections on Donor Failings 181
   Nancy Birdsall

Effectiveness of Policies and Reforms 197
   Kemal Derviş

Index 205

Acknowledgements

This book is based on papers and presentations from the "OED Conference on Effectiveness of Policies and Reforms," held October 4, 2004, in Washington, D.C. The conference was organized by the Operations Evaluation Department (OED) of the World Bank, under the leadership of Ajay Chhibber, Director, and R. Kyle Peters, senior manager, Country Evaluations and Regional Relations. The conference was coordinated by Barbara J. Yale, consultant, OED.

The conference website and CD were produced by Julius Gwyer and information technology support was provided by Tom Yoon and Maria Mar. Special thanks are due to Betty Bain, Nishi Bhatnagar, Yvonne Playfair-Scott, Gloria Mestre-Soria, Helen Joan Mongal, Juicy Qureishi-Haq, Vivian Jackson, Pierre-Joseph Kingbo, Soon-Won Pak, and Aravind Seshadri for their unwavering support.

Debt is owed to the speakers, session chairs, commentators, and conference participants for contributing to the success of this event. We would like to extend our gratitude to H. E. M. Saifur Rahman, Minister for Finance and Planning for Bangladesh for his thought-provoking keynote address. In addition, the conference debate would not have been possible without the insights and experience in the field of development provided by the session commentators: H. E. Donald Kaberuka, H. E. Ljerka Marić, Masood Ahmed, Nancy Birdsall, Willem Buiter, Otaviano Canuto, Pedro Couto, Kemal Derviş, Eveline Herfkens, Ishrat Husain, Tony Killick, Joaquim Levy, Johannes Linn, Kamel Ben Rejeb, Margaret Thomas, Miguel Urrutia Montoya, and Ana Quirós Víquez. We are also grateful to James Adams, François Bourguignon, Pamela

Cox, Danny Leipziger, and Christiaan Poortman for chairing the sessions and to Shengman Zhang for the welcoming remarks.

Ajay Chhibber
R. Kyle Peters
Barbara J. Yale

Foreword

The Operations Evaluation Department was established more than 30 years ago and reports independently to the Bank's Board of Executive Directors on the Bank's development effectiveness. During the first two decades of its existence, OED focused mainly on the development effectiveness of Bank projects. Since 1996, however, it has raised its sights to include the effectiveness of the Bank's policies, programs, and processes at the sectoral, thematic, country, and global levels.

OED's examination of the Bank's effectiveness at the sectoral, country, and global levels reflects the concern of the development community generally with the effectiveness of development assistance in supporting the policy reform and institutional development necessary to support pro-poor growth and sustainable poverty reduction.

Reflected in this publication are the questions addressed by conference: What are the links between good performance and policy change? How can we best use windows of opportunity for reform and how do we recognize a window of opportunity? How can we best judge and encourage ownership of policies and reform programs? How can developed country policies be improved to create a better global environment for development?

OED evaluations—namely, *2003 Annual Review of Development Effectiveness, Poverty Reduction Strategy Study (ARDE)* (World Bank 2004), and various country assistance evaluations (CAEs)—have been used to lead off the discussion and present evaluative evidence and findings on each topic. Expert commentators have then drawn on their own experience and offered their perspectives on these issues.

The main purpose of the OED Conference on Effectiveness of Policies and Reforms has been to provide a forum at which conference par-

ticipants—more than 500 government officials, civil society representatives and Bank staff from around the world—could discuss how to
improve the effectiveness of Bank support for policies and programs.
By publishing the content of the conference, we hope to broaden the
discussion and enhance collaboration and cooperation in the development community on addressing policy change and reforms in development programs.

Gregory K. Ingram
Director-General, Operations Evaluation

Overview

The quest for growth remains as elusive as it was more than a decade ago.[1] While a significant number of countries—from late starters such as Bangladesh and Vietnam to steady performers such as China, India, and Tunisia and even countries affected temporarily by the East Asian Crisis such as Korea, Thailand, and Malaysia—have shown quite remarkable and sustained growth performance, they are a minority. However, our understanding of why some countries do well and other do not has improved.

What marks the faster-growing economies is the important role that policies and reforms have played in boosting economic growth—from China and Tunisia in the late 1970s and 1980s to India in the late 1980s and early 1990s to Bangladesh and Vietnam in the 1990s. But there remains a huge debate on what the right policies are and the timing and sequencing of reforms. There is a growing literature on the importance of institutions for economic growth, and the links between institutions and growth are not yet fully understood.

This overview attempts to summarize some of the key issues and questions that have been raised by OED evaluations and by participants at the "OED Conference on the Effectiveness of Policies and Reforms." There is now clear recognition that the narrow set of reforms epitomized by the term "Washington Consensus" is necessary, but not

---

* Director, Operations Evaluation Department, World Bank Group.

sufficient to engineer growth. But, what should replace or supplement them remains unclear.

The discussion that follows is organized into five sections. Section I asks: what motivates reform? Why did China turn around after a long period of upheaval and decline? Why has India changed course and embraced reforms in the 1980s? What is the role of external pull—as in the case of the European Union's (EU's) pull on Eastern Europe—or pressure from being left behind in generating reforms? In addition, if reforms matter so much for economic well-being, why do they not occur more often?

Section II summarizes the key reform issues as they have emerged from OED evaluations and conference discussions. What is the role of macroeconomic policy? What is the role of sector and institutional issues? What are the lessons on sequencing and timing? How does one choose between selectivity and comprehensiveness? Section III asks what is country ownership and can it be encouraged from the outside? How do countries in different political and institutional settings build social consensus around reforms? And why is this more difficult in certain settings?

Section IV turns to the role of the World Bank and ask how the Bank can be more effective in helping countries undertake reforms and implement policies. How can the Bank improve the country fit of its programs and help build country capacity? How can conditionality be improved to encourage reforms? How can the Bank ensure that its processes encourage rather than detract from country ownership? And how might its governance structure limit the credibility of its advice?

Section V asks whether the Bank needs a different mode of operation in special settings, especially in fragile states, now referred to as "low-income countries under stress," (LICUS) and in countries affected by conflict where more streamlined and simpler procedures may be needed.

The last section turns to a broader set of issues, exploring the legitimacy of policy advice from international organizations such as the World Bank. It considers how to improve their effectiveness and the manner in which advice is formulated and delivered.

I. Why and When Do Reforms Occur?

Why and when reforms occur still remains somewhat unclear. The benefits of reform are by now well documented; yet, many countries go through long periods of stagnation or even decline without being able to create an environment for change,[2] whereas others seem to be able to break the hold of vested interests and start on a path of change. In the past two decades, more and more countries are following the path to reform. Are we seeing a temporary phenomenon, or is this a global trend that will eventually catch on all over the developing world?

Three broad drivers may help explain the increasing tendency to reforms. The first comes from the pressures of globalization, which have created greater opportunities in the developing world, as well as increased demand for change as people are exposed to information and experiences from other parts of the world, that is, a demonstration effect. Countries are afraid to be left behind, and people's expectations are changing: they see how others live and ask why they could not be living better.

The second driver comes from a much better understanding of the development process and which policies work well. We are seeing a greater consensus on broad factors that bring about development, but at the same time, recognition that countries may follow somewhat different institutional, political, and social arrangements on getting there. There is consensus on what is needed, but still plenty of debate on timing, sequencing, and packaging of reforms.

The third driver for change comes from an increase in the frequency of crises[3] in the 1980s and 1990s—akin to the 1920s and 1930s. Crises lead to greater pressure and opportunities for reform as the old methods and structures lose their appeal. The increased frequency of crisis has lately been ascribed to a combination of capital account mobility and pegged exchange rates. In such situations with an implicit insurance against exchange risk, banks and companies have tended to accumulate excessive foreign currency exposure. In many cases these policy choices have been recommended by international agencies, occasionally even after similar policies were known to fail elsewhere. For example, despite the collapse of the peg in Russia, Turkey was advised to adopt a pegged exchange rate with an open capital account.[4]

These three underlying factors help explain why the momentum for reform and policy change is accelerating. Of these three factors, the first two—the spread of ideas leading to demand for change and better understanding of the development process—are likely to continue. The third driver for reform—crisis—will hopefully decline in importance.

The good news on reforms is that more of them are occurring, even though the "why and when" behind these occurrences still remains something of a black box.

Reforms have come in various forms and dimensions, ranging from gradual but steady reforms seen in countries such as China and Tunisia to reform packages that followed sharp economic crisis. Some countries have seen reforms triggered by an economic crisis, followed by steady and gradual reforms, perhaps best exemplified by Chile and India. In other cases, such as East Asia and to some extent Brazil and Turkey, there was a burst of sweeping reforms postcrisis, but with a subsequent slow down. In the 1990s external pull has also been a key factor in generating reforms; the best example of this is reform in EU accession countries. Based on the experience of the past two decades, we can classify reforms in three broad typologies:

Gradual and steady reforms. A number of factors—leadership, desire to catch up with others, and pent-up demand for change—combine to bring about a set of factors that create a consensus for reforms. The consensus is not so much about a particular package of reforms as about the need for change. The reforms need not be comprehensive, but often start slowly by addressing the most pressing areas that need change. As reforms begin to generate benefits, the next set of constraints is tackled and overcome by further reforms.

Crisis-driven reforms. Some countries fail to generate consensus for change unless confronted by a crisis. The crisis creates opportunities for change by weakening the power of vested interests to resist change and exposing the reasons for the crisis. Crisis focuses the mind on the need for reform and is, therefore, a painful but great opportunity for reform. But the consensus that develops in the aftermath of a crisis often does not last. As the economy begins to recover from the crisis, the consensus for further reforms begins to wane. In a few cases, reforms triggered by crisis have been followed by a broader consensus for reforms, as in Chile, but such cases are rare. Conflict and war are one form of crisis, but post-conflict reconstruction is a particular form of reform in which the old structures have often been destroyed and new institutional arrangements take shape.

External pull or pressure-driven reforms. In some cases external pulls or pressures create a consensus for reform. In recent times, the best example of this is reforms in much of Eastern and Central Europe driven by the pulls and pressures of entry into the European Union.

Such opportunities create the consensus that the reforms are needed to achieve certain objectives, even though not everyone may agree with all aspects of those reforms.

Although crises lead to reform, they remain a painful way to get there. It is much better to build the consensus for reform internally before a crisis. But how and when that occurs remains a mystery.

Failure to reform. Even with the evidence that more reform is occurring—especially in the later part of the 1990s—there are a large number of countries where reforms have been avoided or reversed. The power of vested interests in maintaining the status quo despite growing evidence of the returns to reform remains both mysterious[5] and anachronistic.

The failure to reform is not just an issue of vested interests, but also related to at least two other obstacles. First, the issue of time inconsistency arises from the fact that reforms can have short-term costs but pay-offs that come later and beyond the time horizon of the current administration. In this sense, a democratic system can sometimes, paradoxically, hinder reform. Clever and determined leadership is needed to overcome such obstacles by creating short-term wins and displaying the courage to take and explain the long-term benefit of reform. The second obstacle comes from poor implementation of reform, which creates antagonism to reform. Privatization, without careful process in Russia, is often cited as an example of such reform.

II. What Are the Key Policy Issues?

Much greater consensus exists on what policies and institutional changes are needed to foster growth and economic development, but debates continue on timing and sequencing for some issues. We are not only seeing more reform, but a shift in the nature of reforms. Although the bulk of reforms in the 1980s was heavily focused on macroeconomic and trade issues, the recent reforms have increasingly focused on a broader set of institutional and governance issues; these so-called second generation reforms are expanding into regulatory, legal, and broader public sector reforms to create the institutional framework for private sector-led growth. They are more microeconomic and are designed to create a better regulatory and legal framework for investment and growth to occur (figure 1).

Macroeconomic issues are still important, but addressing them is not sufficient for economic development. In fact, the intense and frequent crises in the 1990s have highlighted how costly mistakes are on macroeconomic policy; their effects can shackle economies for years.[6] Re-aligning poor macroeconomic policy is a first step in recovery from a crisis, but the initial bounce back from crisis that comes from correction in macroeconomic policies can be sustained only if the next generation of more micro-oriented and institutional reforms can be tackled. Experience during the past decade shows that the major macro issues under debate relate to the timing of capital account liberalization and the exchange rate regime, in which a combination of open capital accounts and pegged exchange rates increases the propensity of unnecessary crises.

FIGURE 1
Policy and Institutional Improvement from (1999–2003)

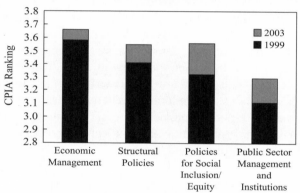

Source: World Bank (2004). This is an adaptation of figure 1.4.
CPIA = Country Policy and Institutional Assessment.

In fact, lack of second-generation reforms has led to greater recurrence of crisis. Lack of regulatory institutions, especially in the banking sector, is ascribed as an important contributory factor to the East Asian crisis. Lack of effective regulation is also seen as a major factor behind the past Russian and Turkish crises. In most cases, premature capital account liberalization without effective regulatory systems in place has also contributed immensely to the increased propensity to crisis.

Behind most macroeconomic crises lies lack of effective institu-tional frameworks, especially for debt management and the financial sector.

It is hoped that these improvements and institutional policy changes will translate into faster growth in the coming decade. The picture on past growth in the developing countries remains dismal. More than two-thirds of the developing countries, however, are growing too slowly, and their average incomes are falling further and further behind the de-veloped world. Overall, during 1990–2003, only 42 of 143 developing countries have experienced growth in per capita income greater than 2.1 percent per capita—the long-run U.S. average (figure 2). And only 29 of 113 countries for which data are available have GDP per capita growth that is faster than 2.1 percent per year for a longer period from 1980–2003 (figure 3). It shows that more than 70 percent of countries in the developing world are not growing rapidly enough to catch up with the richer countries.

Institutions take time to develop, so how does a developing country with weak institutions develop rapidly and in a sustained manner? A wide and growing literature has shown that, in a cross-country frame-work, institutions matter; therefore, institutions are clearly important. But with limited resources and capacity, it is difficult to know before-hand on which institutions to focus and what the best institutional ar-

FIGURE 2
Developing Country GDP Per Capita Growth (1990–2003)

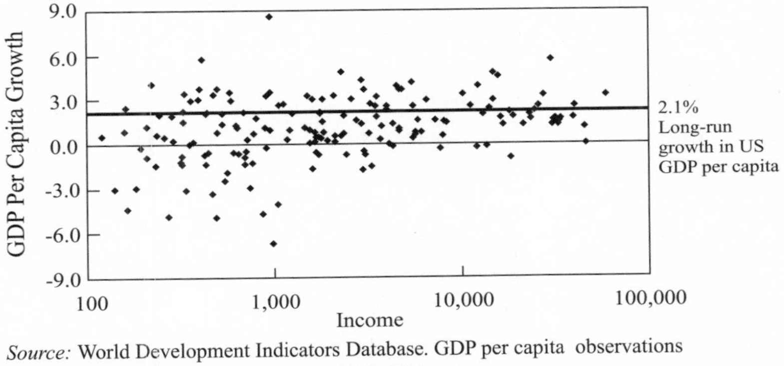

Source: World Development Indicators Database. GDP per capita observations for 143 developing countries between 1990–2003.

FIGURE 3
Developing Countries GDP Per Capita Growth (1980–2003)

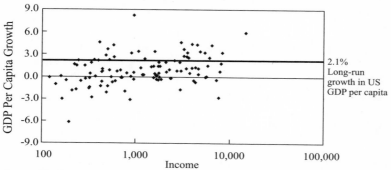

Source: World Development Indicators Database—GDP per capita observations for 113 developing countries between 1980–2003.

rangements in a particular setting are. Moreover, how does a developing country cope with weak institutions and what transition arrangements can be developed as an interim strategy for development? The experience indicates that some of the fastest developing countries are finding ways to cope with weak institutional arrangements.

Countries with very different indicators of institutional capacity have been able to grow rapidly. Table 1 lists 29 countries that have experienced growth rates in the 1990s that are faster than 3.0 percent. It also lists three sets of institutional indicators: one developed by the International Country Risk Guide (ICRG) ratings, another developed at the World Bank Institute, and a third from a World Bank source that benchmarks business development. In general, the institutional indicators show positive change, but again high growth has come in countries with modest and substantial improvements in indicators of institutional quality and, in the cases of Botswana and Malaysia, even with some deterioration in their ICRG indicators.

The fact that high growth has been experienced by countries with weak institutions suggests that more work is needed to understand the links between institutions and growth.

With the shift toward a bigger role for the private sector in provision of infrastructure and utilities—such as energy, telecommunications, and

Errata
Please substitute this page for the original page xix

TABLE 1
Institutional Quality and Investment Climate in Fast-Growing Countries

Country	Growth in GDP Per Capita[a] 1990–2003	Avg. ICRG Ratings[b] 3yr. Avg. 2002–2004	Change in Avg. ICRG Ratings 1990–2004	WBI Governance Indicators[c] 2002	Time Required to Establish a Business[d] 2004
	Percent	Percent of Total	Percentage Change	Percentile Rank 0–100	Days
China	8.6	55.7	2.0	43.2	48
Vietnam	5.8	55.6	17.4	37.2	50
Maldives	4.9	n.a.	n.a.	65.8	12
South Korea	4.8	69.0	38.0	72.5	22
Lebanon	4.3	54.7	71.5	15.5	46
Chile	4.1	62.1	11.0	87.5	27
Mozambique	4.1	56.5	37.4	73.6	153
Mauritius	3.9	n.a.	n.a.	65.2	46
Slovenia	3.9	65.9	n.a.	81.6	60
India	3.8	68.1	86.2	47.9	71
Cambodia	3.8	n.a.	n.a.	29.7	86
Malaysia	3.7	67.3	-4.1	39.5	30
Poland	3.7	59.9	11.7	58.3	31
Thailand	3.7	57.6	17.7	61.0	33
Bhutan	3.5	n.a.	n.a.	56.2	62
Guyana	3.5	61.8	117.4	44.5	46
Sudan	3.4	58.7	92.4	7.4	38
Malta	3.3	76.2	32.9	85.6	n.a.
Lao PDR	3.3	n.a.	n.a.	71.4	198
Sri Lanka	3.3	60.9	48.4	50.4	50
Samoa	3.2	n.a.	n.a.	66.2	68
Dominican Republic	3.2	60.6	41.1	47.3	75
Belize	3.2	n.a.	n.a.	60.4	n.a.
Bangladesh	3.0	49.6	122.5	23.1	35
Tunisia	3.0	64.7	14.3	54.9	14
Iran	3.0	61.4	7.7	28.2	47
Cape Verde	3.0	n.a.	n.a.	60.1	n.a.
Lesotho	3.0	n.a.	n.a.	46.4	92
Uganda	3.0	56.7	41.2	29.0	36

[a] *Source:* World Bank Database. The 29 (out of 143) developing countries with GDP Growth above 3% between 1990–2003.

[b] *Note:* International Country Risk Guide (ICRG) political risk indicators for government stability, corruption, law & order, democratic accountability, and bureaucracy quality. Percentage based on a the total possible rating 34 points.

[c] *Source:* Kaufmann, Kraay, and Mastruzzi (2003). Governance Indicators for 1996–2002: Composite rating of voice and accountability, political stability, government effectivenes, regulatory quality, rule of law, and control of corruption indicators.

[d] *Source:* World Bank: Doing Business: Benchmarking Business Regulations Database. The rate details the average number of days needed to establish a business.

TABLE 1
Institutional Quality and Investment Climate in Fast-Growing Countries

Country	Growth in GDP Per Capita[a] 1990–2003	Avg. ICRG Ratings[b] 3yr. Avg. 2002–2004	Change in Avg. ICRG Ratings 1990–2004	WBI Governance Indicators[c] 2002	Time Required to Establish a Business[d] 2004
	Percent	Percent of Total	Percentage Change	Percentile Rank 0–100	Years
China	8.6	55.7	2.0	43.2	1.3
Vietnam	5.8	55.6	17.4	37.2	1.7
Maldives	4.9	n.a.	n.a.	65.8	n.a.
South Korea	4.8	69.0	38.0	72.5	0.7
Lebanon	4.3	54.7	71.5	15.5	0.8
Chile	4.1	62.1	11.0	87.5	0.7
Mozambique	4.1	56.5	37.4	73.6	5.9
Mauritius	3.9	n.a.	n.a.	65.2	n.a.
Slovenia	3.9	65.9	n.a.	81.6	1.7
India	3.8	68.1	86.2	47.9	2.7
Cambodia	3.8	n.a.	n.a.	29.7	2.8
Malaysia	3.7	67.3	-4.1	39.5	0.7
Poland	3.7	59.9	11.7	58.3	0.8
Thailand	3.7	57.6	17.7	61.0	0.7
Bhutan	3.5	n.a.	n.a.	56.2	1.9
Guyana	3.5	61.8	117.4	44.5	n.a.
Sudan	3.4	58.7	92.4	7.4	n.a.
Malta	3.3	76.2	32.9	85.6	n.a.
Lao PDR	3.3	n.a.	n.a.	71.4	4.9
Sri Lanka	3.3	60.9	48.4	50.4	1.1
Samoa	3.2	n.a.	n.a.	66.2	1.4
Dominican Republic	3.2	60.6	41.1	47.3	2.1
Belize	3.2	n.a.	n.a.	60.4	n.a.
Bangladesh	3.0	49.6	122.5	23.1	0.8
Tunisia	3.0	64.7	14.3	54.9	0.5
Iran	3.0	61.4	7.7	28.2	1.2
Cape Verde	3.0	n.a.	n.a.	60.1	n.a.
Lesotho	3.0	n.a.	n.a.	46.4	2.3
Uganda	3.0	56.7	41.2	29.0	1.7

[a] *Source:* World Bank Database. The 29 (out of 143) developing countries with GDP Growth above 3% between 1990–2003.

[b] *Note:* International Country Risk Guide (ICRG) political risk indicators for government stability, corruption, law & order, democratic accountability, and bureaucracy quality. Percentage based on a the total possible rating 34 points.

[c] *Source:* Kaufmann, Kraay, and Mastruzzi (2003). Governance Indicators for 1996–2002: Composite rating of voice and accountability, political stability, government effectivenes, regulatory quality, rule of law, and control of corruption indicators.

[d] *Source:* World Bank: Doing Business: Benchmarking Business Regulations Database. Rate incorporates the number of procedures required to establish a business and the average number of days per procedure to establish a business.

transport—the type of institutional arrangements needed has changed. The old model typically had a few large state-owned monopolies. In many developing countries, the prevailing approach has been to try to privatize state-run utilities and leave new investment for the private sector. In theory, this makes eminent sense for at least three reasons:

- New technology allows for unbundling in the area of infrastructure
- Poor record of state-run utilities in delivering adequate services and generating adequate return on capital
- Fiscal constraints in the public sector, which force governments to look toward the private sector to meet investment needs.

But in practice, this has been controversial and quite problematic. Although privatization and new private investment has been forthcoming, the experience has been mixed and quite varied. Privatization has not always followed transparent procedures and has acquired a poor reputation in many countries. New private investment has been forthcoming in some sectors, such as mobile telephones, ports, and road transport, but lack of effective regulatory systems has made it less attractive so far in energy generation and distribution and in other areas of infrastructure. Moreover, in a rush to try to attract private investment without adequate regulatory systems in place, fairly expensive and nontransparent contracts were devised, but, although initially successful in attracting investment, these were ultimately unworkable, creating social and political problems.

As it has become better understood that private fixed investment in infrastructure is not likely to be forthcoming in amounts great enough to finance the needs of many developing countries, there is a need to ask what can be done. Returning to the old model of poorly run state utilities is clearly not a solution. Quick fixes in the form of expensive guaranteed take and pay contracts have also not been socially and politically acceptable. In the area of infrastructure provision, with the inadequate response of private financing, use of public financing is needed to meet growing needs, but with more contestable institutional forms and with a greater effort to continue to improve regulatory systems to attract private investment.

Important reforms are underway in the areas of health, education, and social insurance, but they have less to do with the role of the public compared with the private sector, although new private investment is forthcoming in tertiary health care, tertiary education, and some aspects of social insurance. The issues pertain more to adequate design of incentives that will improve the effective delivery of public services under a very wide range of institutional and cultural settings.

III. Building Consensus for Reforms and Their Implementation

Crisis leads to reforms, but such reforms are not necessarily sustained. As soon as the painful memory of the crisis recedes, the momentum for reform slows down. This often leads to further crisis and a highly volatile crisis-ridden economy. Turkey in the 1990s followed this pattern. But sometimes, the reforms get sustained well after a crisis, as in India, Mauritius, and Tunisia. The crisis triggers initial reforms, and as they succeed in improving living conditions and begin to pay off socially and politically, they begin to get more support and become self-perpetuating. Sometimes consensus develops around reforms even without a crisis, as in China.[7] Such consensus building is often a slower, gradual process, but once it develops, leads to effective home-grown reform that has ownership and greater implementability. The ability to generate reform without a crisis is obviously better, as it avoids all the pain associated with crisis.

So, how can a consensus for reform be developed, and how can international lenders such as the World Bank encourage that process? To get a better understanding of how best to support reform, it is wise to get a better idea of the reform process itself.

First, reforms are never linear. They occur in fits and starts, sometimes moving forward at much faster speed, sometimes suffering temporary reversals and then moving forward once more. It is by no means a smooth process, but much more discontinuous.[8] Temporary reversals should not be judged as failures, but periods during which the system is adjusting to the changes taking place.

Second, sustained reform is more like a marathon than a sprint in nature.[9] Patience is needed to build consensus, which, once built up, can accelerate the momentum for reform. Especially in a democratic setup, it is critical to allow for time to build dialogue across different segments of society, especially with labor unions and the legislature.

Third, selectivity, timing, and sequencing matter a great deal. Although an economic development strategy must be comprehensive at any point in time, only certain crucial aspects of reform can be tackled; in most developing countries, the capacity to tackle more than a few well-chosen reforms is limited. It is important to try to fit actions needed to capacity; doing a few things well in a carefully planned sequence is better than doing a lot of things badly.

Fourth, home-grown reforms have a greater chance of success than externally imposed ones, even if they remain somewhat less sophisticated in their depth of analysis and consistency. With unexpected developments in the international economy and the number of variables that remain out of policymaker control, the chances of getting it all right in the beginning are in any case limited.

Fifth, reforms are uncertain. It is not always easy to predict how reforms will turn out or see upfront all the steps that will be needed to get there, as these are often a series of calculated risks that are taken without all the corners covered. The first few moves are known and the end point or goals are usually clear, but how to get there is not necessarily well mapped out.

IV. Improving Bank Support for Policy and Institutional Reforms

Given these features of reform, what should international agencies do (or not do) to encourage reform? If it remains unclear why reforms occur and get perpetuated with time, is there a role for international lenders such as the World Bank? Based on evaluative evidence, is there any attribution possible between the knowledge and lending activities of agencies such as the World Bank to the effective adoption and implementation of reforms and policy change? In other words, where successful reform has occurred, has the World Bank played a role that enhanced its prospects? This is a difficult question to answer, especially in a middle-income country context where the Bank's financial assistance is typically a very small share of overall resource flows. Nevertheless, evaluation does give us some answers.

First, the Bank's economic and sector work, when done well, helps bring about discussion and debate on policy reform. Most countries point to the knowledge of the Bank on development issues as a *reservoir of intellectual capital,* which they can tap for policy advice. Several countries have suggested that the advice could be improved if it is better custom fit to their particular needs and if local expertise is also involved, but most countries acknowledge the value in the Bank's analytical and advisory services. With time a larger share of World Bank assistance now goes to countries with better policies, as measured by the Bank's own Country Policy and Institutional Assessment (CPIA) indicator.[10] Bank assistance is also increasingly going to countries with improving policy and institutional indicators. So the Bank's advisory services and its financial support, when done well, supports policy change. But as later papers show, lack of sufficient knowledge and overoptimism in turn-around situations can lead to mistakes. The Bank jumps in with large volumes of lending in situations in which the prerequisites for reform are not present, leading to delayed reforms and large buildup of debt. Kenya, Moldova, and Malawi can be cited as examples of such overoptimism at various stages in the past decade. Moreover, countries with higher CPIA ratings have grown faster, which has helped reduce poverty, although as shown earlier, countries are finding ways to grow fast even with very low levels of institutional capacity.

Second, be patient, as reforms may take longer than planned and often run into unexpected obstacles. It is important to keep in mind that a hurried reform that does not work can delay and reverse reforms for a long time; a good example is privatization in Russia. The process by which reform takes place and its transparency is often as important as the means, because it determines the legitimacy of reforms and its eventual acceptability and irreversibility.

Third, persuade rather than prescribe. Conditionality as we know it does not work. If the policymakers are persuaded, conditionality is not needed, and if they are not persuaded, conditionality does not work; therefore, it is important to try to shift more to outcome-based support rather than to old style ex ante conditionality.[11] There are instances where even within a reforming government a full consensus may not exist on all aspects of reform, its timing, or sequencing. In such cases, the more reform-minded parts of the government may find conditionality an expedient mechanism to carry their colleagues in government along—there are several instances where this has worked—but it must be used carefully.[12]

Fourth, encourage ownership by consciously avoiding processes that discourage local ownership; the introduction of poverty reduction strategy papers (PRSPs) is a good example of a process that tries to encourage more ownership; but as the evaluation results presented in the conference show, even the PRSPs are hampered by their follow-up requirements on a Washington sign-off. Another mechanism is to try to provide more opportunities for exchange of ideas among countries and play more of the "hummingbird" role of the Bank.[13] One way to help induce greater ownership is to present options rather than single solutions, carefully laying out the pros and cons, and to listen to local options as well. It is typically the combination of best international practice and local custom-fit solutions that work best.[14]

Fifth, focus more on the social, environmental impact of reforms that attempt to include mitigating measures, and carry out better risk analysis of different reform options. The social impact analysis of reform programs needs more care and rigor.[15] Certain interest groups such as labor unions are often excluded from discussions on reform, reducing consensus and subsequently creating problems in implementation. The World Bank and other international lenders are frequently overly optimistic about prospects for reform every time a new government takes office, even when the underlying political and institutional forces are arrayed against it. This overoptimism in turn-around situations must be avoided. Better debt analysis is also badly needed. Providing financial support in situations where the willingness for reform is weak creates moral hazard and hurts prospects for policy change and reform.

Sixth, international agencies such as the World Bank need to find ways to reduce the risks of reforms by sharing in the costs of failed reforms. Reforms supported by international agencies such as the World Bank, in which financial and technical support is provided, are akin to "relational banking."[16] The costs of failed reforms are currently largely and, some would say, disproportionately borne by the borrowing country: failure of reforms creates political and social fallout in the country, but the borrowed funds are still repaid. International agencies often pay in "reputation costs" for failed reforms, but typically do not incur financial costs. Because the risks are largely borne by the country, there is a tendency to be unrealistic about the risks and prospects for reform and policy change, whose outcomes are uncertain.

V. Dealing with Fragile and Conflict-Ridden States?

Much of the previous discussion assumes a functioning system of government; but what about countries in which the state is fragile and the ability to manage policy change is very weak? The preponderant view during much of the 1990s was that aid allocations from the international financial institutions should increasingly go to countries that were reforming and improving their policies. But, it became increasingly evident, especially with the end of the Cold War, that a large cluster of countries were very fragile and in some cases could be classified as failed states.

If a pure policy and institutional performance criterion were to be applied to these countries they would get very limited assistance. Although this might improve the average returns to international assistance, it would leave out very significant parts of the developing world, which with limited assistance, would further decline. In the World Bank, these countries were termed low-income countries under stress and a special approach was developed to help deal with their problems.

With the spread of terrorism, often emanating from failed states, it became impossible to ignore their problems. Many of these countries are also ridden by conflict. Moreover, even before the problems of terrorism leapt to the world's attention, the sporadic outbursts of violence and the spillover of refugees from these areas often caught world attention.

So how does one develop a special approach to these types of situations, that is, where the normal performance criterion would be unworkable, but at the same time, gradually build the country's capacity to move toward normalcy? How does one best ensure that the limited governmental and aid resources are utilized to help people, despite fragile institutional frameworks?

It is, of course, difficult to provide a clear answer as situations vary, but some general lessons from country evaluations can be highlighted:

Engagement. Early and continuous engagement in low-income countries under stress and post-conflict countries is a lesson that comes from many successful experiences with such situations. Engagement does not mean pouring in large resources unmindful of their effective utilization, but it does imply maintaining support for analytical work, emergency-type assistance, and support for rebuilding capacity. In countries such as Armenia, Bosnia-Herzegovina, and the West Bank and Gaza, World Bank engagement has been immensely important in helping make progress so far. Bank disengagement in Rwanda was quite costly in terms of re-engagement. In Armenia and Bosnia, as progress was made from an early emergency to more normal situation, the Bank could gradually step up its technical and financial support for policy and institutional change.

Enclaves. Given limited local capacity in such fragile and conflict-ridden situations, there is always a need to choose where to concentrate those resources. In the early emergency phase, the situation in the country is to some extent direr, but the needs are obvious. Once the initial emergency phase is over and capacity and institution building starts, the choices become more difficult. Increasing the capacity of the central economic agencies is vital for allowing policy options and resource management to occur, but beyond that, how can international assistance best be allocated? Some believe that many of the resources should be provided directly to communities; others recommend building strong enclave-type institutions, which can deliver certain services and become examples for others. These remain open questions, for which no clear answers can easily be provided.

Adaptation of processes and procedures. Because under normal rules of aid allocation and implementation, fragile and conflict-ridden situations will get limited help, rules must be relaxed. But too much relaxation creates the risk of permanent dependency and disincentives to local empowerment and initiative. A common tendency is to use specialized project implementation units (PIUs) to help accelerate policy-making and implementation, but with the risk that capacity building in the rest of the government remains weak.17 The Bank and other donor agencies have not found a clear way out of this dilemma of relying less on external and specialized agencies at the cost of slowing down recovery.

Effective aid coordination and partnerships. Given the large needs and limited local capacity in fragile and conflict-ridden states, aid coordination and partnerships are vital for avoiding duplication and making the most effective use of external assistance. In many successful cases, aid coordination has played a vital role, but has usually resulted from well-publicized political agreements and very effective aid coordination mechanisms on the ground.

VI. Looking Forward

Evaluation is useful in documenting the past and learning lessons for the future. In that sense, the past few years give reason for hope that, as more countries begin to reform and change policies, more developing countries will begin a process of convergence with the developed world.

There is now perhaps less effort being made to find consensus on the best set of policies, in contrast with the 1980s when huge debates took place about what constitutes an optimal set of policies—often termed the "Washington Consensus." There is perhaps a consensus that a consensus is not necessary—that different countries are finding different ways of getting ahead to deliver a better investment climate and social services to their people. For example, China, India, Bangladesh, Tunisia, and Vietnam are different and have all succeeded in reaching policy frameworks needed to achieve growth at the same time.

The new consensus is that consensus on the best policies and institutional arrangements is not necessary; countries can achieve success in different ways by focusing attention on binding institutional constraints, often through innovative transitional improvements.

But this does not mean that every country must find its own unique path to policy change and reform; a deconstructionist approach[18] is also dangerous, because although every country is unique, learning from each other and modifying or adapting programs to fit particular situations is better than trying to find new and unique solutions to every problem.

International experience informs us that certain types of institutions and service provision systems look quite similar across countries, whereas others show greater divergence. For example, although exchange rate policy and the legislated degree of independence can vary, central banks are structured very similarly around the world. Greater convergence is also coming in areas such as debt management: the options for effective debt management are narrowing considerably. Management of ports and road systems are also showing greater convergence. What is common to all these examples is the greater specificity of services to be provided; they are all more easily measurable and, therefore, more common standards and institutional arrangements can be recommended for effective delivery.[19]

In the area of utilities, other options for creating competition and contestability are also possible. For example, finding the best international practice on running an electricity company or public transport is not necessary; improvements in service delivery are possible by simply allowing the private sector to invest and compete with public utilities. But, establishing appropriate regulatory systems is where the choices and options are to be made, and here international best practice offers fewer options that can be made available to countries that are establishing new regulatory bodies.

In other cases, such as social assistance, basic education, primary health care, or rural development programs, such precision and monitorability is more difficult. Here the options are many, and it is very difficult and incorrect to suggest that easily transportable international best practices exist. Countries may find quite unique and home-grown solutions to best deliver such services, and no common policy or institutional arrangements can or should be suggested. In such cases, international agencies, such as the World Bank, can serve as more of a facilitator for exchange of ideas and options among countries, rather than provider of international best practice.

The World Bank must try to restore its preeminent role as the center of excellence in key policy and institutional areas where international best practice is possible, and must become a more effective facilitator for options and ideas where international best practice does not exist.

To be more effective, the World Bank must continue to provide international best practice in those areas where the options for policy and institutional arrangements are limited, but must also better facilitate options among countries where those options are more numerous and no "one size fits all" approach will work. This will help improve the legitimacy of the Bank's advice, which is still viewed suspiciously by many developing countries as a representation of rich country interests. It must also continue to try to find better mechanisms to deal with fragile states and help build capacity under a more long-term approach.

Ownership has been identified as a central requirement for effective policy change and reform. But ownership for the design and implementation of reforms requires capacity: capacity to analyze different options, link those choices to financing arrangements, implement the chosen option, and monitor and evaluate the outcomes. Although many developing countries have adequate capacity, in many situations capacity building (not technical assistance) must be a key objective to helping build ownership.

In almost three-quarters of the developing countries, growth in income remains too slow for any prospect of convergence with the developed countries. The recent acceleration in reforms driven by globalization, regional factors such as EU accession, and crisis will, it is hoped, lead to better outcomes in the future. Large Asian economies are now growing rapidly and are converging, but have a long way to go to catch up. They are also demonstrating that, although institutions are important for growth, it is important to focus on the binding institutional constraints and finding solutions to overcome them, rather than trying to tackle broad, but unfocused institutional reforms across a range of issues. Timing, sequencing, and local adaptation matter as much in institutional reforms as they did in earlier macroeconomic reforms.

In the chapters that follow, a group of distinguished policymakers and experts elaborate on and discuss these and other themes, based on evaluation findings from OED.

Notes

1. The term "elusive" is taken from Easterly (2001).
2. The long decline in living standards in Argentina since the early part of the twentieth century is a well-known example. Several countries in Sub-Saharan Africa have more recently shown a similar proclivity to lack of reform, despite decline in living conditions.
3. See Bordo and others (2001).
4. See Chhibber (2003).
5. Point made by H. E. Saifur Rahman, Bangladesh Minister of Finance and Planning, in his key note address (chapter 1).
6. Emphasized by Kemal Derviş at the closing remarks for the conference (chapter 7, "Effectiveness of Policies and Reforms")
7. Of course, China went through a long period of upheaval and social and political change and decline in living standards before embarking on its economic reforms.
8. Pointed out by H. E. Saifur Rahman, Bangladesh minister of finance (chapter 1), and Ishrat Husain, governor, State Bank of Pakistan (chapter 3).
9. See address by Saifur Rahman, Bangladesh minister of finance and planning (chapter 1).
10. The same result would be found even if we used other indicators such as the ICRG or the Freedom House Index (World Bank 2003).
11. See remarks made by Tony Killick, overseas development assistance senior research associate, in the session on "Effectiveness of Bank Support for Policy Reform" (chapter 2).
12. Ghana, Uganda, and Turkey are examples of countries where conditionality was used by technocratic economic teams to bolster reforms within the government.
13. See remarks by Otaviano Canuto, World Bank executive director, in the session on "Effectiveness of Bank Support for Policy Reform" (chapter 2).
14. See remarks by Masood Ahmed, director general, Policy and International, Department for International Development, in the session on "Effectiveness of Bank Support for Policy Reform" (chapter 2).
15. Pointed out by Ana Quirós, general director, Centre of Information and Advisory Services in Health, in her remarks in the PRSP session (chapter 6).
16. See Aoki and Dinc (1997) on relational banking.
17. As pointed out by H. E. Ljerka Marić, minister of finance and treasury, Bosnia-Herzegovina.

18. I am grateful to Gregory Ingram, director-general, World Bank Operations Evaluations, for pointing this out.
19. For a rich discussion of these ideas see Israel (1987), Pritchett and Woolcock (2002), and Fukuyama (2004).

References

Aoki, Masahiko, and Sedar Dinc. 1997. "Relational Financing as an Institution and its Viability under Competition." Working Paper 97011. Stanford University, Department of Economics.

Bordo, M., B. Eichengreen, D. Klingebiel, and M. S. Martinez-Peria. 2001. "Is the Crisis Problem Growing More Severe?" *Economic Policy* 16 (32). Blackwell Publishing, Oxford, England.

Chhibber, Ajay. 2003. "The Economic Reform of Turkey." Paper presented at the Center for Economic Development. Stanford University, Stanford, Calif. Available at: http://scid.stanford.edu/events/AChhiber%20Paper.pdf.

Easterly, William. 2001. *The Elusive Quest for Growth: Economists' Adventures and Misadventures in the Tropics.* Cambridge, Mass.: MIT Press.

Fukuyama, Francis. 2004. *State-Building: Governance and World Order in the 21st Century.* Ithaca, N.Y.: Cornell University Press.

Israel, Arturo. 1987. *Institutional Development: Incentives to Performance.* World Bank, Washington, D.C.

Kaufmann, D., A. Kraay, and M. Mastruzzi. 2003. *Governance Matters III: Governance Indicators for 1996–2002.* Policy Research Working Paper 3106. World Bank, Washington, D.C.

Pritchett, Lant, and Michael Woolcock. 2002. "Solutions when the Solution is the Problem: Arraying the Disarray in Development." *World Development* (United Kingdom) 32 (2): 191–212.

Rahman, Saifur. 2004. Keynote Address from the OED Conference on Effectiveness of Policies and Reforms, Washington, D.C., October 4.

World Bank. 2004. *2003 Annual Review of Development Effectiveness (ARDE).* Operations Evaluation Department (OED), Washington, D.C.

Part 1

Policy Reforms in the Developing World: Lessons from Bangladesh

Policy Reforms in the Developing World: Lessons from Bangladesh

Minister M. Saifur Rahman *

The World Bank plays a significant role in promoting reforms and formulating policies throughout much of the developing world. This conference is on effectiveness of policies and programs; therefore, reforms are very appropriate and timely.

I would like to start where Anne O. Krueger, first deputy managing director of the International Monetary Fund (IMF) and one of the fervent champions of reforms in her academic incarnation, ended her recent speech on reforms at the University of Nottingham in the United Kingdom. Describing reforms as "dangerous moments" in a nation's life, she concluded, "We do not like admitting that there are things that we do not know and, more important, cannot know. But the reform process is inevitably something of a mystery. We cannot predict the exact outcome. But by proper and effective implementation, we can increase the prospect of success."

I am in broad agreement with her thoughtful comments. To me, however, reforms are not mysterious; lack of reform is. Nobody disputes the fact that unleashing the productive potentials of developing countries is contingent on the removal of existing impediments or roadblocks to growth through reforms.

---

* Honorable Minister for Finance and Planning, Government of Bangladesh.

Experts, such as Ms. Krueger, tell us that unpleasant reforms are usually avoided and are forced by crises. There is no crisis greater or more pressing than the calamity of abysmal poverty in the Third World. This is the crisis that reform should address.

Nowhere is the desire for change so ardent as among the people in developing countries. Yet, much of the developing world continues remains in stagnation. It is indeed a great tragedy that political process in most low-income countries cannot translate into reality the overwhelming desire of people for change.

Much political controversy on reforms relates not to ends, but to phasing, speed, and sequencing of reforms. Obviously, the vested interest groups who lose from reforms oppose them. However—and again, I have to depend on some quotations—what Keynes said about economic policymaking is also relevant for reforms. "I am sure," said Keynes, "that the power of vested interests is vastly exaggerated compared with the gradual encroachment of ideas."

Many policymakers in the developing world, in the words of Keynes, "are usually the slaves of some defunct economists." The intellectual climate in the Third World is haunted by the specter of the nineteenth century economists. The deep distrust of the global economic system that galvanized the struggle against imperialism and colonialism continues to obsess Third World intellectuals. In their mind, the Bretton Woods institutions are also tarred by the same brush. Consequently, much of the economic and sectoral work done by these institutions, irrespective of the level of their professional excellence, is viewed with suspicion.

Ladies and gentlemen, the Bank is also perceived to be indifferent to specific conditions of a particular country, which is true most of the time. This distrust is well reflected in the Operations Evaluation Department's (OED's) *2003 Annual Review of Development Effectiveness (ARDE)* (World Bank 2004a), which states, "But the majority of the respondents also complained that the Bank is too narrowly focused in the analyses and 'best practices' that it presents, with little or no attention to alternative perspectives or to individual country circumstances." Quite often, the Bank believes there is only one view; there is no other view. This is one of the problems that face the institutional people. What they say is true; the other view is not true.

Many respondents expressed frustration about the Bank's insistence that its models and solutions represent the only viable approach to solving economic and social problems in a country. This is what is creating most of the tension on the matter of the Bank's policies and programs. Several said "that the Bank's insistence that its approach is the only correct approach generates mistrust and suspicion of the Bank and substantially decreases receptivity to Bank information overall." In such a hostile intellectual climate, reforms are not likely to be sustainable unless they are designed and owned locally.

The Bretton Woods institutions should lay more emphasis on capacity building for better economic and sectoral work (ESW) by local professionals, rather than relying exclusively on their own experts from Washington. The poverty reduction strategy paper (PRSP) is a step in the right direction for promoting country ownership of reforms. It is, however, hamstrung by uniform requirements for dissimilar countries—countries with different geography, history, political systems, cultural backgrounds, and historical experiences. All are put together and the same solution is given for everybody, which is the weakness of this process.

I fully agree with OED's PRSP evaluation (World Bank 2004b) that "The PRS [Poverty Reduction Strategy] Initiative is an improvement over the policy framework papers of the 1990s, but remains a work in progress and has not yet fulfilled its potential to enhance poverty reduction efforts in low-income countries." The PRSPs should take into account the political economy of the reforming countries—it is very vital—as they are the track records of their governments in policy and institutional reforms and country-specific political and socioeconomic constraints.

Ladies and gentlemen, it is indeed heartening to note from OED's 2003 ARDE that two-thirds of developing countries have improved their development policies. That is good.

The countries with better policies or improving policies, according to this report, grew more rapidly compared with countries with weak policies. The Operations Evaluation Department indicates that the cumulative per capita growth in countries with improving policies during 1998–2002 was two to six times greater than in countries with deteriorating policies and institutional weaknesses. It is also reported that outcomes of World Bank country assistance have been moderately successful 70 percent of the time.

These are indeed encouraging developments; however, economic reform is not a one-shot affair, but a continuous process. In the jargon of athletics, reform is a marathon, not a sprint. We hope that the second- and third-generation reforms in these countries will progress in the same way.

The most frequently used instrument used by the Bretton Woods institutions for monitoring the implementation of reforms is the much criticized "conditionalities" that convert credit into policy tools. The usefulness of conditionalities has been questioned both by the Bank and the borrowers.

From the Bank's point of view, it is argued that conditionality is often ineffective in regulating aid flows, because donors find it difficult to disengage when conditions are not met. The experience is not similar in all cases, however. The borrowing countries complain that very often conditionalities are designed as zero sum games and aid is not disbursed unless all multiyear, complex conditionalities are fulfilled.

Because reforms are often leaps into the dark, it may not be feasible to meet all conditionalities in an uncertain world. We are living in an age of uncertainty. The refusal to disburse aid in case of partial reforms destroys the credibility of ill-fated reformers—sometimes, we become ill-fated reformers in our own countries—who may not succeed despite their best efforts.

In view of these difficulties, single-tranche annual program loans are better suited to developing countries than multitranche credits. Give me one tranche, it is stopped, and then everything is finished. This is one that creates a lot of problems in our experience.

Ladies and gentlemen, the reforms funded by development partners tend to be one-way streets. One can only go forward, and there is no exit. The donors quickly disengage themselves from failed reforms. As a result, the entire costs of a failed reform have to be borne by borrowing countries like us. There is no exit strategy for failed reforms.

Failed reforms can go both ways. They can be either pillars of success by facilitating fresh initiatives for reforms or they can be impediments to new reforms; however, the total disengagement of a development partner from a failed reform in a country may turn out to be counterproductive. The withdrawal of the World Bank in the late 1990s in my country from energy and jute sectors is a case in point. The Bank became a helpless spectator of continued deterioration in these two sectors.

The exit strategy from a failed reform program should not be total disengagement but include continued work in capacity building, advisory and analytical work in the sector, and, where appropriate, technical assistance. By remaining engaged in a limited way, the Bank can then lay the foundation for future reforms even in the failed sector.

The appropriate design of a reform is the most complex problem. Although it is difficult to sustain political support for reforms without immediate benefits—it is very difficult for a reformer to show some benefit—all reforms do not necessarily yield quick results.

In the interrelated economic system, everything depends on everything else. For example, the benefits of financial sector reforms cannot be reaped without judicial reforms, which in turn call for a host of governance reforms. A comprehensive reform strategy is needed in various sectors for producing results in a specific area.

The capacity for implementation, however, is limited in most of the developing countries. In real life, no developing country has the capacity to implement all needed reforms at the same time. This makes the outcome of reforms uncertain.

A related issue is the phasing, sequencing, and speed of reform. Although the borrowing countries consider phasing and gradualness as essential, many donors and development partners view them as excuses for delaying reforms.

What our experience clearly indicates is that reform is bound to be an uneven process, and success is not likely to be uniform in all areas all the time. This is also supported by country assistance evaluations by the Operations Evaluation Department.

It is morally wrong to penalize reformers who fail because of circumstances beyond their control. The petroleum price hike doubling to more than US$60 will put in jeopardy many of the reform measures taken by developing countries with limited resources. So these have to be taken care of.

As the OED report on effectiveness also correctly points out, the Bank "tends to react slowly to deterioration and too quickly to improvement." We must not be impatient for instantaneous results of reforms and remember that in most cases reforms are long, drawn-out processes.

I agree with the Operations Evaluation Department's finding that "institutional reforms and capacity building for effective governance are critical to successful outcomes." Good governance is a sine qua non for a successful reform process or success in the economic agenda of any country. It could be good governance, or it should be institutional governance in sectoral areas.

Institutional reforms and capacity building cannot, however, be carried out in a hurry; it takes time. Capacity building should ideally precede reforms in a sector; it is essential to strengthen the line ministries for implementation of reforms. Unfortunately, the entire burden of carrying out reforms in a program falls on the ministry of finance or economic affairs, which needs the disbursement of aid in the interest of macro stability. It becomes the headache of finance ministers, not the other branches of the government.

Very often, the line ministries, which do not have direct access to financial resources provided for reforms, are not enthusiastic for reforms. These ministries should be motivated through the process of capacity building. Where prior capacity building is needed, reforms will have to be designed gradually, taking this into account.

We welcome the performance-based allocation in International Development Association (IDA). Unfortunately, in practice, this principle is not fully honored, particularly not in all cases. Performance-based allocation is often reduced by caps for countries, such as Bangladesh, that have large concentrations of poor. The largest number of poor live in the South Asian regions, including mine.

One of the problems inherent in the performance-based approach is its primary basis on cross-country comparison. The cross-country comparison of subjective assessment on the basis of a number of criteria does not always give an accurate assessment. The benefits or magnitude of reforms cannot always be quantified. Reforms, to be beneficial, need not always be large. Even small reforms may generate critical mass for further reforms. It is a cumulative process. Instead of imposing too many conditionalities, it is essential to build on successes of small and manageable reforms.

I would like to take this opportunity to draw lessons from my adventures in the economic reform process in Bangladesh for more than a decade. Although Bangladesh's experience with the PRS initiative is not as long as that of many other countries, our government's as well as my experience, particularly in policy and institutional reforms, dates back more than a decade to 1977.

I have been personally associated with wide-ranging reforms in taxation, including introduction of a value-added tax (VAT), credit liberalization, privatization, deregulation, private investment, removal of exchange controls, opening up energy and telecommunications sectors for private investment, reforms in public expenditure, a focus on human development, and poverty reduction and structural reforms in the financial sector. All reforms that have taken place in my country at one stage or another have had to be initiated by the Ministry of Finance, while I was at that ministry.

The reforms have, broadly speaking, contributed to *(a)* growth of GDP at about 4.8 percent annually in the past decade, *(b)* macroeconomic stability, including low inflation, *(c)* significant human resource development, *(d)* deceleration of population growth (we had a population explosion; now we are having less population growth and we have managed very well, I think), *(e)* reduction of infant mortality by half, *(f)* attainment of one of the highest primary school enrollment rates in the developing world, particularly for girl's education, and *(g)* gender equality in primary education. This is the success story of Bangladesh.

According to estimates of the UNDP Human Development Report (UNDP 2004, p. 141), Bangladesh has graduated from the low human development to medium human development category of the United Nations. We are successfully implementing our Interim PRSP (I-PRSP) with the IMF's Poverty Reduction Growth Facility and World Bank's Development Support Credit.

The reforms envisaged in the I-PRSP, especially in sectoral governance and in various sectors—public administration, finance, tax and tariff, expenditure control, energy, and telecommunications—are progressing rapidly.

As a result of these ongoing reforms, autonomy of the central bank has been ensured by changing the law and giving it complete freedom from the Ministry of Finance. Its operational capacity is being improved. Bank-by-bank resolution strategies for nationalized commercial banks have been adopted. Their market share is diminishing, and their ratio of nonperforming loans is declining.

The state-owned enterprise sector is shrinking and their losses are being cut by about 10 percent annually. The Energy and Telecommunications Regulatory Commissions have already been set up independently to create an even playing field for private sector operations. An Independent Anti-Corruption Commission is being set up. Already under the law that has been passed, the commission's budget has been approved, and perhaps the chairman and the members will be nominated today or tomorrow. Maybe it has already been done.

A long-term strategy is being developed for the National Board of Revenue, which is the revenue collector in the country, and it has been undergoing reform since the early 1990s. We have introduced an intelligence unit in the National Board of Revenue, which is a large taxpayer unit; harmonized income tax numbers to be uniform with the value added tax (VAT) number; and used a common number for controlling lapses or leakages in the tax collection.

A police reform project is under formulation to improve law and order in the country. Specific interventions are also improving the economic management capacity of the civil service. We have a cabinet committee in good governance, headed by me, looking into all reforms needed to bring dynamism to the civil service and improve institutions.

The government appreciates the role and support of the development partners, especially the World Bank and IMF, in most of these policy and institutional reform processes on the agenda. Our vision of future policy and institutional reforms will be reflected in the final PRSP due for finalization by the end of December.

We plan to develop a strong partnership with the private sector, nongovernmental organizations (NGOs), and development partners to materialize the vision to be articulated in the full final PRSP. We recognize the sociopolitical impediments to structural reforms in policies and institutions within the framework of our multiparty democratic system. Reform is easier in an autocracy, but it is overwhelmingly difficult in a democracy.

I have worked in both types of governments—autocracy and democracy—and my success in autocracy was much quicker and faster than in democracy. So, you talk of democracy and become impatient when you see reform is not continuing. This is one tragedy we have noted. You want accountable government—democratic government—yet an accountable democratic government requires a lengthier consultation process.

In a country, with bipartisan politics, the reform process becomes very difficult, and the Bank and IMF must have patience to carry out reforms under such a difficult dilemma. If I had to have chosen, I would have had a very harmonized political process, not confrontational. I would have been able to carry out reforms—many of the agendas I have taken up in my hands—within six months. Unhappily, I am road blocked every now and then in my reform process, but this is the price we have to pay for liberty and freedom. We know it very well. So this is one of those tradeoffs between reforms and liberty and democracy.

We also understand the pain of reforms when they hurt the people reforms are targeted to benefit. We also have to appreciate—institutions, such as the World Bank and the IMF, have to appreciate—the constitutional, parliamentary, and judicial frameworks within which reforms are to be implemented. We are a member of the United Nations Charter of Human Rights; it is enshrined in our constitution. Any reform process that hurts any group of people can be taken to a court of law and put under an injunction and stay order, because these people say they are infringed on, whether it is a labor union or even private individuals.

I transferred eight officials from the Board of Revenue; I found them not to be working. They went to the court of law and introduced—brought about a stay order—that their fundamental rights had been infringed. So, this is the elaborate definition of fundamental rights within which we in Bangladesh are working.

I personally feel that, in policy and institutional reforms, a gradualist and incremental approach is more in order and the right choice. The reform process must be based on a carefully built social consensus. It is very hard to gain. All the stakeholders in the reform process should be prepared to be patient in the face of obstacles, which will be temporary, I believe, if the design and sequencing of reforms are right.

In the sociopolitical sector, if the politics of "proposing and opposing" is not there—when a society or politics are too adversarial, the reform process suffers casualties. This is one of my experiences.

Reforms by themselves are difficult. Revolution is easier than reforms; you do one set of changes and get rid of everything, which is much easier. But reform is a very, very difficult task. It involves continuous change, to which we have to adapt ourselves to survive in life and improve ourselves, and is particularly difficult, as I have said already, in a democratic, multiparty environment.

Furthermore, reforms in democratic countries are often reversed or slowed by a change in government. The reforms I carried out in the 1990s through 1995 are being stalled by the subsequent government. As happens in a democracy, governments are temporary. You get out of government, are kicked out by the voters, and then, when the new government comes, they stall reforms that have happened; that is my experience in my own country.

In democracy and reforms, then, there is a tradeoff. We will always opt for democracy, even if it is painful. Despite its inherent limitations, we are fully committed to a democratic way of life, for which we have struggled for centuries. Democracy is still the best form of government, despite its weaknesses and its often imposed roadblocks and so on against good governance and good economic management.

And yet, finally, democracy is the environment in which we have to carry out the reform process. Democracy for us is not a means, but an end in itself. For us, democracy is not only freedom, but also development. It is the democratic way of development to which we in Bangladesh are committed.

References

United Nations Development Programme (UNDP). 2004. Human Development Report 2004. New York, N.Y.: Oxford University Press. Available at: http://hdr.undp.org/.

World Bank. 2004a. *2003 Annual Review of Development Effectiveness (ARDE)*. Operations Evaluation Department (OED), Washington, D.C.

————. 2004b. *The Poverty Reduction Strategy Initiative: An Independent Evaluation of the World Bank's Support through 2003*. OED, Washington, D.C. Available at: http://www.worldbank.org/oed/prsp/.

Part 2

Effectiveness of Bank Support
for Policy Reform

The Effectiveness of World Bank Support for Policy Reform: ARDE 2003

*Robert J. Anderson**

The Operations Evaluation Department's (OED) *2003 Annual Review of Development Effectiveness (ARDE)* (World Bank 2004) examines the effectiveness of Bank support for developing country policy reform. We selected this topic because policy reform objectives underlie almost everything the Bank does and increasingly also the programs of other donors.

I will focus mainly on the conclusions of the ARDE regarding recent trends in developing countries' policies, the linkages between these trends and recent growth and poverty reduction performance, the macro level circumstantial evidence linking policy reform trends to the Bank's programs, and ARDE's recommendations for improving the effectiveness of Bank support. Other sessions will delve more deeply into the specific country-level evidence on the effectiveness of the Bank's programs, as reflected in studies in specific assistance to individual countries and groups of countries with common characteristics.

Given the Bank and other donors' emphasis on policy reform, ARDE 2003 begins by examining recent trends in developing countries' policies. To do this, the report examined four different indicators of developing countries' policies in 1999–2003. One indicator, the Bank's

* Lead Evaluation Officer, Operations Evaluation Department, World Bank Group.

country policy and institutional assessment, is internal to the Bank and used mainly to allocate International Development Association (IDA) resources. The others—the Heritage Foundation's Index of Economic Freedom, the Economist Intelligence Unit's Country Risk Service Rating, and the International Country Risk Guide's Overall Country Risk Rating—are widely used, publicly available indicators.

Despite the differences in content and coverage among the indicators, the picture that emerges from them (figure 1) is remarkably coherent. Overall, developing countries have made modest, but definite improvement in their policies in the past several years. This is true of both low-income countries that are eligible to borrow from IDA and middle-income countries that are eligible to borrow from the International Bank for Reconstruction and Development (IBRD).

FIGURE 1
Developing Countries Have Made Gradual, But Definite Progress in Improving Their Policy Indicators (1999–2003)

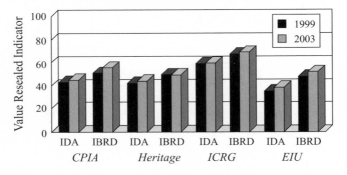

Notes: CPIA = World Bank Country Policy and Institutional Assessment, Overall Rating; Heritage = Heritage Foundation/Wall Street Journal Composite Index of Economic Freedom; ICRG = International Country Risk Guide Composite Index of Country Risk; EIU = Economist Intelligence Unit Country Risk Service Composite Country Risk. All indices were rescaled to range between 0 (lowest value) and 100 (highest value). Note that different indices cover different sets of countries; the CPIA, which covers 134 countries in both 1999 and 2003, is the most inclusive. Sixty-seven countries are common to all three indicators.
Source: World Bank (2004), annex A.

This improving trend has been widespread geographically (figure 2), with improvements, albeit to differing degrees, in all regions of the developing world. The data in figure 2 are for the Bank's Country Policy and Institutional Assessment (CPIA) indicator, but the picture is qualitatively the same for all indicators.

Improvement in policy has also been widespread across policy areas (figure 3). In general, the newer areas on the reform agenda, such as public sector management or policies for social inclusion and equity, started from lower levels at the beginning of the period and advanced more rapidly than policy areas that have long been the focus of the Bank's and others' policy dialogue, such as structural policies and macroeconomic management policies.

FIGURE 2
CPIA Ratings Indicate Policies Have Improved in All Regions
(1999–2003)

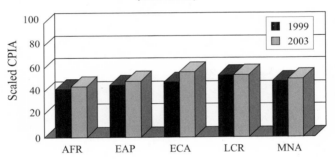

Source: World Bank (2004).

So we concluded, based on these data, that there has indeed been—across countries and across policy—a fairly widespread, recent improvement in developing countries' policies. But policy reform is an instrument, not an objective. The Bank and others emphasize policy reform, because research suggests that aid is more effective in good than in bad policy environments.

FIGURE 3
Policy and Institutional Improvements (1999–2003)

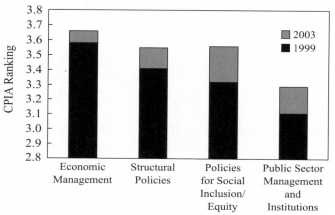

Source: World Bank (2004). This is an adaptation of figure 1.4.

Has recent policy reform, in fact, paid off? The data examined in ARDE suggest that the answer is "yes." Countries with relatively good initial policies, shown in the suite of bars on the right-hand side of figure 4, grew more rapidly than did countries with relatively poor initial policies.

FIGURE 4
Country with Improving Policies Indicators Have Higher Growth Rates

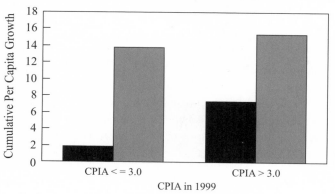

Source: World Bank (2004), annex B, technical note 1.4.

Countries with improving policies, shown in the striped bars, grew more rapidly than did countries with deteriorating policies, shown in the solid bars. Cumulative per capita growth in policy-improving countries in 1998–2002 was more than twice that in policy-deteriorating countries.

But what about countries that have, with time, done reasonably well regarding policy reform, but have had disappointing growth? Countries in Latin America are often cited in this regard.

Interestingly, the same comparative pattern also holds in the Latin America and the Caribbean (LAC) Region (figure 5), although the levels of growth in this recent period were lower. Per capita income in countries with deteriorating policies, and low initial CPIA scores declined cumulatively by an average of almost 11 percent. Countries with relatively high initial CPIAs and improving policies averaged cumulative growth of a little more than 6 percent. The conclusion based on these admittedly limited data is that good policy does indeed seem to pay off.

FIGURE 5
Policy Improvements and Growth in LAC Region

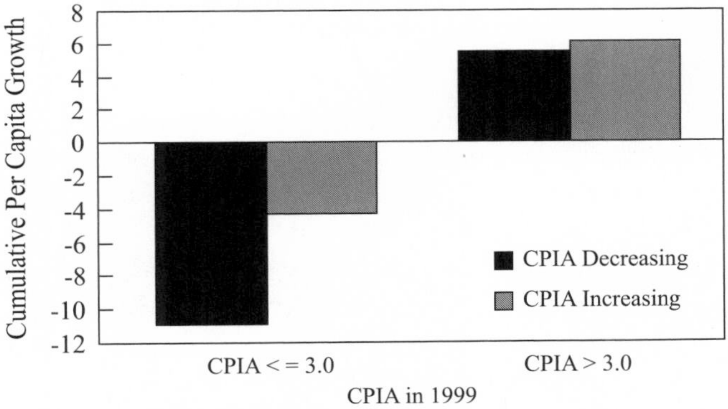

Source: World Bank (2004).

The last point that I want to make on linkages between policy and performance is that we also see the same patterns regarding poverty. During the 1990s, countries with relatively high average growth rates experienced larger reductions in poverty ratios (figure 6). So, there appears to be a poverty payoff to growth as well.

FIGURE 6
Growth is a Major Factor in Regional Poverty Reduction (1990–2000)

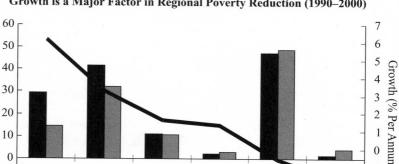

Population Living on Less than $1 a Day (1990)
Population Living on Less than $1 a Day (2000)
Real Per Capita GDP Growth (1990–2000)

Source: World Bank (2004).

What, if any, was the World Bank's contribution to these positive trends? This topic is explored more intensively in other papers in this volume, but there are four points that I would like to make regarding the Bank's role.

First and foremost, these trends clearly reflect a very large number of factors and contributions of many actors, most important, government officials who have been advancing the cause of reform for many years.

Second, one of the most important factors behind these trends in the period that we examined may have been unusually favorable initial conditions for policy reform (table 1). This table shows the countries we identified that had particularly large improvements or degradations in two or more of the four policy indicators examined. One thing that stands out among the improvers, shown on the left, is the strong representation of economies in transition. Nine of the 12 strong improvers were transition economies or 10 of the 12 if one puts Nicaragua in this category.

TABLE 1
Policy Improvement among Transition Countries

Policy Improvement	Policy Deterioration
Azerbaijan	Argentina
Brazil	Egypt
Croatia	Dominican Republic
Estonia	Lebanon
Kazakhstan	Malawi
Lithuania	Panama
Nicaragua	Trinidad & Tobago
Romania	Uruguay
Russian Federation	Zambia
Slovak Republic	Zimbabwe
Ukraine	
Yemen	

Source: World Bank (2004).

This pattern suggests that the initial conditions confronting many developing countries in the years immediately before the period examined by ARDE may have been unusually conducive to reform. During the 1990s, a number of developing countries had been or were afflicted by crises—conflicts, natural disasters, or financial crises. And, of course, we had 20 to 26 countries in Europe and Central Asia that were in various stages of transition to a market economy.

Development research suggests that crisis circumstances frequently lead to episodes of policy reform. The initial conditions for policy reform may thus have been unusually favorable in the period we examined. The group of substantial deteriorators is more diverse, but financial crisis clearly played a role in some, and there are others in the group that have long records of vacillation on policy reform.

Third, regarding the Bank's role, in addition to possibly initially favorable conditions, the data also suggest that Bank support has been a factor. Recent Bank assistance has generally been associated with countries that have been improving their policies. Of total lending in fiscal 1999–2003, 12 percent went to countries in the top quintile of 1999 CPIA ratings and 73 percent to countries that ranked above the median (figure 7).

FIGURE 7

Bank Lending Is Concentrated in Countries with Good Policy Environments (Cumulative Total Bank Lending Fiscal 1999–2003)

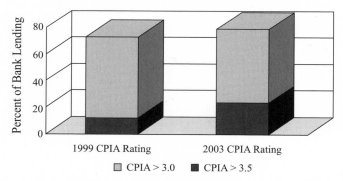

Note: Only the 134 countries with both 1999 and 2003 CPIA ratings are included.
Source: World Bank (2004).

When viewed from the perspective of the 2003 ratings, the concentration of lending on better-performing economies increased. More than 23 percent of the total was committed to countries in the top quintile, and 79 percent to countries higher than the median. This means that the Bank's lending was associated overall with countries that were, relative to others, improving their policies. This is no mean feat, given the fact that several countries in the top quintile of the 2003 ratings chose to borrow little or nothing from the Bank during this period and given the caps and other constraints not related to performance that figure into lending decisions.

Fourth, on the issue of the Bank's contribution to recent trends in developing country policies, country assistance evidence (table 2) also suggests that the Bank's assistance was associated with and contributed to improved developing country policies.

Of 16 of our most recent country evaluations, we found 13 countries where the outcomes of Bank assistance were satisfactory; 11 of these had improvements in policy, as measured by the CPIA. Outcomes of the Bank's assistance were unsatisfactory in three countries, and all three had deteriorating policies.

The full ARDE presents additional statistical and case study evidence on the Bank's contribution to policy reform in a number of countries, and some of this is, as noted earlier, reviewed in other papers in this volume.

TABLE 2
Outcomes of Bank Assistance Associated with Progress in Policy Reform

Outcome of Bank Assistance	Policy Improvement	Policy Deterioration
Moderately Satisfactory or Higher	Armenia Brazil Bulgaria China Croatia Lithuania Mongolia Russia Rwanda Tunisia Vietnam	Guatemala Dominican Republic
Moderately Unsatisfactory or Lower		Haiti Zambia Zimbabwe

Source: World Bank (2004).

Note: Based on CAEs that rate Bank assistance in 2001 or later, the mid-year of the period covered by the CPIA data used in this report.

What accounts for success? In looking behind these aggregates, ARDE finds the factors that tend to distinguish successful Bank programs from unsuccessful ones. One prominent feature of success is diversity. Good results have been obtained with very different mixes of policy approaches, instruments, and sectoral emphases. The key is finding a mix that fits the country situation. This mix frequently evolves with time as country situations change.

Another prominent feature, a corollary of diversity, is that policy-based lending is neither necessary nor sufficient for successful outcomes of Bank support to policy reform. Bank programs have contributed to reforms in a number of countries without use of policy-based lending instruments, and the Bank has made heavy use of policy-based lending in a number of instances with little or no impact on policy, as reflected in no subsequent change or deterioration, indeed, in some policy indicators.

One characteristic, however, seems to cut across successful outcomes—a strong country and sector knowledge base provided by Bank economic and sector work (ESW) and a country program that continually incorporates and adapts to emerging information.

These conclusions concerning success factors led OED to make a number of recommendations in ARDE 2003 that OED believes would strengthen the effectiveness of Bank assistance for policy reform. The overall thrust of these recommendations is to manage better the inevitable risks and uncertainties associated with policy reform.

Regarding improving a linkage between lending and actual policy reform, ARDE recommends that the Bank restrict lending to countries where Bank knowledge is weak or that have no or weak reform track records. With the exception of crisis or emergency situations, the Bank should refrain from large-scale lending until ESW has established an adequate base of country and sector knowledge to guide engagement and actual country performance indicates that policy reform is underway.

In potential "turn-around" countries, policy-based lending should be provided progressively at an equal rate with reform as the Bank's knowledge and evidence of actual country policy performance increase.

Another way in which effectiveness could be improved is through more emphasis on tailoring Bank support to country conditions. ARDE has two specific recommendations to make in this regard. One is to reduce the resources devoted to a search for generic best practices in favor of intensified efforts to customize and adapt the knowledge content of Bank support to specific local problems. The second is to do a better job of calibrating the size and terms of Bank assistance to recipients' debt-carrying capacity. The Bank's debt sustainability analysis needs to examine more critically the realism of and sensitivity to key assumptions that its strategies should adjust to systems as necessary to ensure progress toward and/or maintenance of debt sustainability.

Third, OED recommends consideration of approaches that would link development assistance, in part, to outcome-related results, as well as policy performance. This could improve management of the risk that development lending could reduce the borrower's net wealth and strengthen lender and borrower focus on achieving results.

The Bank should encourage piloting and experimentation with outcome-based lending and other approaches as ways to strengthen country leadership, ownership, and results orientation in willing countries.

References

World Bank. 2004. *2003 Annual Review of Development Effectiveness (ARDE)*. Operations Evaluation Department (OED), Washington, D.C.

Remarks on Effectiveness of Bank Support for Policy Reform

Session Chair: François Bourguignon*

Welcome to this session on "Effectiveness of Bank Support for Policy Reform." It is quite clear that the effectiveness of the Bank through both aid and policy advice is absolutely central to the general debate on what should be done to accelerate development, what should be done to reduce poverty, and what should be done to support efforts of developing countries to achieve the Millennium Development Goals.

The Operations Evaluation Department (OED) has done remarkable work to illuminate the strengths and shortcomings of the Bank's work. OED's 2003 Annual Review of Development Effectiveness (ARDE) (World Bank 2004) and similar reports regularly produced by OED are essential to maintaining our thinking on issues of development effectiveness, keeping the Bank alert and open to change, and creating greater accountability. The report provides a lucid and frank diagnosis of several of the major problems that we face today, both in the Bank as well as the development community more generally, and helps assess the effectiveness of our development efforts.

Improving the Bank's ability to identify, validate, and apply lessons from development experience is particularly important in light of concerns about aid effectiveness, an issue highlighted during the recent International Monetary Fund and World Bank Annual Meetings. Evaluating development effectiveness is extremely difficult, because one cannot rely on direct country evidence or results alone without also addressing the question of attribution. The issues raised in this report and the discussion that follows will help contribute to this important agenda.

* Senior Vice President and Chief Economist, Development Economics, World Bank Group.

Comments on Effectiveness of Bank Support for Policy Reform

*Masood Ahmed**

Thank you very much to the Operations and Evaluation Department for organizing this conference. Having gone through the report, I found that it pulls together interesting material from different sources in a way that is quite compelling. So congratulations to Andy and the team for a nice job in producing it.

I would like to take a few minutes and underscore some points that are in the report or relate to it. First, however, I want to set out a bit of an "a priori" that I have: I am increasingly coming to the view that conditionality associated with the provision of concessional finance is generally a very poor tool for trying to influence the pace or sequencing of reform. I am not at a point where I believe that conditionality is never effective as a tool for influencing policy change, and I can also accept that there are certain very limited situations in which it can be quite effective, but generally, it is a poor tool for influencing policy change.

The reason I start with this point is because it then leads to two sets of issues that are pertinent to your report:

- First, if lending and the conditionality associated with it are not a good tool for supporting policy reform, what are other instruments for supporting policy reform that work?

- Second, if the promise of future policy reform underpinned by conditionality is not effective, what then should be the basis for lending allocations?

Let me take each one in turn:

On the first set of issues—supporting policy reform—you have gone through a number of points in your report. I would like to add two that are worth developing a little further. First, the evidence is now quite strong that in persuading policymakers to adopt a different approach to the problems they face, rather than using a "first principles" analysis of what makes sense in terms of best practice, it is much more compelling to offer them more disaggregated, textured examples of how other

* Director General, Policy and International, Department for International Development.

26

countries faced with similar problems have coped with these issues and what the lessons were of those experiences.

On this point, I would like to suggest that more still needs to be done in terms of shifting the balance of work, including the balance of evaluation work, to pull together the kinds of lessons of experiments that are underway around the world in ways that enable staff from the World Bank and other agencies to share these lessons much more easily with their counterparts. The value added of the Bank and other agencies in a country situation is not to second-guess how the country works. It is to bring cross-country experience to the table that is increasingly based on what other countries are doing in a very disaggregated way, not a theoretical or "first principles" type of analysis.

The second point I would like to make on supporting policy reform is the following: one lesson I have taken away from this report and from the example of some of the colleagues in the room who have been very effective in supporting policy reform is the ability to spot windows of opportunity in the country in areas with political or other momentum building to make actual policy changes and be able to mobilize quickly and effectively the relevant knowledge that can influence those decisions.

I think this is why a decentralized country presence for the Bank is so essential, because that is how effective country directors in the field can support and take advantage of those windows of policy change—by bringing in the best and most relevant expertise to the table. It also means, however, that the Bank and the supporting structure in Washington has to be organized to mobilize effectively and respond quickly to those needs, because those windows of opportunity can sometimes be quite brief. If you do not take advantage of them in time, it is no good coming in later with a weighty document or worthy analysis that is too late to influence outcomes.

Let me turn now to the second set of issues I would like to raise: what should drive the allocation of lending if the promise of future reform underpinned by lending and conditionality is not a good basis for these decisions? I am still convinced that driving basic lending allocation decisions in terms of the relative performance of countries, measured by policies and outcomes, is the most sensible starting point.

The question one must obviously keep examining then is whether the Country Policy and Institutional Assessment (CPIA) or the International Development Association lending allocation is the best representation of the composite of policies that matter. The analysis you have done here suggests quite a good correlation between the CPIA and growth outcomes. Although I am also struck by the slide in your presentation that shows a far stronger correlation between growth and changes in the CPIA, rather than of the absolute level of the CPIA. I think that is an area to keep under review—to see whether you have got the balance right—and I know that some work is underway there.

But, there are two areas in which that basic approach might not work so well. One is in the case of fragile states that have a difficult working environment. I think part of our problem about the effectiveness of lending is driven by the lack of instruments that work in these more difficult circumstances. We are still trying to use the lending and service delivery instruments that were designed for better-performing countries to apply in countries where those environments do not exist. Not surprisingly, they do not work.

There is a lot more work to be done to try to see if there are examples of how other development assistance support instruments—projects, enclave supports, or nongovernmental delivery systems—can begin to have a better rate of return in fragile state environments. I do not believe that we can simply walk away from those environments until they get to the point where they can use the instruments we have got. We cannot let our limited toolkit drive in a dynamic sense where we are involved.

Regarding the second area in which such a basic approach might not work, there is a bit of a tension in terms of the balance between track record and a situation when there is a new government. There is growing evidence that when there is a new government, programs that they formulate, if they are quickly supported, have quite a high probability of implementation. This would lead us to minimize track record requirements for lending in those cases, because you want to support people who are trying to and have the opportunity to make a difference. At the same time, I am aware that there is a history of overoptimism in trying to spot turn-around points. So I think more work on that issue, more work on trying to see how you can effectively take advantage of the window of opportunity that new governments provide, is something that will be well worth taking forward.

In conclusion, I want to say that I am a bit uneasy with the analysis in this report on linking adjustment lending to policy reform. There is sort of an implicit discussion in there about whether adjustment lending is an effective tool for policy reform—whether it is necessary or not.

To me, these are separate issues. Lending conditionality is not an effective tool for policy reform. The value added of adjustment lending or budget support is not based on whether it does or does not accelerate policy reform. It is whether it does or does not empower governments, help to build budget systems, provide better accountability for governments in terms of their own citizens, and avoid having parallel donor projects that fragment and subvert country systems.

I think the arguments for program support are based on quite a different set of issues, and I am uneasy about trying to rationalize whether you should or should not go down that road simply in terms of whether or not that is a better way of influencing policy reforms, because I do not believe that in most cases lending conditionality has much impact on policy outcomes whether you use projects or budget support as the lending instrument.

Comments on Effectiveness of Bank Support for Policy Reform

Otaviano Canuto*

First of all, I would like to say that I share the views of the Board of Executive Directors who have a very favorable view of the work of the Operations Evaluation Department (OED) and about its positive critical contribution to the improvement of World Bank policies. I would also like to thank the organizers for this event and for the possibility of participating here.

I will have to be brief because, in fact, one of my three selected points has already been treated well by both Mr. Ahmed and Mr. Killick: the fact that we have to deepen our understanding of the meaning of country ownership of policies.

Now, it has been fully agreed that country ownership of policies and reforms is a central element for the success of any package of support by the World Bank. But, we have to keep in mind that country ownership of policies and reforms does not imply a dilution of World Bank guidance.

Although we have departed from the old, traditional view, according to which the Bank was the central figure for policy counseling, to which the countries would apply. We are fortunately nowadays far from that.

But country ownership of policies may, in fact, require an even more difficult task carried out by the Bank, which, as aptly said by my predecessors, will be to strengthen the Bank's ability to persuade policymakers.

And so, the key word is "persuasion"—to be able to convince potential policy reformers and the stakeholders involved in the process on how they should align with World Bank guidance.

For that purpose, conditionality, as such, tends to be a very poor tool. We favor the recent evolution of the view on conditionality from the old style ex ante to a more ex post view. Ex post conditionality not only gives a premium on policies that are more appropriate to country circumstances, but also improves incentives to link support to results.

---

*   Executive Director for Brazil, Colombia, Dominican Republic, Ecuador, Haiti, Panama, Philippines, Suriname, and Trinidad & Tobago, World Bank Group.

Ex post conditionality tends to maximize the alignment of World Bank support with country ownership of good policies, because it is not something that is still to be tested or to be established after Bank support. Even the IMF is moving in the direction of dealing more with ex post conditionality, rather than the old kind of ex ante conditionality.

So my first point is simple: the World Bank Group must strengthen its ability to persuade policymakers. My second and third points derive from my first:

Second, we need to complement the qualitative approaches to policy evaluation with an increasingly higher content of quantitative assessment. Of course, OED's 2003 *Annual Review of Development Effectiveness (ARDE)* (World Bank 2004) has shown us a link between support by the Bank and qualitative measures of policy, such as the Country Policy and Institutional Assessment. But we need to go a bit further. I will give you an example. We had a fantastic, beautiful, terrific experience with the Shanghai conference. It was really an amazing event, organized by the Bank—an opportunity during which policymakers around the world could get in touch with each other and know about successful micro experiences with specific projects in different parts of the world. This is part of what I personally like to call the "hummingbird" role of the World Bank Group to collect good knowledge from all around the world and bring it to other parts of the world; this is a very important fertilization role that the Bank can provide.

We have done this first step in terms of qualitative assessment and diffusion and, fortunately, one can nowadays find rich micro databases in many countries, for example, in some of the countries of my constituency: Brazil, Colombia, and the Philippines. We now have a sufficiently rich database with very micro, household information to go a step further in terms of linking policies, projects, and so on to their associated factors to extract more general results in terms of what works and what does not work. Even though country ownership and country specificities, of course, matter, which we now understand, this does not preclude or deny the fact that there are some general lessons to be extracted. Sometimes, community-driven development projects that work in Bahia in Brazil also with some minor adaptations can work in Bangladesh and the other way around. So, to be able to persuade, the Bank has to offer this more quantitatively grounded approach.

Third, to be able to persuade clients, the World Bank must become more competitive in terms of becoming more attractive as a source of funds. And that applies not only to middle-income countries where the Bank has been doing a good job in attempting to become more competitive than it has been in the past few years. But I would extend this also to low-income countries. To strengthen the World Bank Group as a multilateral channel of resources, the Bank must become increasingly attractive as a provider of services.

These two elements, more quantitative assessment of what works and making the Bank a more competitive provider of services should, in my view, be key elements of the search for strengthening the World Bank Group's ability to persuade policymakers.

Comments on Effectiveness of Bank Support for Policy Reform

Tony Killick*

I should say immediately that OED's 2003 Annual Review of Development Effectiveness (ARDE) (World Bank 2004) is a welcome breath of fresh air and further confirmation that important changes are occurring in official thinking in and around the Bank. Without going over the same ground covered by earlier speakers, I would particularly single out the following points:

- The report recognizes that the main determinants of policy choices in borrowing countries are domestic. National politics tends to dominate, so the international financial institutions (IFIs) and other donors can expect to have only limited direct influence over policy decisions. This recognition is perhaps best summarized by the report's remark (pp. 39–40) that "Although adjustment lending has played an important role in many countries that have undertaken reforms . . . its effectiveness is mainly attributable to underlying circumstances in the countries that favored reform." Note also its observation that even in pro-reform countries the Bank is likely to come undone if it seeks to insist on its own priorities.

- The report recognizes a variety of ways in which the Bank and other external agencies can support policy reform and—what I take to be its message—that old style conditionality is likely to be among the least effective of these. In particular, the Bank's intellectual and technical influence should be stressed. The report is surely right, therefore, to insist on the importance of high-quality and country-specific economic and sector work and the avoidance of "one size fits all" best practice approaches.

- The report supports, therefore, moves by the Bank toward greater flexibility in provision of financial and other support for policy reform. I was very interested to learn more about some of its new lending instruments, such as adaptable program loans.

I was also pleased to see further evidence in the report that governments that improve their economic policies tend to be rewarded by faster

---

* Senior Research Associate, Overseas Development Institute.

economic growth and other improved outcomes. There was already a lot of evidence along these lines. It follows that the crucial questions about IFI conditionality are about its efficacy rather than the overall thrust of the policies in question, although in any specific country situation, the devil is in the detail—and the detail has not always been gotten right.

I particularly welcomed the report's explicit acceptance of the tension that often exists between policy conditionality and country ownership, implying a rejection of the altogether too cozy idea of conditionality as simply "an instrument of mutual accountability." The report goes to the heart of the matter when it acknowledges that "Conditionality is often ineffective . . . because the incentive structure makes it difficult for donors to disengage when conditions are not met" (p. 20). I also agree with it that old style conditionality can be effective when it has the effect of tipping the balance within an administration in favor of reformers, but that is an argument that is easily overused and, when we ask about the sustainability of policy changes, tipping the balance is no substitute for the attainment of a broad consensus for change. As the report says (p. 9), "Meaningful policy change . . . does not happen unless a strong enough consensus for change can be forged among the various interests."

As the report recognizes, an implication of the failings of conditionality is the need for the Bank, along with other donors, to be more selective across the countries assisted. It is strong on the perils of "premature lending," and on that, the Bank—or International Development Association—is indeed becoming more selective. Of course, we know that selectivity is difficult to implement, and everyone agrees that selectivity should not mean turning our backs on peoples unfortunate enough to have governments that persist with antidevelopmental policies. But moving toward greater selectivity is surely better than relying on a way of doing business that fails to provide effective assurance that assistance will be put to welfare-enhancing use. In fact, in a possibly unguarded moment, the report (p. 4) includes the subversive thought that the pace of policy reform may have improved in recent years partly *because of reduced availability of aid*. This implies that aid deliveries that rely on the ineffectual instrument of conditionality have, in the past, offered little protection against moral hazard.

I was not asked to be a discussant—just to say how much I admire ARDE and its authors. I do have a caveat, and it is a major one. At an Operations Evaluation Department (OED) conference two years ago,

I asked, in connection with its evaluation of the heavily indebted poor country debt relief scheme, "who is listening?" I think we have to ask the same question here, albeit with a greater sense of the possibilities of improvement.

In its implications for the Bank, ARDE 2003 is actually indicating the need for some rather radical changes in the way the Bank does its business, particularly in low-income countries. Moreover, it is able to point out ways in which the Bank is already adapting: in its shift to greater selectivity and its introduction of more flexible lending instruments. It was also clear from a recent Bank conference in Paris on "Conditionality Revisited" that major changes are already occurring in thinking about this topic within the Bank proper and perhaps within the International Monetary Fund too. The focus of concern is now more to work out what might be put in the stead of a discredited conditionality.

Nevertheless, my sense on this is that there are still large battles to be fought with those who prefer the old ways and that the outcome should not be taken for granted. There are a number of issues here—innocent questions asked by someone who genuinely does not know the answers:

- To what extent have institutional incentives changed to accommodate the new thinking and guard against a situation in which department heads have an incentive to spend their budgets without asking too many questions about the quality of the lending? Also, have the internal politics of the Bank changed decisively in ways that avoid the earlier pressures for a "Christmas tree" cascading of conditionalities, with a multitude of different voices adding their own pet stipulations? Recent reductions in the number of policy conditions per adjustment program suggest that this problem may have been reduced (although the average number of stipulations remains large). If so, how was this achieved and is the process continuing?

- At a more aggregate level, there would appear to be tensions, particularly in African and other low-income regions, between the exercise of greater selectivity and the attainment of targeted total levels of new lending. Is this real, and if so, how is it being managed?

- What about individual staff incentives? Have things changed decisively since the days of the "Wapenhans Report" (World Bank 1992), which pointed out the ways in which staff incentives resulted in giving priority to new lending with seemingly impressive conditionalities, again without many questions asked about quality?

- The Paris conference on conditionality heard reports of continuing large discrepancies between the enlightenment of those in Bank headquarters who want to move toward more ownership-based approaches and those who conduct the Bank's business at the country level. This seemed to indicate so far only limited staff buy-in to the new style. To what extent is this an accurate impression? If so, what is the Bank doing about it, for example, in its training programs?

- To what extent are the major shareholders (especially the United States) in agreement with the new thinking? In earlier periods, the Executive Board of Directors was a major reason for overreliance on conditionality, insisting on getting loud conditionality bang for their bucks. Has this changed decisively? The Board's response to ARDE 2003, as summarized in the report itself (p. 93), seemed underwhelming. I certainly did not glean from it any recognition of the need for more than incremental change.

- There is a question that OED is unable to ask, but an institutionally unconstrained commentator is free to raise: what about the IMF? For a long time, it has seemed to be in denial about the problems arising from the dominance of domestic politics in determination of policy change. I know there are now those within the IMF who are working to change this, and the Paris conference heard the head of the IMF's Policy Development and Review Department say that he regarded the evidence as "overwhelming" that conditionality used as policy leverage was not effective. Nevertheless, I suspect that the IMF and its board are quite a long way behind the Bank in rethinking how best to move away from excessive reliance on conditionality as policy leverage.

This matters, not just because of the importance of the IMF as a lender to poor countries but also because of its "seal of approval" function and the extensive effective cross-conditionality between the Bank's programmatic lending and countries' standing in relation to the IMF.

As I said earlier, my sense is that things are changing in both IFIs, but there are still major battles to be won. I would like to conclude by pointing out that the stakes are high. Aid lending and giving decisions that do not heed the important lessons spelled out in the 2003 ARDE risk continuing the major waste of aid resources that resulted from trying to use financial leverage to induce policy reforms in the 1990s and, perhaps to a lesser extent, through to the present time. I hope those who are really important in these matters are in the mood to listen.

References

World Bank. 1992. *Effective Implementation: Key to Development Impact.* Washington, D.C. (also known as the Wapenhans Report).

———. 2004. *2003 Annual Review of Development Effectiveness (ARDE).* Operations Evaluation Department (OED), Washington, D.C.

Floor Discussion on Effectiveness of Bank Support for Policy Reform

AUDIENCE PARTICIPANT: I agree with Mr. Killick on the moral hazard compared with the essentially hard budget constraint model in spurring policy reform. I wonder what lessons one can take away from ARDE on the more recent proposal to give a 100 percent debt relief to all the heavily indebted poor countries?

AUDIENCE PARTICIPANT: Good Bank country assistance outcomes are associated with policy improvement. I just want to ask why is there this association? Is it that the policy environment is good and it explains why Bank lending in programs work well, or is it that Bank lending programs help create a better policy environment? Which way is the causality?

AUDIENCE PARTICIPANT: There was a comment about the importance of spotting opportunities for reform and that this could possibly be worked into criteria for changing the amounts of lending. I think this is a very interesting and important comment, and I wonder if the staffing of the World Bank is appropriate for assessing windows of opportunity for reform. Does this require just economists or a mix of economists and social scientists? And I wonder if OED has done any specific work on what has been the track record on this.

AUDIENCE PARTICIPANT: I have a question about conditionalities. Policy reform is clearly essential, and if as an IFI, we have to leave it up to the countries to do those reforms, very often they do not happen. At the same time, we know that conditions do not work if country ownership is not there. So I am wondering: is there is any in-between solution?

Mr. Killick talked about the incentive structures being such that it is very hard to disengage, which is true. But perhaps we need to think of solutions that are somewhere in between the harsh consequences of not following up on the conditions and not doing anything at all when the conditions are not being followed up on.

MR. ANDERSON: On the question regarding the direction of causation between Bank assistance and policy change, the ARDE is very careful to describe this as an association, without commenting specifically on causation in the large. I think, however, that if you delve into the stories in the country assistance evaluations, you will see a line of argumentation and evidence presented that, in my opinion, leaves you with the impression and supports the conclusion that the Bank was helpful and did contribute in some way.

I think opportunities for reform and turn-arounds do exist, but the problem with them is you really only understand them and know them well after the fact. In ex post evaluations, you are likely to find the success and the failure cases evenly divided between both. If you use the words "window of opportunity," there might actually be a lower probability of success, but that is a hypothesis.

But, certainly, we do observe these things, and the Bank as the institution has an obligation to try to be helpful. The question is what can we do to improve our ability to judge turn-around situations? Will decentralization help? Will having a different staff mix improve diagnosis of subtle political economy trends? Maybe, but the predictive power of political analysis is not great, just watching the inherent uncertainties that Bangladeshi Minister M. Saifur Rahman described earlier of policy reform.

On turn-around, it certainly is true that newly elected governments have better implementation records than ones that are not newly elected, but track record is also a very important predictor of better outcomes.

MR. AHMED: I will just pick up on one point, which is the issue of what you do in a turn-around situation. There is no doubt that track record matters, because that is from where the new government is starting. But the track record is in the past. So the question at any time is whether looking forward matters? Is there a probability that if a new government comes in trying to change things that they are more likely to succeed, and what should the Bank do about it?

I also want to say, in that context, that it is not obvious that seizing windows of opportunity is about providing money. The most effective ways in which good country directors have taken advantage of windows of opportunity for reform is by mobilizing the right information and the right cross-country evidence that enables policymakers to make the most informed choice and to influence those choices. Often at that point, it does not require coming in with additional funding.

And the most important thing for me is that, increasingly, the Bank has to think about lending allocation decisions as being separate from the nature and focus of the policy advisory work and how it is best delivered.

MR. KILLICK: Just on the question that was raised about selectivity compared with debt relief, I think the crucial question is whether the money for debt relief is additional to what will be forthcoming as regular development assistance?

The earlier evidence suggests that it has not been additional, and in those situations there is obviously an opportunity cost between using it for debt relief or using it for other forms of development assistance. It seems to me, on that basis, that because there is a correlation between poor past policies and indebtedness, allocating aid according to indebtedness is a pretty bad idea.

If you want to see the arguments against further extending debt relief as a form of using aid, read the OED report of two years ago on this subject (World Bank 2003). Of course, the latest version of debt relief when it finally emerges may not replicate the many deficiencies of the existing arrangements, and redesign will be really important. But, basically, I fear that as it is now being discussed, the extension of debt relief is a pretty bad idea.

MR. CANUTO: I will touch on the direction of causality issue. It is, of course, from the analytical standpoint a very interesting question; but in terms of policy support, it matters less. What matters, in fact, is that good policies receive the kind of incentives—positive incentives—that the Bank can provide. If the link is because of the Bank or because of the countries, it matters less.

In terms of windows of opportunity for reform, this is, of course, one of those realms in which political economy usually prevails. And certainly, it is mostly the country that has something to say in that respect, not the Bank.

To conclude, let me pick up on a point that comes out clearly from the report and the discussion about the need to have a better information set to use when we evaluate policies—when we evaluate our actions. It is important to have this information set for various reasons. First, it is always interesting to know what works, what does not work, or what works better or worse than other solutions. But it is also extremely important in terms of incentives. It is part of the incentives to be able to analyze the result or the outcome of a specific project or policy reform in light of other experiences and what we know about this reform in other circumstances in other countries. And it is always much better to approach a government with a catalog of things that have been done elsewhere—have been properly evaluated or at least evaluated in the best way possible in other countries under other circumstances—to tell those actors that this is what we know. This is the kind of catalog from which you can choose; these are the kinds of combinations of policies or kinds of designs of a project from which you can choose.

With this kind of information at hand, things are becoming very different in terms of the effectiveness of our actions. This kind of analysis was started in the field of specific projects—micro-oriented projects. But it is also important to have the same kind of approach in more macro-oriented programs, more macro-oriented policy reforms. We totally agree that it is difficult, but we must make the effort, and we must make sure that, at the time the advice of the Bank or the international development community spills over into the country, somebody is trying to make sure that we have all the information on the precise experience of the country and the impact of that particular policy reform has been in terms of results. This is extremely important, and I believe that as a community we can set this as a goal for the future.

References

World Bank. 2003. *Debt Relief for the Poorest: An OED Review of the HIPC Initiative.* Report No. 25160. Operations Evaluation Department, Washington, D.C.
———. 2004. *2003 Annual Review of Development Effectiveness (ARDE).* Operations Evaluation Department, Washington, D.C.

Part 3

Lessons from Country Program Evaluations

Lessons from Country Program Evaluations[†]

R. Kyle Peters[*]

The World Bank's Operations Evaluation Department (OED) began evaluating Bank country assistance programs in fiscal 1995. These country assistance evaluations (CAEs) assess how well Bank assistance programs have met their objectives within an extended period, normally a decade.[1] By the end of fiscal 2004, OED had issued CAEs assessing the impact of Bank assistance to 58 countries.[2] These evaluations cover roughly 41 percent of borrowers and 65 percent of total net commitments. This note summarizes some preliminary findings and lessons from the 25 CAEs completed in fiscal 2001–03, but also includes some insights gained from the additional eight CAEs completed during fiscal

---

[†] This paper is excerpted from the "Country Assistance Evaluation (CAE) Retrospective," (World Bank 2005), which was prepared by Poonam Gupta, Chandra Pant, Kyle Peters, and Rene Vandendries in OEDCR. Individual country assistance evaluations can be found on the OED website at http://www.worldbank.org/oed/ (publications).

[*] Senior Manager, Country Evaluation and Regional Relations, Operations Evaluation Department, World Bank Group.

2004.[3] The first section presents overall findings and lessons for development extracted from CAEs. The second section reports on nine major lessons specifically for the Bank. Three of these are general lessons, emphasizing the importance of government ownership and political economy considerations, the role of institution building, and the interdependencies in reform efforts. Three other lessons have implications for Bank instruments: one each for economic and sector work (ESW), investment/technical assistance (TA) lending, and adjustment lending. The last three lessons relate to strategy formulation by the Bank and its response to downside risks and turn-arounds in country situations.

Findings

This CAE retrospective draws primarily on the findings and lessons generated from 25 CAEs completed during fiscal 2001–03. The group of 25 CAEs produced during this period is clearly not a random or rep-

TABLE 1
Characteristics of the 25 Countries with CAEs

A.	Income level		B.	IBRD, IDA, or Blend	
	Low	10		IBRD	14
	Lower middle	12		IDA	8
	Upper middle	3		Blend	2
		25			24[a]
C.	Post conflict or not		D.	CPIA level	
	Yes	4		Above average	13
	No	21		Below average	11
		25			24[b]
E.	Region		F.	OED outcome ratings	
	Africa	12		Highly Sat.	2
	EAP	2		Sat.	9
	SA	1		Mod. Sat.	8
	ECA	5		Mod. Unsat .	3
	MNA	3		Unsat.	9
	LAC	2			31[c]
		25			

a. For West Bank and Gaza, the financing comes through a World Bank Trust Fund and is on IDA or grant terms.

b. No CPIA for West Bank and Gaza.

c. Four countries received different ratings for subperiods.

Source: World Bank (2005).

resentative sample. CAE countries are selected based on several factors. The most important factor is the timing of the Bank's next country assistance strategy (CAS), but other factors are also considered, for example, OED's ability to collaborate with other international financial institutions,[4] regional balance, and whether a previous CAE had already covered a country. So, although the group of countries cannot be called a sample of Bank borrowers, these 25 CAEs do constitute a reasonable basis for this "findings and lessons" discussion (table 1). There is a good mix of low- and middle-income countries and of International Bank for Reconstruction and Development (IBRD) and International Development Association (IDA) borrowers, and all regions are covered. In addition, four post-conflict countries are included. But, the coverage of Latin American and South and East Asian countries is small, primarily because evaluations of countries in these regions were fairly complete before fiscal 2001. The sample also contains a good mix of countries with outcome ratings that were satisfactory (about three-fifths) and unsatisfactory (about two-fifths). It is also fairly evenly divided between good performers and weak performers, as measured by the Bank's Country Policy and Institutional Assessment (CPIA) rating. As noted in OED's *2003 Annual Review of Development Effectiveness (ARDE)* (World Bank 2004), a positive correlation exists between CAE outcome ratings and policy performance.[5]

TABLE 2
CAE and Project Outcome Ratings

Country Portfolio Outcomes	CAE Outcome Ratings	
	Percent Satisfactory	Percent Unsatisfactory
Satisfactory	53	33
Unsatisfactory	7	7

Source: World Bank Database.

CAE outcome ratings can deviate from the aggregate performance of project outcomes. In about a third of the CAEs, the outcome rating of the country assistance strategy was unsatisfactory, but the aggregation of project outcomes in a country during the CAE period was satisfactory (table 2). This is not surprising; the CAE is a comprehensive evaluation of the Bank's program in a country that comprises projects, as well as analytical and advisory services. Moreover, CAEs must make an assessment of overall Bank strategy, including the size, sectoral composition, and type of lending; thus, the CAE outcome may be unsatisfactory if, for example, there are critical omissions in the Bank's overall assistance strategy, even if the outcomes of individual projects are rated satisfactory.

CAEs found that Bank programs were more successful in education and health than in other sectors, and least successful in private sector development, rural development, and social protection (table 3). These results are also largely reflected in aggregate project ratings for the same set of 25 CAEs (table 3). The only divergences between sectoral ratings in CAEs and project outcome ratings were in the case of private sector development (PSD), rural development, and public sector management (PSM), where the relatively unfavorable outcomes in CAEs contrast with the high proportion of satisfactory outcomes at the project level.

TABLE 3
Sectoral and Project Ratings for FY01–03 CAEs

	Project Outcomes % Sat*	CAE Sector Outcome Ratings (%)**			
		Satisfactory	Unsatisfactory	Mixed	Not Assessed
Education	100.0	48	8	4	40
Health	86.5	40	20	8	32
Social Protection	37.9	12	24	20	44
Environment	25.5	16	16	24	44
Rural	87.2	12	36	28	24
Financial Sector	81.6	24	16	32	28
Infrastructure	87.7	36	16	24	24
Public Sector	99.9	24	32	28	16
Private Sector Development	60.1	12	24	44	20

*   This is the percentage of satisfactory project outcomes by sector (commitment value) for the countries where CAEs were completed during FY01–03.

** These columns are ratings by CAE task managers and a desk review of CAEs of the outcomes by sectors. In most case, explicit ratings by sectors were not included in the CAEs and thus, these ratings should be treated as indicative only.

Source: World Bank Database and OED staff estimates.

The relative success at the project level and lack of it at the sector level in the case of PSD, rural development, or PSM could reflect several factors:

First, the political economy of reforms in these sectors is more problematic, and opposition from potential losers and vested interests is likely to be more focused and sustained. Individual projects may be successfully implemented, but it will take a longer and more sustained effort to overcome political opposition and achieve successful outcomes at the macro level.[6]

Second, even if there was no strong political opposition, these areas are crucially dependent on institutional reforms and capacity building, which take time and are not always captured even in the relatively longer time frame of the CAE. For example, private sector development depends on an effective judicial and court system, which takes time to develop. Civil service reform takes time to implement, and the results take even longer to materialize; thus, successful outcomes at the sector level will take time to materialize.

Third, outcomes in these areas depend more on economywide developments and exogenous factors; thus, the growth of the private sector depends not just on the legal and regulatory framework for private sector development, but also on progress in other areas of economic policy, such as macroeconomic stabilization, infrastructure, and financial sector. Noneconomic conditions within the country, such as law and order, and external events, such as prevailing market sentiment in the region, also play a major role in PSD. Rural development and reforms in the public sector are also influenced significantly by economywide developments.[7]

Lessons

Lesson One: An understanding of the political economy of reforms, including government's commitment and ownership of reforms and the degree of political support or opposition to them, is essential for developing realistic country assistance strategies, specific assistance programs and projects, and analysis of risks.

Often economic reforms failed, either because the government was not committed to them or because the government underestimated opposition to reforms and was unable to carry them through. An insufficient understanding of the political economy of reforms and the nature of the state may have led the Bank in some cases to push reforms that stood little chance of success. For example, in Zimbabwe, one of the principal motivations behind the government's economic and social policy was to ensure indigenous ownership of productive assets. A proper appreciation for the importance of this issue might have led the Bank to give priority to land reforms. The government's reluctance to undertake parastatal and civil service reform would also have been better understood. Privatization and civil service reforms in Peru are threatened by opposition from the middle class. Their opposition could have been lessened by a different sequencing of reforms and social protection measures to mitigate the adverse consequences of privatization and civil service reforms.

Lesson two: Institutional reforms and capacity building for effective governance are critical to successful outcomes. Because capacity building takes time, these reforms need to start early and be followed through for several years.

Institutional development is at the core of development effectiveness.[8] Successful reform outcomes are often undermined by weak institutions or the absence of important institutional arrangements. For example, in the transition economies of Central and Eastern Europe and the former Soviet Union, the existing institutions were not designed for a market economy. As the command economy collapsed and market-oriented reforms were implemented, the right institutions emerged only after a lag, preventing the full benefits of reforms from emerging.[9] Institutional reform goes beyond changing organizational structures and rules; it also involves the discarding of long-established habits and patterns of behavior—a complicated and lengthy process. Major institutional changes may have to be spread across several years.[10]

Lesson three: Successful outcomes from reforms in a sector often depend on complementary reforms and success in other sectors. The sequencing and packaging of reforms need to take account of this complementarity.

Several CAEs noted that more successful outcomes could have been achieved had more attention been given to the complementarity of reforms in different sectors. Private sector development cannot be assured simply through privatization. It depends as well on reform of the public sector through deregulation, changes in taxation policy and administration, anticorruption reforms, and so on. For example, in Mongolia, important measures were implemented to promote PSD (such as enabling private property, removal of price and margin controls, reduction in trade barriers, simplification of tax regime, and improved framework for foreign investment), but not enough was done to lighten the heavy hand of the state on the economy. Inefficient government regulatory and oversight functions continued to hamper PSD. And as several CAEs noted, the growth of the private sector depends very much on an effective judiciary and court system. Other experience showed that the effectiveness of financial sector reforms in improving financial intermediation depended critically on reforms in the enterprise and public sectors.[11]

Lesson four: ESW must be timely, of good quality, and be fully integrated into the design of Bank strategy and programs and projects. Timely ESW is particularly important for first time or renewed borrowers and for "stop-go" reformers.

ESW can play an important role in developing the Bank's assistance strategy and in enhancing its effectiveness. Two-thirds of the CAEs that reported favorable outcomes also reported that the ESW was timely. The same CAEs reported unfavorable outcomes when the ESW was not timely. In Brazil, timely ESW helped the Bank to direct lending toward education, health, and rural poverty projects in the Northeast with maximum impact on poverty reduction. And in Vietnam, ESW demonstrated that rural poverty was strongly associated with inadequate economic infrastructure, helping orient the Bank's lending program toward economic infrastructure. Examples of less satisfactory contributions of ESW include the case of Kazakhstan, where a social protection project sought to mitigate the social impact of privatization by strengthening the institutional capacity of unemployment services to streamline procedures for registration and payment of unemployment benefits. The poverty assessment that came two years later, however, showed that policies to facilitate labor mobility and equip workers for changed circumstances were required, rather than strengthening the capacity of unemployment services. In Bulgaria, a timely poverty assessment might have enabled a social protection loan to address more effectively the targeting of social assistance to the needy.

In a few countries, ESW was timely and of high quality, but findings were either not fully taken into consideration in designing the strategy or used selectively, thus reducing their relevance and effectiveness. For example, in Jordan, Bank lending during the 1990s did not address the high level of government expenditures, despite analytical work identifying how these expenditures could be reduced and better targeted. In Peru, the Financial Sector Reform Loan (fiscal 1999) did not address fundamental problems in the sector, which had been correctly identified in an ongoing assessment of the financial sector.

ESW can build a good knowledge base and help the Bank engage the government in its policy dialogue. It can also assist the government to understand the costs and benefits of reforms and help design its reform program. The long-term impact of ESW should also be borne in mind, as it initiates debate on policy issues and serves to familiarize civil society with reform issues. But it goes without saying that ESW cannot catalyze policy change when governments lack commitment to reform.

Lesson five: Specific investment and technical assistance loans can be useful vehicles for promoting institutional reforms, but for benefits to be sustainable these operations should be part of a broader macro-stabilization and economic reform strategy.

About 22 of the 25 CAEs provide strong evidence of the role of specific investment lending and technical assistance loans in promoting institutional development in both low- and middle-income countries.[12] Twenty of these countries also received adjustment loans. In many countries, specific technical assistance and institution-building loans were linked closely to adjustment loans, helping build capacity to formulate and implement policy changes supported in adjustment loans. Strong government commitment and clearly articulated priorities remained a key factor in the effectiveness of these instruments in promoting institutional development. In this environment, the longer time frame of investment loans allowed the Bank to build relationships with counterparts and to combine advice with financial assistance, especially to sector ministries. Conversely, when strong and sustained government commitment to institutional reform is absent, Bank assistance is not likely to be successful.[13]

Lesson six: Adjustment lending in the absence of sustained progress on reforms only saddles the country with additional unproductive debt and can weaken the incentives for reforms in the future.

Adjustment lending can be successful, especially when combined with a strong government commitment to macrostabilization and structural reform; however, the Bank should resist pressures to persist with adjustment lending in the absence of the government's commitment to and a satisfactory track record in implementing reforms. The rationale for adjustment loans was to provide financing to alleviate the cost of adjustment that occurred when structural reforms were implemented; however, the review of CAEs for this retrospective showed that adjustment lending was appropriately delayed in only two countries (Bulgaria and Brazil) when reforms stalled. But in as many as seven other countries, the Bank went ahead with adjustment loans, even though little progress was being made toward the Bank's assistance objectives and corporate goals.[14] In these countries, there were pressures to lend for a variety of reasons: exploit a unique "window of opportunity" (Kenya), show support for the government (Morocco), maintain relationships (Zimbabwe), avert a potential crisis (Peru), avoid a return to communism (Russia), and prevent negative net flows (Zambia). Although these factors may well have influenced the Bank, there is little doubt that in some of these countries, the pressure to reform may have been further diluted by the Bank's decision to lend, saddling these countries with unproductive debt.[15]

Lesson seven: Thorough, hard-headed, and realistic risk analysis is important to increase the realism of country strategies.

The Bank needs to be more realistic and hard headed in its country assessments and country strategy formulations, including assessing borrower commitment to reforms and implementation capacity, receptiveness to Bank advice, and the impact of reforms on growth and poverty alleviation. Consistent errors of overoptimism on the part of the Bank regarding borrower receptiveness to Bank advice, its willingness to undertake difficult reforms, and the government's capacity to implement reforms plagued Bank strategies in many of the countries evaluated (Zimbabwe, Kenya, Paraguay, Haiti, Zambia, Kyrgyz Republic, Peru, Jordan, Kazakhstan, Lesotho, and Morocco). This optimism often persisted in the face of contrary evidence[16] and contributed to lending decisions by the Bank that failed to meet their objectives.[17]

Country assistance strategies in many countries assumed a much stronger growth performance than warranted by past country experience or experience of other countries facing similar constraints and prospects. Evaluations pointed to unrealistic growth projections in several countries (Zambia, Kazakhstan, Jordan, and Kyrgyz Republic). Unrealistic growth estimates contributed to inappropriate Bank assistance strategies and entailed real costs for the country. Had growth estimates been realistic, the Bank would have likely concentrated more analytical work on the sources and constraints to growth, as well as on poverty reduction measures. Realistic growth projections would also have more clearly illustrated debt sustainability issues, and greater efforts would have been made to seek debt relief or other forms of concessional financial assistance in order not to impose too high a burden of external debt on the country;[18] countries may also have been persuaded to undertake deeper reforms to accelerate economic growth.

Lesson eight: The Bank should be more prepared to reduce the level of planned assistance when faced with clear evidence of policy slippages.

In addition to identifying risks, the Bank needs to be prepared to modify its assistance program to reflect wavering government commitment or policy slippages. A positive example is Bulgaria in the mid-1990s, where lending was scaled down and a major adjustment loan was put on hold in the face of rising macroeconomic risks and a lack of government commitment to address reform issues. But, the review of CAEs suggests this did not happen in a number of cases. In Peru the Bank's program did not contain triggers to reduce lending if risks materialized. In Kenya the 1998 strategy also recognized risks and the program contained CAS benchmarks, but the Bank did not follow through when the benchmarks were not met.

Lesson nine: The Bank should be prudent in turn-around situations. Realistic country assessments, rather than wishful thinking, should inform its assistance strategy in turn-around situations.

The Bank typically has difficulty in identifying "turning points" and calibrating its response to changing country conditions. It tends to react slowly to deterioration and too quickly to improvements.[19] To overcome this, the Bank needs to keep its ears closer to the ground through its resident missions, its contacts with civil society, and relevant ESW, including a better understanding of the political economy. As far as possible government commitment should be assessed on the basis of its track record in implementing reforms, not declarations of intent. Levels of assistance should be initially prudent and calibrated to measurable outcomes and meeting concrete benchmarks. This is especially the case in situations with long-standing issues of implementation failures. Kenya and Zimbabwe in the late 1990s are prominent examples.

ATTACHMENT A

Completed Country Assistance Evaluations, Fiscal 1995–2004

1995 (1)	1996 (2)	1997 (2)	1998 (10)	1999* (12)	2000 (10)	2001 (8)	2002 (9)	2003 (8)	2004 (8)
Ghana	Argentina	Morocco	Albania	Azerbaijan	Argentina	Paraguay	West Bank & Gaza	Peru	Tunisia
	Zambia	Poland	Bangladesh	Cambodia	Burkina Faso	Kazakhstan	Lesotho	Zambia	Bhutan
			Bolivia	Croatia	Cameroon	Morocco	Chile	Eritrea	China
			Côte d'Ivoire	Ecuador	Costa Rica	India	Vietnam	Zimbabwe	Bosnia
			Kenya	Ethiopia	Egypt	Kenya	Haiti	Lithuania	Armenia
			Malawi	Indonesia	Ghana	Kyrgyz	Bulgaria	Brazil	Moldova
			Mozambique	Jamaica	Papua New Guinea	Mexico	Mongolia	Dom.Rep.	Croatia
			Philippines	Maldives	Tanzania	El Salvador	Russia	Jordan	Rwanda
			Thailand	Nepal	Uganda		Guatemala		
			Togo	Sri Lanka	Uruguay				
				Ukraine					
				Yemen					

*A Country Assistance Note for Honduras was prepared in fiscal 1999, but was converted to a Fast Track Brief following Hurricane Mitch.

Note: The shaded area represents the 25 CAEs that were reviewed in preparing the CAE Retrospective.

Source: World Bank Database.

Notes

1. For a brief discussion of the methodology for CAEs, see http://www.worldbank. org/oed/oed_cae_methodology.html.
2. See attachment A for a complete list of completed country assistance evaluations.
3. OED has distilled lessons from CAEs in the past. The *Annual Review of Development Effectiveness (ARDE)* distills lessons from the most recent CAEs completed at the time of the ARDE. In 2002, lessons for four African countries were discussed in a workshop organized by the Africa Region. In the same year, OED prepared a note on lessons for low-income countries under stress (LICUS) and LICUS-like countries for the Committee on Development Effectiveness (CODE). In 2003, lessons from evaluations in transition economies were synthesized for OED's transition economies study.
4. In the sample of 25 countries, one CAE was jointly undertaken with the African Development Bank (Lesotho), one with the Islamic Development Bank (Jordan), and one in parallel with the Inter-American Development Bank (Peru).
5. See World Bank (2004), page 15.
6. For example, in transition economies, the historical antipathy to private business on the part of the nomenclature had strong ideological roots and is not easily overcome. Despite legal and regulatory reforms, there remains an ingrained bias against private business in many of these countries. In the less developed economies of Asia, Africa, and Latin America, major rural development initiatives often involves conflict of interest among powerful groups (big farmers versus laborers, rural dwellers versus urban population) that takes time and political acumen to resolve.
7. This is not to say that outcomes in other sectors do not depend to some extent on such factors. It is a matter of degree.
8. One measure of the importance of institutions for development effectiveness is that stronger institutions are associated with a 20 percentage point increase in the likelihood of a project's outcome being rated satisfactory (see World Bank 1999).
9. For example, in many of these countries macroeconomic stabilization was undermined because of poor revenue collection reflecting weaknesses in tax and customs administration. Financial intermediation suffered, because it took time to develop an efficient payment system and newly privatized banks lacked capacity to make commercial credit decisions. Central banks lack capacity to regulate banks. Private sector development is hampered because the judiciary and courts system is often incapable of implementing key legislation for private sector development, including private property rights, creditor rights, bankruptcy legislation, antimonopoly laws, and so on.
10. The Bank has developed several new instruments, adjustable program loans, learning and innovation loans, and programmatic adjustment loans to support reforms involving a long learning process, which seem to be well suited to the situation in some economies.
11. For example, experience shows that as long as enterprises are being bailed out by the public sector (through explicit or implicit subsidies and build up of tax arrears), they have less incentive to borrow from banks. On the supply side, banks are reluctant to lend to enterprises that survive only because they are subsidized by the public sector. Either way, financial intermediation is stunted.
12. Examples included *(a)* strengthening of state secretariats of education, implementation of information and evaluation systems for primary education, and implementation of minimum operational standards in all schools in Brazil, *(b)* develop-

ment of a legal and regulatory framework, exploration and development rights, and environmental regulations in Peru, *(c)* introduction of a performance-based private management contract for water supply in Jordan, *(d)* strengthening of the General Directorate of Roads in Guatemala, *(e)* capacity improvements in the Ministry of Finance and the central bank in Mongolia, *(f)* development of administrative capacity to adjust utilities' tariffs, enforce cash collections, and monitor performance in Russia, and *(g)* strengthening of the Ministry of Agriculture in Zambia.

13. Bank interventions in Brazil, for example, in health, education, and infrastructure were relatively successful, because the government defined primary education, health, and infrastructure as clear development priorities. On the other hand, in Morocco, the government had not yet established clear priorities or an agenda for implementation in education. Two education projects, which closed in recent years, had unsatisfactory outcomes and negligible institutional impact.

14. OED's IDA review and 2003 ARDE, however, found that the link between countries' policy and institutional performance and lending levels has been strengthened. According to the 2001 adjustment lending retrospective, in the past few years, most—but not all—adjustment lending has gone to countries with above-average policy performance for sectors where there was a track record of progress (World Bank 2001).

15. In Zambia, withholding disbursements until preconditions for the Bank's "high case" scenario were being met would likely have forced issues of governance, structural reform, and debt forgiveness to the forefront at an earlier stage. In Zimbabwe, a Bank stance in 1997–2000 rooted in implementation of reforms, rather than mere expressions of good intentions, would have sent a strong message to the Zimbabwean leadership. In Russia, although the Bank's shift to policy-based lending in 1996–97 was to address systemic reform issues, the message sent to the Russian authorities was that geopolitical considerations would keep the international community's funding window open, regardless of missteps and hesitation in adopting the reform agenda.

16. For example, in Paraguay, the Bank's strategy in 1993 was too optimistic about the potential for reform and country implementation capacity, given Paraguay's poor track record in these areas. In Zimbabwe, strategies overestimated government receptiveness and willingness to undertake parastatal and civil service reforms. In Haiti, the 1996 strategy did not adequately recognize the risks posed to achievement of objectives from unresolved political and governance issues. In Lesotho, despite its experience with the 1993 elections, the Bank was too optimistic in assuming that democratization and stability could be accomplished shortly after the May 1998 elections. As a result, the Bank's assistance strategy did not include contingency plans in the event the democratization process fell apart, as it did.

17. In Kenya, for instance, the appointment of a Change Team in July 1999 and initiation of long-standing economic governance and policy reforms were rewarded with an adjustment loan when conditions for such support as specified in the 1998 country strategy were only partially met. In Zambia, overoptimism led to less results-oriented or vaguely worded conditions in adjustment lending. In Morocco, the Bank provided a policy reform support loan in the late 1990s as a way of rewarding the country's movement toward a more open political system and commitment to reform. The loan was too unfocused to have a major impact on any of the critical reform areas identified in the country strategy. Many of the actions taken before Board presentation were first steps, sometimes in the form of studies or plans, and many others did not show concrete results.

18. OED's heavily indebted poor country evaluation (World Bank, 2003) found that unrealistic growth projections led to debt problems.
19. In the Dominican Republic, the Bank failed to recognize an upturn during fiscal 1992–95 and failed to support the government during a crucial period of successful economic reform. This mistake cost the Bank its influence in the country. The Bank failed to recognize the downturn in Peru in 1997 and continued the support it was rendering earlier when reforms were implemented. In Kenya, initial steps toward reforms in mid-2000 were prematurely identified as an upturn and rewarded with increased lending; in the event reforms remained stalled.

References

World Bank. 1999. *1998 Annual Review of Development Effectiveness*. Report No. 20180. Operations Evaluation Department, Washington, D.C.

———. 2001. *Adjustment Lending Retrospective*. Operations Policy and Country Services Working Paper, Washington, D.C.

———. 2003. *Debt Relief for the Poorest: An OED Review of the HIPC Initiative*. Report No. 25160. Operations Evaluation Department, Washington, D.C.

———. 2004. *2003 Annual Review of Development Effectiveness*. Operations Evaluation Department (OED), Washington, D.C.

———. 2005. Country Assistance Evaluation (CAE) Retrospective: OED Self-Evaluation. Operations Evaluation Department (OED), Washington, D.C.

Comments on Country Program Evaluations

*Willem Buiter**

A lot can be learned by watching the World Bank at work in its programs in 27 countries in Central Europe and the former Soviet Union and from this very systematic evaluation of World Bank programs in the region.

Let me first point out that the European Bank for Reconstruction and Development (EBRD) only undertakes project lending. It does not provide programmatic or policy lending. Also, about 75 percent of its lending and financial activities involve the private sector. The remainder is with sovereign or subsovereign states.

On the effectiveness of conditionality, the shortcomings of traditional forms of World Bank and, even more so, International Monetary Fund (IMF) conditionality are now well known, even though it is not clear what to do about it.

One of the adverse incentive effects from aid is a poor policy environment. Aid becomes an excuse for a failure, rather than incentive to reform. The same applies to debt forgiveness. If one cannot differentiate between bad luck debt and bad policy debt, using indebtedness as a criterion for debt forgiveness creates serious adverse incentive effects, regardless of whether the money is additional or not. Even if the money is additional, an incentive effect exists. So it is important to target aid, and targeting on existing debt is not sensible.

There is the inherent problem of coordination among donors: multilateral and bilateral agencies. Harmonization is an attempt to address the problem, but there still is a long way to go. The burden imposed by the bilateral and multilateral agencies, which may make different, often conflicting demands on the poorest countries, which have limited implementation capacity, is still unacceptable, despite recognition of the problem and progress on its solution.

In the transition countries, the record of policy conditionality is questionable, including EBRD's sovereign project loans. Performance criteria for fiscal aggregates tend to be mixed in countries with weak revenue systems. The transition countries are exposed to frequent shocks; as a result, structural benchmarks are also often missed, either because

---

*   Chief Economist, European Bank for Reconstruction and Development.

the macroeconomic program is off track or because insufficient revenue undermines the implementation capacity for the reforms.

The EBRD's experience in private sector project conditionality has been better, although things can still go wrong. Even meritorious projects, such as small and medium enterprise microcredit lines through local participating banks, can lead to misdirection and misappropriation of funds, unless a commercially oriented banking sector free of public sector pressures and an independent regulatory and supervisory framework exist. So it is easy to do more harm than good, if we are not careful.

But, on the whole, experience with the private sector has been better. Commercial conditionalities in contracts are more easily understood. These conditionalities are based on a simple business logic, which tends to be quite effective.

Transition conditionality or development conditionality is harder to do, but tends to work if it is front loaded and if financial incentives encourage compliance. So, financial incentives—such as step-ups in interest rates if certain targets or monitorable benchmarks are not met, or nondisbursement of later tranches—do work, but they need to be applied consistently.

More severe options, such as calling loans or putting the equity to the sponsor for nonfulfillment of transition conditionality, do not work. So it is better not to threaten their use.

Country ownership, which is not a favorite term of mine, seems to imply that something is approved and supported by a small number of people who own the country, and that is not what we are after.

The new trend among international financial institutions (IFIs) and to some extent bilateral donors is toward programmatic budget support. There are obvious benefits if it means buying into a nationally drafted and nationally supported strategy, which is widely supported throughout society and rewards existing and past policies as an indicator of possible future success and as a selection device.

The poverty reduction strategy paper (PRSP) process is such a process that tries to foster a national strategy. But, the jury is still out on the effectiveness of these programs. There are ten PRSPs in transition countries, but they have only been in effect for, at most, three years. And, many are now being revised, so it is too early to come to any firm conclusions.

There is some important work on budget management reform supported by the World Bank and bilaterals, which is ongoing as part of the

PRSP process. But the priorities that derive from a participatory process are questionable when no tradition of legislative checks and balances, civic engagement, or private sector dialogue with official bodies exists. In this situation, a participatory PRSP process may still not come up with sensible policies and programs.

Moreover, it is apparent that whatever priorities are set in the PRSP, the allocations in the national budget are often different. It is also hard to match actual financial allocations to policies in countries with poor budget management systems or inadequate systems of financial and/or political accountability.

Furthermore, channeling loans or grants of fiscal institutions is always highly risky in any country, be it in the European Union or Sub-Saharan Africa. So, it is something that must be monitored carefully.

In conclusion, I would like to make two brief points. First, information and knowledge are among the most important products our institutions provide. Technical cooperation or technical assistance funds are often immensely valuable. Some very positive achievements have been accomplished through these activities with participating banks in creating the knowledge base for self-sustaining SME lending efforts.

It is also very important that countries at all stages of regulatory reform benefit if they can engage with international standard-setting bodies. There is a role for the rest of the world even if policies are country owned. International standard-setting bodies can be agencies of restraint, as Paul Collier noted, setting broadly recognized standards, while limiting the scope for poorly conceived domestic policies. This was apparent in the case of European Union accession for the Central European countries. The adoption of the regulatory and legal framework of the accession was, with the notable exception of the common agricultural policy, extremely beneficial for these countries.

This was also true, to some extent, with the process of World Trade Organization (WTO) accession in Georgia, Moldova, and the Kyrgyz Republic. WTO membership conditionality has been very beneficial.

My second point is that the EBRD has another form of conditionality that is not present at the World Bank or other IFIs. This is political conditionality. EBRD has a political mandate that directs it to operate in countries committed to multiparty democracy, open societies, and human rights. This limits EBRD's ability to do business in a country when its government is inept, incompetent, corrupt, or repressive. As a result, EBRD no longer works with the public sector in three countries—Belarus, Turkmenistan, and Uzbekistan—although, it still works with the private sector in these countries. But, much of the private sector is adversely affected by failures in state and private sector reform. So, if the mandate is taken seriously, one ends up doing less business than one could. Stopping doing business is the ultimate form of conditionality, but it is the conditionality of impotence.

Our institutions can collectively do better, especially in those countries where the institutional and political climate favors reform; in this way, we can help reduce poverty.

Comments on Country Program Evaluations

*Ishrat Husain**

The Operations Evaluation Department (OED) has done all of us a great service by carrying out evaluations of Bank country programs in a systematic manner using a common framework. The findings of these studies should be of value not only to the Bank's own operational staff, but also to the economic managers of the client countries. As someone who has had the good fortune of working on both sides of the table, I would like to share some of my thoughts with you on the findings of these studies.

First, I find myself in agreement with some of the conclusions of the 2003 ARDE (World Bank 2004) in at least three broad areas:

• Aid is neither necessary nor sufficient for good policy. Aid can complement and catalyze the political and administrative processes by fostering and reinforcing the development of ownership, but aid in itself is no substitute for ownership.

• Conditionality in itself is ineffective in linking aid with reform, because the incentive structure makes it difficult for donors to disengage when conditions are not met. The donors should avoid micromanagement and focus on results.

• The relationship between policy reform and growth is even stronger than indicated in the OED report. Strong empirical evidence exists at the country level (not clearly sorted out in cross-country regressions) that this relationship is indeed robust. The experience of Pakistan since 2000 demonstrates that prudent fiscal balances, appropriate exchange rates, open trade regimes, and so on do lead to good growth outcomes and absence of these policies in the 1990s decelerated growth and raised poverty levels.

Having agreed with these broad findings let me elaborate on some other nuances and lessons that should be taken seriously at the time of formulation of policy reforms.

• The policy reform process is not always linear, and slippages, setbacks, and reversals should be expected during implementation. This should not throw donors off, and they should not decide to disen-

---

* Governor, State Bank of Pakistan.

gage, withdraw, or reduce planned assistance. The donors should stay the course if the long-term direction, framework for action, and overall strategy pursued by the country is clearly defined, followed, and shared by them.

- Donors, including the World Bank, have a vast array of instruments at their disposal, and they should use the appropriate instruments judiciously and imaginatively at different stages to support the strategy. For example, if it is determined by World Bank advisory and analytical work (AAA) that a particular institution is not ready for lending because it is in bad shape, the appropriate response is not to wait until there is a turnaround in the institution, but to deploy technical assistance, capacity building, advice, best practice dissemination, and dialogue to prepare the institution so that it is ready to become eligible for lending.

- A convergence of interest exists between the sectoral ministries in the country and their counterpart sectoral departments of the Bank. So they form a lobby group and agitate for a higher allocation of resources for their respective sectors and projects in an additive mode. Little effort has been taken to explore tradeoffs in a constrained resource situation and to assign weights to the outcomes, which can contribute to achievement of the strategy and desired results. On the other hand, complementarities and linkages between different sectoral programs and interventions are not fully exploited and the planning and sequencing of different forms of reforms do not always reflect the synergies arising from such complementarities. For example, those who design education policy interact with those responsible for labor policy only at a superficial level, but not in an integrative manner.

The behavior, response, and advice extended by the donors to the countries should be countercyclical in nature. When there are good days and boom periods, they should not be carried away by excessive affection for the country manifested in the form of higher lending, AAA work, and all kinds of assistance. Donors should desist from the temptation to shine in the glory of their countries. It is during these times that donors should render advice of caution to the country and exercise prudence in their assistance. But when the country faces bad days or difficulties, it is incumbent on donors to continue engagement and not pull the plug. They should not sound tough at those moments, but work with the country's reformers to get the country out of the difficult patch.

The trust and goodwill generated during these times will foster closer relationship between the Bank or other donors and the authorities of the country on a long-term sustained basis.

Comments on Country Program Evaluations

Miguel Urrutia Montoya*

First, I would like to start with one important topic not discussed in the report: the relationship between macroeconomics and Bank programs. This was also mentioned by Governor Husain.

On the one hand, in middle-income countries, cycles in capital flows create macroeconomic instability. Bank programs need to be calibrated to these cyclical flows. For example, in Latin America in 1998 and 1999, sudden reversals in private capital flows generated serious increases in poverty and unemployment, which in some countries rose to more than 18 percent. It has been very difficult since then to reduce unemployment and poverty. Although recently, unemployment has decreased, the shock was very costly in terms of poverty. In these circumstances, the increase in funds from multilaterals was very important.

On the other hand, the flows from international organizations may at other times actually generate problems. During boom periods, such as the present situation in some countries with oil exports, a sudden increase in flows generates serious problems in foreign exchange rates, as currencies appreciate in response. The resulting overvaluation of the exchange rate, which is not permanent, disrupts efforts for export diversification. So, a case exists for having the World Bank design programs that adapt to the economic cycle.

In addition, during cyclical downturns, some Bank projects should be directed to generate countercyclical support, as has been the case in Eastern Europe and Latin America. For example, projects can be developed that are designed to support families that are unable to keep their children in school. A recent evaluation of such a program in Colombia indicates that programs of this type can be very successful.

So, in summary, a need exists for ongoing economic and sector work to identify projects that can be used in the different phases of the cycle. In addition, nothing is wrong with net payments to international organizations in boom times. The Bank, however, should be careful not to withdraw resources during times in which downturns in resource flows are already generating macroeconomic problems.

---

* General Manager, Central Bank of Colombia.

Other points are already covered in OED's 2003 ARDE (World Bank 2004). One of the more interesting recommendations is for the forward-looking type of reforms. Reforms are easier to carry out before pressure groups against them become organized. One example is the issue that many developing countries already face or will face in the future: pension reform. As populations age, older voters become very powerful and politically effective at blocking pension reform. In such circumstances, it is crucial to push for reform early before a crisis in social security leads to a fiscal crisis, by which time reform will become very difficult due to the strength of the pressure groups against it. Many countries, especially in Latin America, have allowed the problem to grow for too long. Although studied, solutions have been developed too late. This emphasizes the importance of the conclusions in the CAE Retrospective (World Bank 2005) regarding economic and sector work.

Support should be given to the idea presented by His Excellency Saifur Rahman this morning of putting greater emphasis on economic and sector work by local researchers. These professionals remain in the country as permanent supporters of the reforms suggested by the studies. A number of examples of this exist. Many people who have worked on issues such as tax reform in Latin America later became ministers of finance; as a consequence of their work, they are much better prepared to continue the reform process.

In addition, as the report mentions, dissemination of economic and sector work is important. Dissemination of the results of policy studies is greatly facilitated by the local experts, who were involved in the study and are able to discuss these reform issues with the press and civil society. Positive experience has been gained not only with local experts undertaking economic and sector work, but also with joint research projects in which Bank staff train people on the ground who later continue pushing for reform. Moreover, local experts also have a better understanding of the political economy of reform, which will make the proposals easier to implement not only then, but also later.

Windows of opportunity are created by new governments, because in democracies, reforms can be put through much more effectively in the first months of office. Not only is the government popular, but governing coalitions are still solid. Two or three years down the road, this is not usually the case. Although new governments do present opportunities to support reform, often the reforms of new governments are not very consistent or technically well thought out. In such cases, it is crucial that the Bank use its previous economic and sector work to convince policymakers of the need to make the necessary changes in the reforms or influence changes in those reforms that will make them operationally effective. In other words, although it is difficult to engage new governments about potential problems with proposals made during the electoral campaigns, this has to be done. Otherwise, unless adjustments are made, the Bank should not support this "window of opportunity."

In defense of conditionality, it is useful if it is self-imposed, in other words, if it is proposed by the country itself. Why is this of any use? One of the most difficult things in a country is to coordinate policy across different ministries to ensure that a government's program is coherent. The government, therefore, sometimes finds it useful to accept or even suggest certain conditionalities precisely to make governance more effective and commit the entire government to a set of reforms. Only in this case, can conditionality can be useful.

Observations on Country Program Evaluations

Session Chair: James Adams*

I would like to make a few concluding observations. First, the focus on the country level is an important change; it reflects the broader movement of the Bank and indeed the donor community. But what have emerged are some interesting examples of tensions between the sector, as mentioned by Governor Husain, and project levels, as well as between project and country results. These tensions will continue, and we need to continue to deal pragmatically with these issues.

Second, continuing the discussion from the first session, a lot of concerns exist on conditionality. As noted in the Development Committee communiqué, the Bank, under the leadership of the Operations Policy and Country Services (OPCS) Network, will undertake some work on conditionality, as it is recognized that the existing system is not satisfactory. I agree with Governor Urrutia's point that conditionality only works when reformers are in the government who feel that the specified conditionality is part of what they need to deliver on their own reform program.

Third, this session raised interesting discussion on several important topics: *(a)* managing cycles in middle-income countries and how they should be handled, *(b)* the role and importance of analytic work, and *(c)* a subtle message about the importance of local capacity, which is an area in which the Bank needs to do more.

Fourth, the session raised concerns on how to deal with difficult partnerships, especially with low-income countries under stress (LICUS). What we do when progress is limited and how we manage it is a new challenge the Bank is taking on. As yet, there are no definitive answers, but the Bank is actively thinking through the questions in a more systematic way.

The Operations Evaluation Department (OED) is also going to assess the Bank's work on LICUS in the past couple years. This will provide us with additional results and observations on this important topic. It is important that this analysis focus not only on what the Bank, but also the broader development community, is doing. One of the interesting things

---

*   Vice President and Head of Network, Operations Policy, and Country Services, World Bank Group.

that we have learned about these difficult partnerships is that the issue is engaging the entire donor community, and everyone is struggling in different ways. So, we are now engaging in a broader discussion across the development community on these issues, not to reach one answer, but at least to have an ongoing and more constructive dialogue.

References

World Bank. 2004. *2003 Annual Review of Development Effectiveness.* Operations Evaluation Department (OED), Washington, D.C.
———. 2005.Country Assistance Evaluation (CAE) Retrospective: OED Self-Evaluation. Operations Evaluation Department (OED), Washington, D.C.

Part 4

Middle-Income Country Programs: Lessons from Brazil, China, and Tunisia

Middle-Income Country Strategies for Development[†]

S. Ramachandran [*]

Unlike low-income countries that are struggling to overcome economic stagnation, middle-income countries (defined as those with real per capita incomes between US$3,036 and US$9,385) would appear to be proceeding well along the development path. But historically, sustained and balanced growth is relatively rare[1]: policymaking is fragile in many middle-income countries such as Argentina and Turkey. And the progress of countries that consistently adopt sound policies is often interrupted by shocks in their terms of trade and/or capital flows. The 1997 crisis showed both the vulnerability of countries, such Korea and Indonesia, that have decades of impressive progress and the difficulties of getting assistance from multilateral banks after an extended absence: the Bank's knowledge of Korea was outdated, and even in Thailand, many affected sectors were poorly understood.

[†] This note was prepared as background information for the session "Middle-Income Countries: Lessons from Brazil, China and Tunisia" for the OED Conference on "Effectiveness of Policies and Reforms," Washington D.C., October 4, 2004. The individual country assistance evaluation reports for these countries can be found on the OED conference website at www.worldbank.org/oed/conference2004/.

[*] Senior Evaluation Officer, Operations Evaluation Department, World Bank Group.

The Bank has played a useful role in such middle-income countries, but it is a different role than when the Bank is usually the main or only source of external finance and advice. The Bank's overall lending has fallen considerably in recent years, although countries' total borrowings (i.e., from non-Bank sources) have not declined, and the decline in Bank lending is particularly pronounced for most middle-income countries. This prompted the Bank to set up a task force in 2001 to examine how well it was meeting middle-income country needs; the task force's recommendations on how to tailor the Bank's assistance and products better and streamline its procedures have been approved by the management and Board[2] and are under implementation. The "cost of doing business" with the Bank could be reduced; but what some see as costs may actually be the benefits.

Although the Operations Evaluation Department (OED) has not been directly involved in these efforts, its many evaluations illustrate some of the germane issues. Evaluations of individual loans in the past 30 years have emphasized the importance of sound analytical work as the basis for lending, adequate project preparation and supervision, and country ownership of all programs. OED also began evaluating the Bank's assistance with a country (as distinct from a loan) focus in 1995, and the country assistance evaluations (CAEs) examine whether the Bank engaged effectively in relevant sectors and what effect it had on the country's development.

Recent CAEs for Brazil, China, and Tunisia illustrate the issues that arise and what the Bank should and could learn from them: not just about what the Bank does, but how it engages the country and *how* it could do so more effectively.

China

China turned to the Bank for help and advice from the beginning of its transition to a market economy. In the early phase starting in 1981, Bank reports were keenly read and influential. The Bank also brought in renowned experts to brief China's leaders on the needed changes in policies and their implications—without forcing the pace or sequence of the reforms. The Bank earned the trust of China's economic reformers, especially when it continued to be engaged after the events of 1989, but although it remains effective in many areas, the Bank's prominence has since waned. This was inevitable as the Chinese became more knowledgeable and the private sector grew more important; but the CAE (World Bank 2004b) also describes how the scope and content of the Bank's work did not always keep pace with China's changing needs and increasing complexity of policy issues.

The CAE covers 1992–2002 when the Bank's assistance strategy had four main objectives: *(a)* promoting market-oriented system reform and better macroeconomic management, *(b)* reducing poverty, *(c)* supporting infrastructure development for growth and market integration, and *(d)* protecting the environment.

OED found the Bank's approach of building trust and supporting new techniques through lending and promoting policy reform through economic and sector work broadly effective. The Bank helped establish successful models of targeted interventions through integrated rural development projects and helped promote better project management. Instituting competitive bidding for procurement, for example, greatly reduced project costs and probably also reduced corruption; such procedures were welcomed and adopted in non-Bank projects also. Other procedures, such as those for resettlement of people displaced by a project created resentment and suspicion with counterparts. One such project was referred to the Bank's Inspection Panel, which found serious shortcomings with the Bank's handling of resettlement issues.

Such concerns have eroded, but not entirely eliminated the openness and candor that characterized the early phase of the Bank's assistance to China. The change is felt in all sectors, and the Bank's work on poverty illustrates the issue. Although poverty has decreased in China, the rate of decline is not commensurate with its economic growth[3]. Eastern and coastal areas (where manufacturing growth and exports originate) have prospered economically, but poverty is *largely* rural and concentrated in central and western provinces. The Bank correctly identified these issues in a 1992 report and helped improve the measurement of poverty, but it was only after the mid-1990s that policies to tackle this became discernible (e.g., the system of taxes and subsidies was regressive). The Bank's 2000 China rural poverty assessment (World Bank 2000), however, repeats the official view (based on statistics that fail to capture undocumented migrants in cities) that poverty is *entirely* a rural phenomenon. But although the assessment endorses the government's strategy and is silent on urban poverty, it is critical of its inadequate targeting, noting that nearly half of the poor live outside the targeted area, and urges increased investment in health, education, and nutrition.

In a large country with many programs, it is inevitable that the Bank is more effective in some areas than in others: infrastructure project management improved with the Bank's involvement, but environmental protection was mixed. The Bank's work could have been more effective in the areas of enterprise and banking reforms, for which advice continued to be generic, although a few staff were aware of the complexities in practice. The Bank's advice was at a very general level in the early years, for example, the importance of separating central banking functions from commercial banking, but as qualified technocrats were trained as well as Bank staff rose in the bureaucracy, they needed more specific advice, and the Bank did not always meet these needs.

Even so, China still values the Bank's help, which is why it continues to borrow despite having substantial foreign exchange reserves, access to commercial funds, and having lost access to International Development Association (IDA) facilities. Although China is the Bank's largest borrower, the Bank is not China's main lender; its influence is more through persuasion and example, not loan conditions. Indeed, China only borrowed once through an adjustment loan.

It is not just the relations with the Bank that changed with the years, but also China's own internal decisionmaking. The de facto control that various levels of government exercise varies by region and personalities involved. The Bank does not always know the inner workings of the government, and counterparts may sometimes have sought the Bank's involvement to further bureaucratic interests than for the advice per se. There are also many issues in which the authorities do not wish the Bank to be involved. So the Bank's role became more complex in ways that Bank staff did not always understand. But both the authorities and Bank staff are cognizant of the constraints under which each other operates and acutely conscious of avoiding friction.

Ideas concerning policies and the pace and scope of reform ebb and flow in very different ways than even a decade ago. OED, therefore, suggests that the Bank broaden the audience for its work. Although open debates are difficult when sensitive decisions are to be made, the analysis of issues could be discussed with a broader group than just the project counterparts; OED suggests that they include researchers and other stakeholders, especially because they are increasingly influential in the country. Such researchers, even if as well qualified as Bank staff, are not always as knowledgeable about China because information does not easily *flow* within the country; so partnering with the Bank would help. This could be done in many areas such as poverty, water, health, agriculture, and rural development, whereas one must be more careful with sensitive issues such as privatization or banking.

The Bank was particularly successful in doing precisely this in Brazil, and the CAE notes that "The Bank's strategy was underpinned by high-quality analytical work on poverty and growth done with substantial participation by top Brazilian researchers." We now turn to how this was done.

Brazil

Brazil entered the 1990s suffering the consequences of the "lost decade" of high inflation and low economic growth. Its earlier transition to democracy from military rule was peaceful, but the political difficulties of limiting spending to tax receipts resulted in periodic bouts of inflation. Much of the Federal government spending was nondiscretionary and its difficult financial relations with the provinces made expenditure control difficult. So curbing inflation was a major achievement, but the accumulation of debts, both domestic and foreign, makes its continued stability especially vulnerable to market sentiments. In addition, trade and exchange restrictions instituted over decades had misallocated resources and created vested interests, while years of low public investment made infrastructure a development bottleneck.

The CAE (World Bank 2004a) again looked at the period of 1990–2002, when the Bank's central objective was the alleviation of poverty. The Bank had learned a great deal from its earlier mistakes. Traditional agriculture projects (irrigation and extension) had excessively unsatisfactory outcomes in the 1980s as did energy projects, and the Government of Brazil also had reservations with the Bank's involvement in resettlement.[4] So the Bank's strategy during the 1990s was not to lend significant amounts (net disbursements were negative between 1986 and 1995), but to focus on the poor Northeast and on activities that addressed the roots of poverty: education and health and the provision of basic services (water, sanitation, rural electricity, and so on) to the poor. To do this, the Bank had to deal directly with the states and municipalities; it did so by increasing its field presence, not just in Brasilia, but also in the Northeast.

By the early 1990s, the proportion of Brazilians in extreme poverty had risen from 16.5 to 19 percent, but it was more than 41 percent in the Northeast. The Bank funded and helped improve the efficiency of education spending with impressive results: primary school enrollment rose from 72 to 93 percent in the Northeast, *compared with* 84 to 96 percent nationally, and youth illiteracy declined from 22.7 to 9.6 percent in the Northeast, *compared with* 9.8 to 4.2 percent nationally. Similarly, infant mortality declined in the Northeast more than the national average: from 73 to 44 *compared with* 48 to 29 per 1,000 live births.

The Bank's assistance underwent three phases: the first phase contracted lending for the social sectors and environment (1990–94); the second (1995–98, after the successful stabilization under the 1994 real plan) increased lending to support structural reforms; and the third (1998–2002) expanded lending to support stabilization. This third phase included several adjustment loans to support reforms in fiscal/public administration, social security, the financial sector, and energy. These have since given way to programmatic lending.

The CAE notes that, although macroeconomic stabilization greatly contributed to the success of various projects, the success did not flow from stabilization alone: the Bank's role in redirecting spending and project management was important. The second component of the Bank's program was less successful: although Brazilian states are better able to manage their infrastructure, poor regulation stymies the contribution of the private provision of infrastructure and public investment remains low.

The Brazil program shows the importance of a sustained involvement, but with an approach that evolves with the country's circumstances. When projects were less than satisfactory, the Bank changed its design and/or curtailed lending to the sector, but did not disengage from the country. It was also important to engage authorities with the right level of responsibility (states, not just Federal) and to support the needed technical work on numerous details of policy and implementation. The CAE notes that "Government officials indicate that the Bank is a multilateral institution that the Government mostly resorts to for technical advice. The Government has also indicated that the Bank can play an important "pedagogical" role in the country, informing Brazilian society about long-term structural issues, their potential solutions and the tradeoffs involved." But despite the success, the CAE continues that to ". . . play this role effectively . . . the Bank must make a greater effort to disseminate its work among several potential audiences and to the population at large."

Tunisia

Tunisia, with a current population of 9.8 million, is far smaller than China or Brazil and faces different development issues, although its income also falls in the same range. A former French colony, Tunisia retained ties to Europe, but adopted many dirigiste policies. Even so, it grew rapidly during the 1970s in the wake of the petroleum boom, but declining prices and reserves created problems during the 1980s.

Although the Bank had long lent to Tunisia (the recipient of the Bank's first education loan), macroeconomic problems in 1987 prompted necessary changes in economic policies. The Bank and IMF helped the government put its finances in order and advised on opening its economy to trade. These changes, begun in the mid-1990s, have paid off: although the state still plays a large role, manufacturing has developed in addition to tourism. Although Tunisia also borrows commercially, it did not do so between 1997 and 1999 in the aftermath of the East Asian crisis. Some 80 percent of its external debts are public and publicly guaranteed, but being long term makes it less vulnerable to bond market sentiments that plagued Brazil. Real gross domestic product has grown faster in recent years: from 3 percent per year in 1985–90 to 5 percent in 1996–2002. Per capita income is now US$2,000, and absolute poverty fell from 40 percent in 1970 to 4 percent in 2000.

The CAE (World Bank 2004c) reviews the Bank's substantial assistance to Tunisia, both financial (some 5 percent of external inflows, although net transfers are slightly negative) and advisory. The bulk of the Bank's lending (39 percent) was for economic, financial, and private sector policies, but it also supported education and health (21 percent). Tunisia benefits from its free trade agreement with the European Union; the Bank's analytical work (e.g., private sector assessments and updates) helps to ensure policies that benefit the economy. The Bank's economic and sector work increasingly focused on education and health and on infrastructure modernization.

The OED evaluation found that, although Tunisia is a relatively small country, the Bank respected the government's pace of reforms: so although these proceeded slowly, there were no reversals. Its competent civil service ensured that agreements with the Bank were fully carried out, and this fostered trust on both sides. The CAE recommends that the Bank follow through on programs that further private sector development, because unemployment remains high, and continue support for the social and rural sectors.

What Can the Bank Learn from Assisting Middle-Income Countries?

The Bank offers its member countries a package of services; although the package details differ by country and evolve with time, funds are tied to advice. The Bank's relations with middle-income countries are a litmus test of whether the package is appropriate, because they could instead borrow commercially.

The Bank's advice covers policies relating to the economy or particular sectors and to procedures that apply only to the Bank's projects and funds. Some of the advice is sought, sometimes it is heeded, and occasionally it is resented. That countries such as China still borrow despite losing access to IDA funds suggests that the Bank's package is valuable; but overall value could hide problems with its components. So it may be useful to look at four of these in turn:

1. The Bank as a Funding Source

Although the Bank remains the primary source of external funds for some (especially Sub-Saharan African) countries, it is not so for most others. Middle-income countries generally have access to commercial borrowings, but such borrowings create problems as well: countries could be caught in a squeeze when market sentiments change and debts cannot be rolled over on similar terms as before. Brazil's predicament illustrates this situation well: Argentina's default in 2001 made nervous markets more jittery. The higher interest rates that were required to roll over Brazil's debts that were maturing threatened its macroeconomic stabilization program. Borrowing from the Bank and IMF helped, both to calm markets and lower interest costs, allowing the government to pursue its development efforts.

Countries with access to international capital markets are a diverse group. The Bank's task force put 69 such middle-income countries into four categories: *(a)* 22 had good policies and investment-grade access to capital markets, *(b)* 10 had poor policies and impaired credit worthiness (e.g., Venezuela and Indonesia), *(c)* 20 had generally satisfactory policies, but volatile market access (e.g., Brazil and Turkey), and *(d)*

17 IBRD-eligible (including blend) countries had satisfactory performance, but insignificant market access and, therefore, depended on Bank or other multilateral development bank (MDB) financing.

Even countries with good policies and access are vulnerable to changes in market sentiments. The speed with which such changes occur requires the Bank to act quickly when the need arises; but it can lend responsibly only when it knows the country well. The 1997 crisis in East Asia showed the dangers of neglecting "graduating" countries such as Korea and Thailand. Continuing to work with these countries not only benefits the countries[5] in times of crises but also others through the transfer of knowledge (the "Knowledge Bank").

2. The Bank for Economic and Sector Work and Policy Advice

The CAEs illustrate the added value the Bank brings to policy discussions—even when much of the analytical work is done by or in partnership with local staff. The Bank brings not just technical skills, but also experience and perspective and, as in China, provides access to data and/or policymakers that a country's internal structure does not otherwise allow.

The quality of the Bank's policy advice is sometimes questioned: Vaclav Klaus, when finance minister of the Czech Republic, asked the Bank's country director "Why should we pay hard money for soft advice?" Disagreement with the advice should not be confused with its value; in numerous instances, the Bank's advice was initially spurned but later adopted.

The three CAEs underscore that the *process* is also important: that involving the country, both official counterparts and others, increases country "ownership" and often improves its quality. But China also illustrates the problems that sometimes arise when officials are accustomed to operating in secrecy. Yet, this is an important aspect of institution building and is the spirit behind the PRSP in low-income countries.

Good economic and sector work (ESW) requires effort and expense. Funding ESW is easier when the country borrows. But when circumstances do not justify lending, as with Brazil during much of the 1990s, continuing the ESW pays off later. The real dilemma arises not with episodic reductions in country borrowings, but when there appears to be a secular decline as was the case with pre-1997 Korea and Thailand when the Bank scaled down its activities. Should the Bank be lending if it reduces what more "needy" countries could borrow? And if it does not lend to prospering countries, how should it fund its ESW? Some high-income (oil-rich) countries reimburse the Bank's costs without borrowing; but other countries are less willing. Besides, lending allows the Bank to "push" for changes in myriad ways that "purchased ESW" cannot. The Bank is grappling with such questions in countries such as Hungary with increasingly rosy prospects.

3. The Cost of Doing Business with the Bank

The Bank's procedures for disbursement, procurement, and so on are meant to ensure that the funds are used for their intended purpose and apply only to the Bank's project and/or own funds. But some procedures have become obsolete and archaic: the old practice of the Bank choosing the currency disbursed, while ignoring its likely depreciation when setting interest charges, for example, was changed. Other sensible procedures (such as procurement through competitive bids) should apply to all of the government's procurement, not just that "traceable" to Bank funds.

The Bank responded to middle-income country concerns of administratively burdensome requirements by moving to "fiduciary assessments" that a country's general procedures and safeguards are adequate. If so, different procedures for Bank projects and funds would not be required. But such simplification and harmonization may not always be possible: a huge chasm could exist between current practice in some countries and what the Bank desires. "Ring fencing" is the term used; but fungibility could make the fence become perverse as explained below.

Most Bank procedures are meant to benefit countries that borrow (after all, the government guarantees repayment regardless of the project's financial return); but, some may also reflect the views of its non-borrowing shareholders. Many of the environmental and resettlement safeguards, for example, are viewed thus; but even if they ultimately benefit the borrower, they may not immediately perceive these benefits. As with recommended policies about which the authorities are not convinced, the procedures would only be grudgingly accepted for Bank projects or funds, not adopted for all its activities.

Regardless of the merit of the procedure and/or safeguard, the real danger of imposing such requirements on unconvinced countries stems from fungibility: countries could use the Bank only for projects that entail fewer procedural safeguards, but proceed with the contentious projects using other funds. China built the Three Gorges Dam without involving the Bank, whose environmental and resettlement safeguards did not apply.

The Bank must, of course, follow its procedures, but we must also recognize that countries will follow only if they are convinced, which requires persuasion. Sound analysis and explanation go further than attempts at imposition.

4. The Bank as a Learner and Conduit

One often hears the term "best practice," and however tempting it is to think that this could be identified and propagated, the very notion is contrary to what we also know to be important: local adaptation and experimentation. We have, for example, sought to establish "best practice" independent regulatory authorities—whether for electricity price setting or for banking—and are constantly disappointed when they do not act as independently as their U.S. counterparts. Successful countries do not just have good policies and practices, but also good mechanisms that permit them to respond to shocks and learn by doing. Such "institutional development" is the result of trying variants, not the blind mimicking of Organisation for Economic Cooperation and Development (OECD) models or rigid adherence to standards set elsewhere.

The success of middle-income countries may make them a more useful model for low-income countries; the Bank could be an effective conduit to convey such knowledge. The Bank's international staffing and use of consultants familiar with many countries allow this; voucher schemes to assist farmers in Central America have been adapted to Turkey, and so on, but it could be done far more often.

So, the Bank clearly still has a lot to learn.

Notes

1. See World Bank (2005).
2. See World Bank (2001). Indonesia, Russia, and China accounted for about 60 percent of the lending decline, but the decline was widespread. The task force report charts the decline by sector, region, and instrument and identify the many factors that may have been responsible.
3. See World Bank 2004b.

4. The Bank cancelled a power transmission loan in 1992, because of the government's unwillingness to adjust tariffs. In 1992, when reviewing the environmental effect of Bank projects, OED noted that the cost of rural resettlement in the Itaparica project exceeded US$63,000 per family.
5. China borrows from the Bank, despite the loss of access to IDA and its large foreign exchange reserves, in part because it allocates such borrowings to the provinces where the projects are located. This internal accounting mechanism encourages provincial and municipal fiscal discipline and a similar notion across line ministries.

References

World Bank. 2000. *China: Overcoming Rural Poverty*. Report No. 21105. Washington, D.C.

————. 2001. *Report of the Task Force on the World Bank Group and the Middle-Income Countries*. Operations Policy and Country Services Network. Washington, D.C. Available at: http://siteresources.worldbank.org/COUNTRIES/Resources/mictf.pdf.

————. 2004a. *Brazil: Country Assistance Evaluation*. Report No. 27629. Operations Evaluation Department, Washington, D.C.

————. 2004b. *China: Country Assistance Evaluation*. Report No. 29734. Operations Evaluation Department, Washington, D.C.

————. 2004c. *Republic of Tunisia: Country Assistance Evaluation*. Report No. 29669. Operations Evaluation Department, Washington, D.C.

————. 2005. *Economic Growth in the 1990s: Learning from a Decade of Reform*. Poverty Reduction and Economic Management Network, Washington, D.C.

The Role of World Bank Lending in Middle-Income Countries[†]

Johannes F. Linn*

I will focus my comments specifically on the role of World Bank lending in middle-income developing countries (MICs).[1] I will make six interrelated points:

- There has been a substantial decline in World Bank lending to MICs.
- MICs still face a significant development challenge.
- The declining role of Bank lending is a problem for the MICs and the Bank.
- There are many reasons for the decline in Bank lending to MICs.
- There is good news, as some progress has been made to facilitate lending to MICs.
- There is still much that can and needs to be done.

1. There has been a significant decline in World Bank lending to MICs.

For fiscal 1990–97,[2] lending by the International Bank for Reconstruction and Development (IBRD) fell within the range of US$15–18 billion. After a dramatic, but brief spike in lending in response to the East Asia financial crisis, IBRD lending dropped to about US$10–11 billion during fiscal 2000–2003. This decline took place in all regions, except South Asia, and in all sectors, except education and health. The drop was particularly dramatic for infrastructure and financial interme-

---

† For the comments I draw on my four-year engagement as the World Bank's vice president for financial policy and risk management and my eight-year experience as the Bank's vice president for the Europe and Central Asia Region. I also draw on my involvement in two internal World Bank task forces, which during the past three years assessed the Bank's role in middle-income countries. The factual evidence cited draws on the work of these task forces. The positions I advocate here are consistent with those I have advocated as a member of these task forces. The views expressed in these comments are entirely my own and should not be seen to represent views of the World Bank or Brookings Institution.

* Visiting Fellow, Brookings Institution.

diation loans[3] and especially affected lending for investment projects (as against balance of payments and budget support loans), for which lending roughly halved when comparing the same periods (from about US$12 billion to US$6 billion). The decline in lending was found in both well- and badly performing countries. It occurred at a time when private capital flows to MICs collapsed and while lending by regional development banks (such as the Asian Development Bank, European Bank for Reconstruction and Development, and Inter-American Development Bank) expanded.

Why would one worry about this declining trend in World Bank lending to MICs? Is it not a good thing if the Bank works itself out of a job in countries that, one might think, should in any case stand on their own feet?

2. MICs still face significant development challenges.

About 80 percent of the population of developing countries lives in MICs and 70 percent of poor people in developing countries live in MICs. In addition to poverty, MICs face many important development challenges:

- Significant shortfalls regarding the potential to achieve Millennium Development Goals
- Vulnerability to macroeconomic and financial crises
- Serious weaknesses in the private investment climate and public governance
- Shortages of physical and social infrastructure
- High rates of unemployment and social security systems that are under stress
- Vulnerability to environmental damage and natural disasters.

These challenges affect not only the well-being of people in MICs, but also carry major worldwide risks that endanger the well-being of people in industrial countries as well as in low-income countries. These risks include:

- Global macroeconomic imbalances and financial instability
- Global political instability
- Migration
- Global environmental damage.

3. The declining role of Bank lending is a problem for MICs and the Bank.

Many MICs need the Bank's financing to help address these challenges:

- After the East Asia crisis, net private financial flows to MICs turned from an average annual inflow of about US$140 billion per year during the 1990s to zero or negative flows in the early 2000s. In late 2003 more than one-third of 82 IBRD borrowers had no market access at all, and most of those who did have some access had to borrow at spreads that typically ranged from 100 basis points to more than 500 basis points, compared with about 40 basis points that IBRD borrowers usually pay on World Bank loans.

- It is standard practice in industrial countries to channel sizeable financial flows to backward regions to support convergence in regional production and incomes. This holds for the structural and cohesion funds in the European Union and is a very common characteristic for intergovernmental transfers from national to regional and local authorities within industrial countries. The same rationale applies to channeling funds from industrial to developing countries, including MICs, whose per capita income still amounts to as little as 10 percent of the per capita income of a typical industrial country.

- The World Bank's package of financial and advisory support through IBRD loans (along with its free-standing analytical and advisory services) is in principle well suited to supporting the structural and institutional changes along with investments in physical, social, and environmental infrastructure that are needed in the MICs.[4]

For the Bank and its shareholders, the decline in IBRD lending carries a number of serious risks:

- The Bank's role as "transmission belt" carrying low-income countries through middle-income status into the ranks of high-income countries will be at stake. This is somewhat ironic, because, on balance, the Bank has probably been more successful in helping middle-income than low-income countries.[5] Part of the "transmission belt" function of the Bank is to convey the lessons of MIC development experience to low-income countries.

- The ability of IBRD to continue making sizeable contributions to the Bank's soft-loan and grant window—the International Development

Association (IDA)—and for transfers to the debt reduction initiative for the poorest heavily indebted countries will be endangered, because these financial windows are financed in part from the income generated by IBRD loan charges. This would mean a sizeable reduction in financial flows to the poorest developing countries.

- If the Bank is no longer seriously engaged in supporting MICs, its role as a global development organization that helps address global economic, social, and environmental challenges on a worldwide scale will be at risk. No other organization can currently perform this function credibly.

4. There are many reasons for the decline in Bank lending to MICs.

The decline in Bank lending to MICs reflects a complex mix of factors at the country and sector levels and in terms of the Bank's own attitude and procedures.

At the country level, various factors have caused a reduction in MIC borrowing: some MICs have formally or informally graduated from IBRD lending, as has been the case with some Central European countries. Others have dropped from IBRD to IDA borrower status due to financial and economic crisis and mismanagement (Indonesia and Nigeria). Others have high oil revenues and, hence, temporarily little need for external borrowing by the government (Kazakhstan and Russia). Some are constrained by severe limits on their ability or willingness to service loans due to financial crisis (Argentina), and in yet other cases the Bank's strict exposure limits constrain lending to high-risk or high-exposure countries.

At the sector level, there has been a particularly severe decline in infrastructure and financial intermediation lending. This is due to a number of factors:

- During the 1990s there has been a deliberate shift away from physical infrastructure and financial intermediation lending toward lending for social sectors on the grounds that the private sector can be relied on to finance infrastructure and financial services and that social sector spending contributes more directly to poverty reduction. Recent experience has shown that private sector financing for infrastructure is often not sustainable even in the MICs and that banking institutions in MICs are not equipped to intermediate adequate financial resources for private investment. The importance of these sectors for supporting economic growth, employment, and poverty reduction in MICs has now, therefore, once again come into focus.

- Constraints of excessively rigorous and demanding fiduciary and social/environmental safeguards attached to Bank projects has slowed down Bank lending and increased its effective cost to borrowers. Fear of running afoul of such stringent requirements and the ensuing sanctions both inside and outside the institution has also encouraged risk-averse behavior among Bank staff and management. These factors help explain in particular the reduction in investment lending.[6]

- The number of skilled project staff in the Bank's Regional operational units has declined, which can be explained in part by an overall reduction in staff numbers; a shift of staff to fiduciary, safeguards, and quality management functions; and a shift of senior staff to central sector units engaged in places away from frontline operational work.

- In contrast to some of the regional development banks, the World Bank is constrained from lending to subnational governments, because it always requires a sovereign (national government) guarantee on its loans and traditionally has been able to make only foreign-currency denominated loans (which are not well suited for lending to subnational governments, which generally cannot effectively manage currency risk). As the Bank has encouraged its client countries to decentralize and strengthen subnational government capacities, its own lending practices have prevented it from supporting a corresponding shift in loan commitments to subnational authorities.

In addition, some fundamental attitudinal factors have been at work: During the 1990s and into the new millennium, the Bank shifted its focus from viewing itself primarily as a financial institution providing loan services, albeit combined with high-quality advice, to an institution principally providing development knowledge and advisory services and engaging in development advocacy, especially for the world's poorest countries and related global causes. At the risk of drawing something of a caricature, one might conclude that the institutional culture has moved from a focus on the "business of lending" to one that focuses more on the functions of a "knowledge bank" and "development advocate." At the same time, lending has become mostly restricted to the dual role of a "crisis lender" alongside the IMF and a "development finance boutique" that finances only the highest-quality projects, while minimizing risks at great cost to the borrower and the Bank. This tendency was reinforced by the externally imposed need to perfect the loans, maximize policy conditionality, and minimize risks (both the risk of project failure as well as country risk). It was reinforced by the Bank's organizational matrix structure in place since 1997, which permits the "churning" of project design and approval decisions, as many units have an opportunity and even incentive to stop a project from going forward. Whatever the reasons, I have no doubt that during the 1990s the incentives for staff and managers in the operational departments were clearly biased toward lending less and more slowly, rather than lending more and faster.

It is notable that some of the principal regional development banks (e.g., the European Bank for Reconstruction and Development [EBRD] and the European Investment Bank [EIB]) have had very different priorities, processes, procedures, and attitudes, which have enabled them to maintain or even expand their lending to MICs at a time when the World Bank's lending has declined.[7]

5. There is good news as progress has been made to facilitate lending to MICs

The good news is that the Bank's senior management has recognized the challenge posed by the declining trends in lending to MICs and has begun to address it seriously. There have been two recent management and Executive Board reviews of the issues and possible solutions, and some progress has been made in addressing some key constraints:

- There is now a clear managerial focus on setting stretch targets for lending and monitoring the delivery of loans, not only in terms of quality, but also amounts and timing.

- A programmatic approach to lending allows more flexible and scaled-up support that combines budget support loans, sectorwide investment loans and advisory work in individual sectors for longer periods.

- Efforts have been underway for some time to simplify and streamline loan procedures, reduce the cost of fiduciary and safeguard requirements, and encourage some transparent and justifiable risk taking in project design. Improvements in and increased reliance on local fiduciary and safeguard systems are now pursued in MICs. This builds local capacity and facilitates speedy World Bank lending.

- There is now a clear effort to revitalize traditional lines of lending, especially for infrastructure programs.
- More flexibility is being introduced into the way managers can adapt the lending envelopes embodied in the country assistance strategies approved by senior management and endorsed by the Executive Board.

6. There is still much that can and needs to be done to ensure responsive and dynamic Bank lending to MICs.

The steps taken to date give one a sense that a turning point has been reached and that the pendulum, which had moved too far against lending, is beginning to swing back toward a more sensible position.[8] But I believe more can and needs to be done to ensure that the constraints and risks that the Bank faces in supporting the legitimate needs of its MIC shareholders are adequately addressed. The following list contains some proposals that should urgently be considered and implemented by the Bank's management and Board:

- Make sure to keep the attention of the Bank's senior management, Board, and stakeholders on this high-priority matter. Strongly advocate for a "sunrise," rather than "sunset" role for the Bank in MICs!
- Be ready to learn from others, especially some of the dynamic regional development banks, such as EBRD and EIB. (The next three recommendations reflect areas in which these banks have been more active in maintaining or expanding their lending to MICs.)
- Expand the scope of financial intermediation lending.
- Adapt the instruments for lending to subnational governments by introducing options for local currency lending and lending without sovereign guarantees.
- Integrate the lending activities of the World Bank and the International Finance Corporation, which lends to and provides equity to private investors, under the direction of World Bank Group country directors. This will allow for a more effective and flexible response of the Group to the needs of its MIC clients.
- Staff up the frontline regional units with senior sectoral and technical experts by shifting resources out of central units to the operational front lines.

- Ensure full implementation of project simplification directives (including the reduction of policy conditionality in investment loans, adoption of programmatic and sectorwide lending approaches, streamlined fiduciary and safeguard administration, and so on).

- Introduce more flexibility and risk taking in the allocation of country lending envelopes reflecting IBRD's development mandate and superior financial risk-taking capacity.

- Reduce or eliminate the IBRD's front-end fee for low-risk borrowers.

- Perhaps most important, look at all proposed organizational and procedural changes through the eyes of a MIC borrower and judge whether a proposed action really makes the Bank more attractive to the borrower as against merely shifting around the internal procedural "deckchairs."

Concluding Remarks

In short, the role of the World Bank in MICs is as essential as it has been threatened in recent years. It is urgent that the initial steps taken by the Bank's management and Board be maintained and reinforced. The pendulum had clearly swung too far from "pressure to lend" in the 1970s and 1980s to "pressure not to lend" during the past 10 years.[9] In doing so, one needs to be aware of the possibility of the pendulum swinging too far again in the opposite direction, risking a loss of hard-won gains in improved quality and the Bank's enhanced focus on social and environmental aspects of programs and projects. But at the moment, the Bank is more at risk that it might fail supporting and enhancing worthwhile projects and programs in MICs than it is at risk of lending too much with too few safeguards.

I believe that the Bank's Operations Evaluation Department can be part of this momentum of change by focusing not only on the narrow questions of "quality" of Bank-financed projects and programs, but also by considering more broadly whether the Bank is delivering effectively on its broad mandate as a development *finance* institution in the MICs. In this regard, one key performance criterion should be whether the Bank takes sufficient financial risks and adequately applies its considerable financial resources in support of its MIC clients' development aspirations and the global development objectives of all its shareholders.

Notes

1. As is commonly done in analyses of World Bank lending trends, I equate middle-income countries with countries borrowing from the International Bank for Reconstruction and Development.
2. The World Bank's fiscal year runs from July 1 through June 30.
3. Financial intermediation loans are loans to banks in borrowing countries, which in turn lend on these funds to final borrowers.
4. This is in contrast to the situation in the low-income countries, where grants may be a more appropriate way of providing financial assistance, especially for the poorest and most debt-ridden developing countries.
5. Important exceptions, of course, exist: China, India, South Korea, and Turkey at one time were IDA-only borrowers, but now have either graduated from IDA (and even IBRD) borrower status or have moved into IBRD/IDA blend status.
6. Sebastian Mallaby in a newly published book (2004b) argues that this is in large part due to inappropriate pressures by northern advocacy NGOs. See also his *Foreign Policy* article (2004a). More generally, the position taken in my comments here is closely in line with those by Mallaby in regard to constraints and risks that the Bank faces in its lending to MICs. I read his book with great interest after making my own comments on October 4, 2004 at the Operations Evaluation Department conference.
7. One of the reasons is that these banks were less of a target for NGO pressures. See Mallaby (2004a and 2004b).
8. I am indebted to Sebastian Mallaby for the image of the "pendulum swung too far," which he expressed at a seminar organized by the Center for Global Development in Washington on October 2, 2004.
9. The one exception to this trend was the temporary pressure by the G-7 on the Bank's senior management to engage in high-stakes crisis lending with exceptional and exceptionally large balance of payments support loans in the immediate aftermath of the East Asia crisis of 1997–98. If anything, this further weakened the Bank's capacity for delivering its line of standard investment and sector loans for long-term development programs.

References

Mallaby, Sebastian. 2004a. "How NGOs Hurt the Poor." *Foreign Policy* (September/October 2004), pp. 50–58.

———. 2004b. *The World's Banker*. New York: Penguin Press.

Comments on Middle-Income Country Programs: Tunisia[†]

*Kamel Ben Rejeb**

I would like to thank the Operations Evaluation Department (OED) for having given me the opportunity to come and present the case of my country, Tunisia.

Tunisia, as you know, is a relatively small country. We have 10 million inhabitants, and our per capita income is about US$2,000 right now. But before reaching this stage of development, Tunisia went through various stages. After its independence, Tunisia became a member of the World Bank. Our relations are excellent, and the dialogue is always of very high quality. This brought about a level of cooperation and commitment, as the Bank financed more than US$5 billion through approximately 121 loans.

At the time of independence, in the 1960s, Tunisia chose centrally planned economic and social policies. It was a fundamental choice, and I think had good results, especially pertaining to education. As soon as Tunisia became independent, it made a conscious choice to invest in its human resources, because natural resources were quite scarce. The second decision behind the good results was family planning. Had we not made this decision as early as we did, the population of Tunisia would be more than 50 million now. So there would be more difficulties on solving various issues.

The third choice that we made was to emphasize the role and status of women. More than 5,000 women are heads of corporations, 55 percent of higher education teachers are women, as are 40 percent of scientists, 60 percent of pharmacists, 50 percent of teachers, 40 percent of civil servants, 33 percent of doctors, and 25 percent of magistrates. So, women have contributed greatly to the development of our country.

Tunisia, however, also went through lots of ups and downs. As I said, economic and social policies during the 1960s were centrally planned and state directed. Starting in the 1970s, Tunisia started to liberalize its economy, and investment rose to approximately 30 percent of gross

---

[†] Comments have been interpreted from French.

[*] Director General, Tunisian Ministry of Development and International Cooperation.

domestic product, especially in the manufacturing sector. Real gross national product (GNP) has increased by about 7.4 percent per year.

All this was when there were high oil revenues; but when oil prices fell and production decreased, we maintained a high level of investments and major cracks appeared in Tunisia's economic performance. In 1984 inflation reached 10 percent, the current account deficit was almost 11 percent of GNP and a balance of payments crisis seemed imminent by 1985.

The authorities became very concerned by these developments, and the Bank and the IMF encouraged the authorities to do something about it. The World Bank had conducted a mid-term review in connection with the sixth development plan. Many countries abandoned planning, but we never gave up our development plans; we have had about ten of them. We always maintained our mid-term vision so that we could set our targets and decide on how to reach those goals.

The mid-term review of the sixth development plan and a similar analysis in the International Monetary Fund (IMF) led the authorities to adopt a macroeconomic stabilization program and structural adjustment process. This allowed us to avoid a crisis, but the economy remained vulnerable to external shocks, such as a drought and fallout from conflicts in the region.

The high-quality exchanges with the Bank resulted in a series of structural adjustment loans. The first was for agriculture in 1986 to deal with agricultural prices and public investment in the sector. This first sectoral loan was followed by an industrial and commercial policy adjustment loan in 1987.

These ambitious measures had mixed results. Seventy percent of production had deregulated prices. The budget deficit decreased as a percentage of GNP, but not as much as planned, because some subsidies continued. But customs duties were rapidly reduced from a 5 to 235 percent range to 15 to 41 percent range. A value-added tax was introduced, and investors took on exchange rate risks.

A third structural adjustment loan in 1988 supported continued reforms that included the financial sector in terms of better banking regulations and procedures to international standards.

Since 1997, the Bank's contributions to Tunisia have become more formal with the country assistance strategy, but the Bank continues to support Tunisia's opening of its economy more broadly, especially after the 1995 free trade agreement with the European Union.

The two country assistance strategies (CASs) covered 1997–99 and 2000–02. The first country assistance strategy had the following goals: strengthening of structural reforms to encourage competition, development of human capital, modernization of key infrastructure services, and improvement of environmental management. To reach these goals, the Bank reoriented its lending instruments toward more sectoral investment loans and fewer traditional projects and gave greater importance to nonlending instruments that included 18 reports, sectoral notes, and workshops devoted to trade, development of the private sector, public expenditures, education, transportation, water, and agriculture. The activities financed through grants helped prepare projects and complemented the analytical and sectoral work.

The second CAS built on the experience of the first and supported *(a)* consolidation of long-term development of activities in many of the traditional intervention sectors such as human resources, management of natural resources, transport, and rural and urban development and *(b)* economic reforms to strengthen resources and develop new areas of expertise such as information technology and mobilization of external financial means.

The structural reforms and prudent economic policies created favorable conditions for development of the private sector and improved competitiveness of the economy. The economy grew at 5.5 percent in 2003 and great progress has been made in health, education, and social protection. Tunisia is at the top of the list of countries with similar income and in an excellent position to reach the Millennium Development Goals. Life expectancy is now 72 years, and poverty has been reduced from 8 percent of the population in 1995 to 4 percent in 2000. Tunisia has also made tremendous progress in terms of education for young girls, reduction of fertility rates, and greater protection of women's rights. The country has also committed itself to sustainable environmental development.

Regarding the lessons learned from our experience, I can only agree with the team of OED that undertook this year an evaluation of the Bank's aid to Tunisia in the past 20 years in terms of economic management based on a general political consensus, a vast human resource basis, and a stable macroeconomic environment.

The second lesson is the pace and the breadth of reforms. They can vary, depending on the area concerned, and depend on the political or technical difficulties that exist. When they exist, external development partners must be flexible and support reforms that can be implemented, all the while keeping in mind that it is the impetus of reform that must be maintained.

Another lesson to mention is the necessity of keeping a good sense of perspective and stepping back when a political measure has been implemented. This is especially true for the development partners; it is necessary to measure the progress within the framework of a more balanced and global vision.

The most important lesson that has always brought about the most controversy with the Bank is that of the pace of reforms. We noted that the gradual approach that was applied in Tunisia was very good. Also, Tunisia decided to have a broad political consensus in sensitive areas. But this also brought about a certain slowness; however, this judicious approach allowed us to develop the necessary consensus and served the general goal of reform remarkably well.

Comments on Middle-Income Country Programs: Brazil

*Joaquim Levy**

It is very good to be here, I think this meeting is extremely good and timely. The work of the Operations Evaluation Department (OED) is very interesting and brings us a number of important lessons. I also think that Mr. Linn addresses some key issues for the Bank and for middle-income countries.

Since the beginning of the Lula government [in Brazil] last year, we have been gladdened by the level of Bank support and praise from Mr. Wolfensohn, as well as the local representatives, with whom we work very closely. But the net flows from the Bank have been negative. Brazil is repaying more to the Bank than it has received in new loans during the past two years. And this raises questions about how appropriate the Bank's mix of procedures, products, and policies is toward middle-income countries.

The good news is that there is an open and deep dialogue between the Brazilian Government and different groups in the Bank about these and other issues relating to the future. Not all of you may be familiar with the details of the situation of Brazil, but in a nutshell, the main issue is that the old type of Bank lending does not mesh with fiscal constraints in the country or even its institutional framework.

As mentioned earlier, since 1998 there has been a shift toward more programmatic and policy support loans, which has been extremely positive. We Brazilians have a very good knowledge of local conditions and the local market, but the great asset of the Bank is having people from different places with knowledge of international and cross-country experiences.

We have had a very good cooperation with Bank staff in a very difficult time. In the government, we started to rethink the liberalization of the market that began in 1995 and made a lot of progress in the years since the program began. The Bank aided in this process by implementing a loan—a programmatic loan. It was great to have all these Bank experts, but we also had very good use for the US$500 million loan when Brazil was under some stress in the international financial markets.

---

* Secretary of the National Treasury, Ministry of Finance, Brazil.

This combination of technical assistance, the programmatic loan, and dialogue was valuable, especially at a time when the government changed and there was so much worry and concern about the new policies of the new government. Such Bank support helped us continue to build on what had been started before.

These second-generation reforms are a very difficult and long process. The more you involve the private sector in infrastructure, the more difficult things are, because you have to think about competition, the many details of market structure, and appropriate institutions, such as regulation. This is hard work, and the support of the Bank has been unflagging in this area.

So the Bank can have a very important role in middle-income countries. Some Brazilian experts are giving advice to other countries, for instance, in China. This kind of exchange of experiences is good for a number of countries.

The massive intellectual input that the Bank can provide is valuable, but this should not be the only resource available from the Bank. If that were the only resource, we would have problems even financing the institution. So coming back to some of the points mentioned by our earlier speakers, which I think were very clear and precise, the Bank has been very successful in Brazil in engaging public discussion, sometimes with a lot of repercussions, so it is important to deepen the discussion. For instance, we recently had a Bank report on the business environment, and some of the figures in it became a bit controversial. So, it is important to explain the report and its findings in detail and reach out to everybody so that they understand the Bank's analytical work. The more such analytical work is understood, the more powerful it becomes.

Let me illustrate how difficult changes are with the example of increasing literacy in the poorest region in Brazil. A lot has happened in the past ten years, and as was mentioned, the contribution of the Bank increased; but this did not happen by chance. It happened mainly because the government directed resources and changed laws so poor states had the support to pay for teachers and cover the cost of improving basic education.

We now have very good results, but these policies have also given rise to serious questions. To achieve this level of commitment, the instrument used was earmarking of some tax revenues. But Brazil is now at another stage: we have plenty of money to fund elementary schools, but not enough for middle schools and high schools, which the generation that has gone through elementary school now wants to attend. Because all the money was earmarked for elementary schools, we now face new issues. So even the best policies sometimes have unintended consequences. But discussions in these areas are important.

One of the other issues mentioned was for the Bank to be flexible. We have a situation now in which, for instance, we sometimes have difficulty borrowing more for the private sector. We cannot spend all the money in the public sector, and this is one of the reasons why the flows are negative. Everybody wants to have more engagement of the private sector, but this raises issues in integrating risk assessment and the levels of lending from the International Finance Corporation and International Bank for Reconstruction and Development. So we need a fresh look at the best way to manage risk in the Bank group. This is more feasible now than in the past because, in the case of Brazil, the more we progress in terms of institutions and fiscal stability, the more appropriate it is to bring in private capital into areas such as infrastructure. When the environment was not ripe, privatization and other measures led to problems later on; but the time may now be right for changes, and it is important to have Bank support.

I can really sympathize with what I heard here from earlier speakers. Environmental issues were mentioned, and we are also experiencing this. We were glad that last year—actually this year—the Bank took some risk in supporting Brazil's environment initiatives, which were controversial. It may have been more convenient not to get involved— not take a stand—but the Bank recognized the government's efforts and the progress made since last year, and we have an important programmatic loan to support this.

This brings me to an issue that may be related to the general questions at this conference: how can conditionality best be used, especially with middle-income countries? I think that, more and more, conditionality has to strengthen the domestic institutional capacity of countries. We have learned in the past ten years working with the Bank in Brazil that a policy matrix should not be used to force policies. This will never work.

My experience with a number of loans, especially programmatic loans, is that it is best when the Bank recognizes progress that has already been made, especially in difficult areas, and shows its support with a loan. Then we agree on some common ground, and we can discuss what we would like to see as priorities. So basically, the policy matrix works as a way to list what we should expect to see in the future. It should not be tied to a second tranche of the loan or things like that, but rather used as an opportunity to meet together some time later and evaluate progress. Evaluations are increasingly important, but although there is progress in ex-post evaluations, a formal framework to evaluate the success is some years down the road.

This is constructive and builds institutions. This also supports good policies and is the way to go. I say this, not as a wish, but as a result of many years' experience with the Bank. We have had some programs that progress in stages—phase one, two, and three—and there is no pressure to move from one to the other. At the right time, however, we have the incentive to move. As my Minister Palocci says, one should never hide behind a multilateral, be it the IMF or the Bank, to do what we have to do.

We have to grow domestic support for our programs. Leaders must build support, form a consensus, and then move ahead. That is the way to have enduring reforms. Real ownership is the key to success in dealing with the multilaterals. And ownership brings with it accountability and transparency. This is the way that Brazil has dealt with the multilaterals in the past few years and continues to do so with very good results.

I would like to congratulate the Bank again for this process of evaluation and for listening to its constituents. As Mr. Linn said, the financial part is an integral part of the Bank if it is to have a meaningful role in middle-income countries. The Bank's support is part of the common agreements and discussions that, like similar discussions with academics and congress, ensure that good policies are followed. The results will be improved performance in our economies and in our social indicators.

Floor Discussion on Lessons from Middle-Income Country Programs

AUDIENCE PARTICIPANT: One thing I would be interested in hearing about from perhaps the Bank officials and also Mr. Linn, if he wants to respond, is how the Bank is going to measure its success in helping middle-income countries, because speakers in other sessions as well as this one have stressed that the Bank contributes not just through financing, but also through its knowledge products and diagnostic work and policy advice.

There is obviously some tendency to focus on just the gross flows to these countries. But, given their needs and the importance of developing the private sector—which is not going to entail IBRD lending, but maybe the IFC or policy lending that helps leverage the private sector—how is the World Bank going to tell whether it has been successful in these countries?

MR. RAMACHANDRAN: I guess the proof of the pudding is in the eating; much has to do with if, in the view of the country officials involved, the Bank added value in its work. And because the work is so complicated, the evaluation will also be complicated.

This is exactly what the country assistance evaluations (CAEs) try to attempt. I would urge you to read any of the CAEs; they suggest ways in which the evaluation can be done, the limitations of the review, and the difficulties involved.

MR. LINN: I think you obviously face a complex problem, as we all know. There are a lot of places where you are struggling with how to measure success, not only in middle-income countries. But, if you have laid out a strategy in the country assistance strategies that is fairly specific—both in terms of the instrumentalities that you are proposing, priorities you are setting, sequencing and effects you expect, together with a sense of commitment from the government—if three to four years later, you can say there are benefits both in terms of growth and social impacts—girls are in school, the social support system is actually reaching out further, land reform in agriculture or incentive reforms are progressing, you have macroeconomic stability, and your debt crisis is more or less under control—you can then look back and say it worked.

Now, if you fail, it is more difficult, obviously, because then you have to trace back why did it fail—where did we go wrong—and make the tough assessment that OED very often helps us with.

So, I think that is how I would look at it. The country assistance strategy is obviously key. And by the way, in the future I would hope that the example of Kazakhstan is being followed— that we call it a country partnership strategy, rather than assistance strategy. That generally goes down much better in middle-income countries.

AUDIENCE PARTICIPANT: There has been much talk about policy reform, but it seems to me that policy reform contains a lot of things. Should there not be more discussion about what the priorities are and sequencing of things regarding policy reform?

MR. RAMACHANDRAN: If I can just quickly say, policy reform and priorities and frequency—and I agree with the sentiment expressed in the question that it is not all policies—is what do you do first and what is most important. Again, the country assistance evaluations attempt to deal with these issues. I cannot summarize one without going into more detail, so I would urge you to read them.

MR. LINN: Here let me refer to examples. I think that the best example in the Europe and Central Asia Region of where the priorities and sequencing was well done—and I am not saying this because Ajay Chhibber is now here at OED or because there is a country assistance evaluation coming up, so I say it with some trepidation—is Turkey.

My sense was that there was, first of all, priority setting in terms of broad areas of engagement or reforms of the government, then broad areas of engagement, a focused response of the Bank—not all over, but in a few areas—and then a programmatic approach that combined policy lending and investment lending in a multi-year framework that actually worked out remarkably well.

There were times when crises and whatever got in the middle of it, including earthquakes, and one had to adjust. But I think if you look back now, together with a sequence of governments, starting with Kemal Derviş' government and now the current government, reforms have been owned and supported in a very consistent and strong way. The "dangling carrot"—the umbrella of EU accession—also combined to help set priorities and get the sequencing right in a programmatic framework. That had a very important role for lending both on the investment and the policy side.

Part 5

Lessons from Post-Conflict Countries

Lessons Learned from World Bank Experience in Post-Conflict Reconstruction

*Fareed M. A. Hassan**

Introduction

Since 1980, more than 50 countries have experienced significant periods of conflict with severe and lasting effects in terms of destruction of physical assets, disruption in trade links, displacement of people, and loss of income and life (genocide). For example, Rwanda was scarred by the genocide of 1994, in which around one million people were killed, three million people displaced, the gross domestic product halved, and poverty worsened. Damage estimates from the 15-year (1975–90) civil war in Lebanon have been as high as US$25 billion (150 percent of gross domestic product). In Bosnia-Herzegovina the cost of reconstruction has been estimated at US$5.1 billion (100 percent of gross domestic product). Lebanon's post-conflict real per capita income was estimated at about one-third its 1975 level. Similarly, post-war incomes in Bosnia-Herzegovina have recovered to only about 70 percent of pre-war incomes.

The proportion of official development assistance devoted to relief increased from 2 percent in 1989 to 10 percent in 1994 and further to 27 percent in 2003. Official assistance to post-conflict countries, however,

* Senior Evaluation Officer, Operations Evaluation Department, World Bank Group.

varies widely: although Bosnia-Herzegovina received US$3,652 million in fiscal 1996–99 or US$246 per capita per year, Eritrea received US$589 million in fiscal 1994–97 or US$41 per capita per year (attachment A). U.N. peacekeeping operations alone cost the international community US$3 billion in 1995 and US$2.6 billion in 2002.

The World Bank is engaged in 38 post-conflict countries and areas.[1] A fifth of Bank commitments were devoted to those countries in fiscal 2004 (table 1). When Bank commitments to Bosnia-Herzegovina are compared with the Bank's response in other post-conflict countries, the exceptional nature of the Bosnia-Herzegovina case stands out starkly (figure 1 and attachment B). The Bank created a new Post-Conflict Unit in 1998 and instituted a new grant facility, the Post-Conflict Fund, to reinforce its capacity to respond to reconstruction situations. Twenty-two conflict-affected countries have ongoing Post-Conflict Fund grants. Drawing on the experience of the Bank in post-conflict settings and in recognition of the unique nature of post-conflict situations, the role of the Bank, and the risks involved, in 1997 the Bank's Board of Directors endorsed a policy framework paper on the role of the World Bank in post-conflict reconstruction; this was followed in 2001 by Operational Policy and Bank Procedures 2.30 on Development Cooperation and Conflict.[2] The Bank has also forged partnerships with other donors, as they play a vital role in the reconstruction process.

TABLE 1
World Bank Commitments for Post-Conflict Countries in Fiscal 2004

	Commitments in millions of US$	Percent of total commitments
International Development Association (IDA)	2,581	29
International Bank for Reconstruction and Development (IBRD)	1,217	11
Total	3,798	19

Source: World Bank Database as of August 2005.

This paper examines the World Bank's experience in post–conflict reconstruction with the objective of extracting lessons for future assistance. The paper draws on the considerable work completed by the World Bank's Operations Evaluation Department (OED): *(a)* a post-conflict report assessing Bank experience in nine countries (Bosnia-Herzegovina, Cambodia, El Salvador, Eritrea, Haiti, Lebanon, Rwanda, Sri Lanka, and Uganda [World Bank 1998]) and *(b)* eight in-depth country assistance evaluations (CAEs) on post-conflict countries and areas: Bosnia-Herzegovina, Cambodia, Croatia, Eritrea, Haiti, Rwanda, Uganda, and West Bank and Gaza. These studies assess the effectiveness (i.e., relevance, efficacy, and efficiency) of Bank lending operations and emergency grants and evaluate the Bank's role in providing analytical and advisory services, including economic and sector work, policy advice, technical assistance, and donor coordination. The paper also draws on the 1997 policy framework paper on the role of the Bank in post-conflict reconstruction as well as Bank strategy, economic and sector work, project, and program documents.

FIGURE 1
Average Annual Per Capita IDA Commitments for Post-Conflict Countries

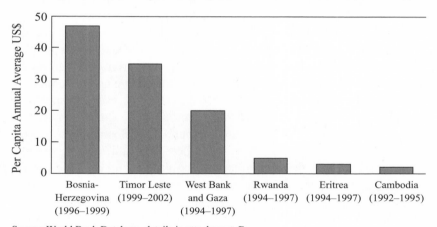

Source: World Bank Database, details in attachment B.

Lessons Learned in Light of the Experience Gained

Four lessons emerged from the Bank's experience with post-conflict reconstruction, including the need for: *(a)* early engagement in post-conflict situations, *(b)* strong and continuous field presence, *(c)* adaptation of Bank services and products to post-conflict situations, and *(d)* effective aid coordination and partnerships with other donors. Adhering closely to these lessons helps enhance donor and Bank effectiveness in post-conflict settings.

Early Engagement in Post-Conflict Situations

The need for early engagement in post-conflict countries is strongly indicated by Bank experience, as time is of the essence in post-conflict situations. Windows of opportunities often exist within which significant progress is possible, but these opportunities can quickly pass. In general, the Bank has responded quickly and flexibly in initiating contact and preparing or participating in preparation of strategy and funding packages. Experience in Bosnia-Herzegovina and West Bank and Gaza, for example, illustrates the critical value of early planning and preparation of reconstruction programs. The Bank was involved in West Bank and Gaza even before the 1993 Oslo Accord, preparing a comprehensive analysis of the development needs of the area (World Bank 1993). Although this early involvement has now become an integral part of the Bank's guidelines, at the time, the Bank's role was unusual. Although the Bank initially hesitated to engage in a territory in a highly visible and politicized context, representing neither a sovereign state nor a member country, OED noted that the Bank took an appropriate risk, given the importance of sustaining the peace process to achieve any development effectiveness (World Bank 2002b). Also, the Bank moved quickly to support reconstruction in Bosnia-Herzegovina.[3] The Bank approved an exceptional level of IDA/Trust Fund resources for Bosnia-Herzegovina in 1996–2003, committing a total of US$983 million, which, on a per capita basis, is more than any other post-conflict country to date. On the other hand, the failure of the international community as a whole to provide early and adequate support to Rwanda during the first three months of genocide (April–June 1994) had undermined stability and development efforts (Steering Committee of the Joint Evaluation of Emergency Assistance to Rwanda 1996). The Bank responded to the conditions created by the genocide with an Emergency Assistance Grant (US$20 million) in August 1994, which was implemented through four United Nations (UN) agencies (U.N. Children's Fund [UNICEF], U.N. High Commissioner for Refugees [UNHCR], U.N. Food and Agriculture Organization [FAO], and World Health Organization [WHO]); however, it took nearly two years following the genocide for the Bank to become fully re-engaged in Rwanda, a situation discussed below.

Many factors constrain the Bank's early engagement in post-conflict situations, including the presence of "stateless societies" and arrears to the Bank. The lack of a government counterpart for the Bank when states collapse and no clear authority emerges, as in Somalia, constrains the nature and size of Bank assistance. In other cases, where the outcome is fairly clear, the Bank has creatively worked within the existing framework to provide resources to governments even before their states are recognized as formal members of the Bretton Woods institutions, as occurred with the emergency loan for Eritrea via an agreement with the Ethiopian government.[4] Other solutions were found in the cases of West Bank and Gaza and Bosnia-Herzegovina. In the case of West Bank and Gaza the World Bank executive directors agreed that assistance to nonmembers was warranted "for the benefit of members."

Outstanding debt and arrears to the Bank constitute an additional complication to the Bank's early engagement. Because access to resources from the Bank and other international financial institutions (IFIs) is important for most post-conflict countries' medium- and long-term development, planning financial normalization is crucial. Normalization will depend on a variety of factors, including the size of the arrears and the amount of support available from the international donor community to assist with financing. The resumption of Bank lending to a number of post-conflict countries has depended on resolving the issue of outstanding debt. For example, before Bosnia-Herzegovina could join the Bank in 1996, a solution had to be found for the stock of Bank debt (US$621 million) that the country had assumed as its share of the debts of the former Socialist Federal Republic of Yugoslavia, of which 80 percent was in arrears. The Bank renegotiated this debt as three new Bank loans on relatively concessional terms. In the case of Lebanon, despite the conflict, repayments on loans were made without undue delays, such that arrears were not a problem for Bank re-engagement. For countries in nonaccrual status (e.g., Haiti), the Bank has prepared Country Re-engagement Notes to position the Bank to provide assistance when conditions permit.

In a number of post-conflict countries, however, Bank support began with little or no sustained contact between the Bank and the country for critical or extended periods. For example, the Bank was absent for significant periods before reentry in Cambodia (20 years) and Lebanon (15 years). In such instances, the Bank's absence from a conflict country for extended periods has restricted the Bank's response capacity once the conflict has receded. For example, the quality of the Bank's portfolio in Lebanon has been low and has deteriorated since 1997. OED evaluated four completed projects during fiscal 1997–2004 and concluded that only one project was rated as moderately satisfactory in terms of outcome, and the Bank performance was only satisfactory in half the cases. Even absences during shorter but critical intervals (e.g., Rwanda in 1994 and 1995) have had an impact on the Bank's ability to interact effectively with a new government and adversely affected the ability of staff to recognize, in a timely fashion, opportunities to support the transition of a country out of conflict.

Strong and Continuous Field Presence

The need for a strong and continuous field presence is the second lesson to emerge from Bank experience. Post-conflict situations are complicated and involve a multitude of players and organizations. Field presence is essential to monitoring Bank programs and projects, maintaining coordination with other donors (see below), and responding quickly and flexibly to changes. Bank field missions need to be strengthened to meet post-conflict roles. An expansion of field presence and the devolution of authority to managers in the field have proved to be a critical aspect of Bank programs in the West Bank and Gaza and in Bosnia-Herzegovina and should be considered strongly for other countries where local dynamics are similarly complicated and in flux. West Bank and Gaza was the first program to be decentralized to the field in 1994, before the practice was mainstreamed throughout the Bank.[5] It provided a model for transferring decisionmaking and accountability to the field.

To enhance the effectiveness of its intervention in Bosnia-Herzegovina, the Bank opened a Resident Mission there in early 1996 (despite concern over personal safety), hired competent local professional staff to help supervise projects, and established project management units (PMUs), all of which enhanced the effectiveness of Bank interventions. Almost all of the reconstruction projects had successful outcomes, and the Bank performance was judged both timely and highly relevant and should serve as an example of good practice in post-conflict reconstruction. Although project management units (PMUs) helped the Bank implement its projects in a transitional/ emergency phase, long-term measures should be undertaken to strengthen the country's institutions, as discussed below. The Bank has met the need for strong field presence through other mechanisms. When the Bank first began work in Eritrea, for example, it worked through the United Nations Development Programme (UNDP) office to organize the first economic report and emergency recovery program.

In contrast, the absence of a strong field presence reduced Bank effectiveness in a number of reconstruction programs. The absence of Bank representation in Haiti reduced the ability of the Bank to work with key donors, such as Inter-American Development Bank and the U.S. Agency for International Development, which are more decentralized, as well as government and civil society; any decision to gear up the Bank program may necessitate an increased Bank presence (World Bank 2002a). Also, the results of the Bank's working relationship had been mixed in the aftermath of the Rwanda genocide due to the lack of a fully staffed Bank country office for two years after the genocide (World Bank 2004c). The OED evaluation of Bank assistance in Rwanda also reported that some government implementing agencies believed there was a shortage of operational staff in the Kigali country office. The comments made by the government on the evaluation emphasized that strengthening the local Bank office is vital in early stages. As indicated earlier, a limited Bank field presence can be supported by partnership with U.N. agencies with significant presence in the country or through the use of extended Bank missions by task managers. The evaluation of Bank assistance in Rwanda concluded that the Bank did not put as many resources into supervision as were required by complex project design and should continue to coordinate its effort with other donors closely. Similarly, frequent changes in Bank staff reduced the effectiveness of Bank programs in Eritrea and Haiti.[6]

Adapting Bank Services and Products to Post-Conflict Situations

The uncertainties inherent in post-conflict situations, suggest a different approach is required, as it is not always feasible for the Bank to define an overall country assistance strategy (CAS) beforehand. Rather an "opportunistic" approach is needed, building on what is feasible. When conditions do not warrant a full CAS, the Bank has recently adapted its approach and prepared transitional support strategies for nine countries, including Afghanistan (2003), Angola (2003), Burundi (2002), Democratic Republic of Congo (2004), and Eritrea (2000), that are consistent with the Bank's post-conflict policy.[7] The Bank has also used flexibility in implementing these strategies, reviewed and revised its existing services and products to facilitate an appropriate and efficient response in light of the experience gained. For example, the Bank has appropriately adapted its strategies to the changing circumstances in West Bank and Gaza, initially focusing on infrastructure development, shifting to emergency support for employment creation in response to the 1996 economic crisis, and, as the situation stabilized, then shifting to medium-term institutional development (World Bank 2002b). Similarly, in the intermediate postgenocide period in Rwanda, emergency assistance dominated, but this was later replaced by assistance for economic policy reform with emphasis on poverty reduction, reconciliation, and improvement of basic social services and institutions (World Bank 2004c).

Most of the Bank's lending to post-conflict countries has been in rebuilding physical infrastructure, such as roads and buildings, carried out under the Bank's guidelines for emergency lending.[8] The overall reconstruction effort has, however, been the Bank at its best (World Bank 2004a). In fiscal 1985–95, 14 emergency projects were approved to support reconstruction in countries emerging from conflict. During fiscal 1996 and the first half of fiscal 1997, 16 additional emergency projects were approved for Bosnia-Herzegovina alone, representing a total International Development Association allocation and Trust Fund commitment of US$356 million. For the first time in the history of the Bank, most of a portfolio in a country is being implemented under emergency provisions. Similarly, Rwanda's emergency and reconstruction period lasted until 1998, but normal development activities have predominated only since 2001. It should be noted that these emergency recovery loans do not address long-term economic, sectoral, or institutional problems and do not include conditionality linked to macroeconomic policies. They include only conditions directly related to emergency recovery activities and to preparedness in the event the disaster recurs. Although such an approach is valid for reconstruction following natural disasters, post-conflict reconstruction requires a broader approach that takes into account the multifaceted impacts of long, violent conflict.

Recent Bank responses have included operations specifically designed to promote economic adjustment and recovery, social development, and, to a lesser extent, institution building. With Bank support, Bosnia-Herzegovina's education and health services were restored, a degree of pension reform achieved, and some cross-entity cooperation realized.[9] The Bank has made a positive contribution to employment generation and poverty alleviation in West Bank and Gaza. Recent lending operations also involve unique post-conflict elements, including demining operations (e.g., Bosnia-Herzegovina and Croatia) and demobilization and reintegration of ex-combatants and refugees (e.g., Cambodia, Rwanda, and Uganda). Demining is one area where the Bank's record is less than satisfactory, but given the Bank's experience with a relatively small number of operations, this finding should be viewed as preliminary.[10] The Bank's support for demobilization and reintegration has been largely successful with a couple of exceptions. In Rwanda, for instance, more than 19,000 combatants have been demobilized through the Bank-supported Demobilization and Reintegration Program.

In a number of highly visible and politically charged post-conflict situations, however, the Bank found itself operating in ways that were inconsistent with its more traditional role of supporting long-term economic and social development. For example, the Bank administered the financing of recurrent budgetary expenditures for a number of years in West Bank and Gaza, something it had never done before, and developed a program of emergency employment creation, which initially involved nonproductive activities (such as street sweeping), although this was quickly converted to support for more productive activities. More important, OED's evaluation of Bank assistance in Bosnia-Herzegovina, Haiti, Rwanda, and West Bank and Gaza found that the Bank has not always been successful in using leverage (conditionality, delayed program/project funding, and overall levels of funding) in support of the implementation of important reforms, particularly in governance and public sector management and in sound economic policies; political pressures of other stakeholders and the fragility of the whole situation were simply too great to allow the Bank to operate as it would have in a more normal setting. For instance, the 2002 Rwanda CAS was frank in citing weaknesses of past Bank postgenocide strategies, including the lack of attention to public sector capacity building and relatively little analytical work to underpin Bank assistance. The Haiti CAE concludes that the development impact of Bank assistance to the country since 1986 has been negligible, as the critical constraints to development—governance and public sector capacity and accountability—have not diminished (World Bank 2002a).

Building on the CAE recommendations, Bank assistance in post-conflict settings should give priority to governance and institutional issues in almost all sectors. The West Bank and Gaza evaluation recommends that the Bank should try to ensure a competent, transparent, fiscally sound governing structure that will be at the heart of the sustainability of the development effort. The Cambodia and Bosnia-Herzegovina CAEs find that the Bank could have done more to address problems of governance, particularly weak customs administration, tax evasion, and smuggling, and should rethink its approach to private sector development (e.g., imposing hard budget constraints on public enterprises, removing legal and institutional barriers to privatization, and strengthening privatization agencies). Similarly, the West Bank and Gaza and Rwanda CAEs recommend that Bank assistance should be centered on enhancing the enabling environment for private sector development, emphasizing the rule of law and property rights development. Bank assistance should also focus on helping Rwanda resolve the technical and institutional constraints to development of the agriculture sector, which dominates the economy; 90 percent of the population resides in rural areas. In addition, the Haiti CAE notes that without improved governance and institutional reforms, the Bank and other donors will be able to accomplish very little.

Overly ambitious Bank program and weak country capacity. In a post-conflict setting, in particular, when considerable uncertainty exists, assistance programs should not be ambitious and their objectives should include capacity building. The Rwanda CAE recommends that project design should be simple and sufficient Bank resources should be allocated to ensure close project supervision. The recommendation is based on the CAE finding that project lending regularly failed for two reasons: overly ambitious design and inadequate supervision given the country need.[11] Government comments on the Rwanda CAE noted that in designing projects and programs, limited capacity should be assumed and compensated for until steady state is attained. Likewise, the significance of weak capacity has to be recognized and provided for in the case of Eritrea (World Bank 2004b). Also, the Haiti CAE concluded that the Bank and other donors erred by offering traditional assistance programs to the country without identifying the fundamental governance and political barriers to development and by overwhelming fragile absorptive capacity (World Bank 2002a). Similarly OED's post-conflict report found a total mismatch between the levels of foreign aid to Haiti and government capacity (World Bank 1998). In such instances, lending could be channeled through piloting activities, possibly through the use of learning and innovation loans, which would contribute to institution building, or through adaptable lending instruments.

A flexible approach to technical assistance. In post-conflict situations, the challenge of delivering effective technical assistance may be even greater. In Cambodia, Eritrea, and West Bank and Gaza, for example, delivering effective technical assistance has been plagued with difficulties. These findings reinforce conclusions from experience with technical assistance projects in more normal settings. First, within broadly defined priorities, flexibility should be built into technical assistance provided in post-conflict situations. Second, the Bank should make particular effort to ensure adequate resources and staff continuity for supervision. It is preferable to take a flexible approach to providing technical assistance, start with modest amounts of funding, and be prepared, as in the case of West Bank and Gaza, to commit large resources to close supervision.

The use of PMUs has been an issue in many post-conflict situations. The establishment of PMUs has served the Bank well in the immediate post-conflict period, as the CAEs for Bosnia-Herzegovina, Eritrea, Haiti, and West Bank and Gaza point out. The short-term benefit of good project implementation, however, has a direct tradeoff with long-term institutional development of line ministries. Sometimes the existence of a PMU creates tensions and jealousies among government officials. The Bosnia-Herzegovina CAE recommends that the use of PMUs be discontinued and PMUs should be absorbed into government structures (World Bank 2004a). This recommendation is endorsed by the government in its commentary on the CAE. Similarly, the Eritrea CAE recommends that PMUs should be used with an explicit exit strategy (World Bank 2004b). To reduce dependence on PMUs, certain PMU activities (particularly procurement and financial management) could be contracted out to safeguard the Bank's fiduciary obligations, until significant strengthening of government procedures and processes take place.[12]

Effective Aid Coordination and Partnerships with Other Donors

Effective aid coordination in a reconstruction program improves Bank responsiveness to the realities of post-conflict situations. The Bank collaborated with the IMF in developing a stabilization program[13] and played a catalytic role in supporting, mobilizing, and coordinating aid for the reconstruction effort. At the request of international donors, the Bank has played a key role in coordinating international aid in the West Bank and Gaza, Bosnia-Herzegovina, and other transitional situations through the Holst Fund (US$270 million pledged by 26 donors) and other mechanisms. The Bank has successfully mobilized additional assistance to post-conflict countries. For example, in fiscal 1994–2001, the West Bank and Gaza program secured an extraordinary amount of cofinancing/parallel funding—US$541 million against US$326 in Bank commitments—a ratio of US$1.66 on every Bank dollar. Similarly, donors funded more than 50 percent of the cost of projects that the Bank prepared in Bosnia-Herzegovina. The Bank's expertise has proved to be a critical aspect of the Dayton talks on Bosnia-Herzegovina, contributing a reconstruction and development perspective and providing practical advice on intermediate matters such as the implications for economic governance, budgets, economic incentives of proposed government structures, and taxation and demobilization arrangements. On the other hand, had the Bank played a more formal role in the negotiations leading up to the El Salvador Peace Accords of January 1992, a clearer, more realistic picture of the costs of the various provisions might have emerged earlier (World Bank 1998).

Partnerships with the United Nations and other donor agencies need to be forged as soon as possible, as they play a critical role in delivering aid and services in post-conflict situations. Early agreement should be reached at a high level, however, on the respective roles of the main players and especially on who will have the lead role in each sector. Early Bank involvement helps to define its role to ensure that its comparative advantage is put to its best use within the international community, ensure realistic planning on the part of the Bank, and facilitate integration of the goals of the peace process into Bank strategies. OED noted in general that an understanding was reached on which institution would take the leading role in specific sectors in reconstruction programs. In Bosnia-Herzegovina, the Bank and the donor community expected the Bank to take a leading role in reconstruction. The Bank organized a consultative group meeting in Haiti in 1997, which designated lead donors in priority sectors; included NGO, civil society, and media; and was considered a model for other post-conflict programs (World Bank 1998). There are indications that the overall response of the international community is enhanced by cohesive multi-donor funding strategies. In the case of West Bank and Gaza, the Bank worked closely with U.N. agencies in the field, which proved to be an effective partnership, but in the cases of Haiti and Rwanda, while partnering effectively with other donors at the higher levels, the Bank did not promote effective coordination on the ground (World Bank 2002a, 2002b, and 2004c).[14] The Bank took an appropriate risk in assuming the role of administering donor funds to West Bank and Gaza. Also, the Bank's strategy and objectives for Bosnia-Herzegovina were timely and relevant for the country situation and were closely integrated with the approaches of other donors (World Bank 2004a).

In collaborating with other donors, the Bank's main role is to help close the gap between relief and development. Fostering a better understanding of the operational implications of this transition would help avoid negative patterns that can jeopardize later reconstruction and development efforts. The Bank should have a clear appreciation early in the process of how its assistance will engage and take over from emergency operations. The Bank managed to close the gap between relief measures and long-term development in many instances in West Bank and Gaza, for example, by converting the short-term emergency assistance program into community development projects.[15] Several voluminous reports, including recent Bank analytic work, *Development Under Adversity: The Palestinian Economy in Transition* (Diwan and Shaban 1999), analyzed challenges and policies needed for long-term growth. In the case of Rwanda, however, the relative paucity of Bank analytical work in a country transitioning from enormous social, political, and economic upheaval is striking (World Bank 2004c).[16]

Concluding Remarks

Lessons that emerged from Bank experience with post-conflict reconstruction included:

- Engage early and deploy a strong field presence
- Coordinate aid, establish partnerships with other donors, and agree on respective roles of each donor
- Adapt services and products to post-conflict situations.

These lessons are relevant for effective Bank and donor assistance to post-conflict countries.

ATTACHMENT A
Average Annual Per Capita Official Assistance (Net Disbursements)
for Post-Conflict Countries

Country Name and Years	Total Cumulative Amount (US$)	Average Population (millions)	Per Capita Annual Average (US$)
Timor Leste (1999–2002)	800	0.8	264
Bosnia-Herzegovina (1996–99)	3652	3.7	246
West Bank and Gaza (1994–97)	2112	2.5	215
Rwanda (1994–97)*	2115	5.9	89
Eritrea (1994–97)	589	3.6	41
Cambodia (1992–95)	1394	10.2	34

Note: Official assistance includes both emergency relief and development assistance. Figures are from Organization for Economic Cooperation and Development (OECD) Development Assistance Committee (DAC) databases and are considerably higher than World Bank and IMF data.

*Underestimated, because considerable assistance channeled to refugees outside Rwanda.

Source: OECD/DAC and World Bank Databases and World Development Indicators.

ATTACHMENT B
Average Annual Per Capita IDA Commitments for Post-Conflict Countries

Country Name and Years	Total Cumulative Amount (US$)	Average Population (millions)	Per Capita Annual Average (US$)
Timor Leste (1999–2002)	107	0.8	35
Bosnia-Herzegovina (1996–99)	698	3.7	47
West Bank and Gaza (1994–97)	194	2.5	20
Rwanda (1994–97)*	127	5.9	5
Eritrea (1994–97)	49	3.6	3
Cambodia (1992–95)	100	10.2	2

Source: World Bank Databases as of February 5, 2004 and World Development Indicators.

Notes

1. Of these 38 countries, six are in nonaccrual status, four have prepared country re-engagement notes, nine have a transitional support strategy, seven have prepared interim poverty reduction strategy papers, nine have prepared full poverty reduction strategy papers, and the remaining had a country assistance strategy as of March 2004 (World Bank data).
2. The 1997 paper drew on a draft of a World Bank report (1998).
3. The rapid response of the Bank, in the case of Bosnia-Herzegovina, was possible in part because, beginning in late 1994, Bank staff met frequently with officials outside the country. After October 1995, Bank staff were able to work with the government and agencies in the country to develop estimates of reconstruction needs and prepare specific reconstruction projects. In early 1996, the Bank established a US$150 million trust fund for the country and opened a resident mission in Sarajevo.
4. The 1993 Recovery and Reconstruction Project for Eritrea became effective in advance of Eritrean Bank membership.
5. More than two-thirds of Bank country directors are now in the field.
6. For example, a reorganization in 1991 moved Haiti to a different department, and between 1994 and 1997, Haiti had three directors and three country operations division chiefs.
7. According to the Operational Policy and Bank Procedures 2.30 on Development Cooperation and Conflict when a conflict leads to significant changes in the environment for Bank assistance, the country director, determines whether *(a)* continued assistance in accordance with the CAS is feasible, *(b)* conditions warrant initiating a transitional support strategy, or *(c)* continued assistance is no longer feasible and a watching brief should be initiated.
8. The Bank's policy on emergency recovery assistance is set out in Operational Policy 8.50 (OP/BP 8.5).
9. Customs harmonization is one example.
10. Although strong economic and humanitarian reasons exist for demining, the main lesson learned from the OED post-conflict report is that Bank involvements should focus primarily on indirect, nonclearance activities, such as coordination, information and mine awareness, training, and institution building. Consistent with the February 1997 "Bank Operational Guidelines on Demining," support for landmine clearance should be provided always as an integral part of a specific development activity, for example, road construction (World Bank 1998).
11. Sixty percent of disbursements for investment projects were evaluated as having unsatisfactory outcomes (World Bank 2004c).
12. The Haiti CAE noted, however, that the nearly constant state of crisis and recurring instability in the country have blocked any long-term strategy to reduce dependence on PMUs (World Bank 2002a).
13. For example, there was tension between the IMF and the Bank about stabilization in Uganda, in particular how large the budget deficit could be and whether expected donor inflows could be counted on. As a result, the Bank arguably pushed for raising taxes prematurely (World Bank 1998).
14. The Bank did not play as active a role in aid coordination as it might have at the beginning of the post-conflict period in the summer and fall of 1994, particularly within Rwanda itself. It was hampered in this regard by the absence of a resident representative until January 1995 and by the resident representative's intermittent presence until June 1996.

15. These projects supported small-scale labor-intensive works, but involved communities more proactively in the selection and implementation of projects, and maintained its focus in other areas on long-term objectives.
16. The Bank undertook two large public expenditure reviews, as well as smaller analyses of public expenditure in the health and education sectors. The only other postgenocide analytical work was a strategy note for the agriculture sector (World Bank 2004c, p. vi).

References

Ishac Diwan and Radwan Shaban. 1999. *Development under Adversity: The Palestinian Economy in Transition*. Washington D.C.: World Bank.

Steering Committee of the Joint Evaluation of Emergency Assistance to Rwanda. 1996. *The International Response to Conflict and Genocide: Lessons from the Rwanda Experience*. Copenhagen: Danish International Development Agency (DANIDA); London: Overseas Development Institute.

World Bank. 1993. *Developing the Occupied Territories: An Investment in Peace*. Report No. 12360. September 1993.

———. 1998. *The World Bank's Experience with Post-Conflict Reconstruction*. Report No. 17752. Operations Evaluation Department (OED), Washington D.C.

———. 1999. *Uganda: Country Assistance Evaluation*. Report No. 22120. OED, Washington D.C.

———. 2000. *Cambodia: Country Assistance Evaluation*. Report No. 21354. OED, Washington D.C.

———. 2002a. *Haiti: Country Assistance Evaluation*. Report No. 23637. Washington D.C.

———. 2002b. *West Bank and Gaza: An Evaluation of Bank Assistance*. Report No. 23820. OED, Washington D.C.

———. 2004a. *Bosnia and Herzegovina: Country Assistance Evaluation*. Report No. 29824. OED, Washington D.C.

———. 2004b. *Eritrea: Country Assistance Evaluation*. Report No. 28778. OED, Washington D.C.

———. 2004c. *Rwanda: Country Assistance Evaluation*. Report No. 27568. OED, Washington D.C.

Comments on Post-Conflict Country Lessons from Rwanda

Minister Donald Kaberuka*

I would like to begin by congratulating my colleague Minister Marić on the excellent results achieved in Bosnia-Herzegovina. Rwanda is also cited as a successful post-conflict case. In my view, not yet.

At the outset, I would like to note that I agree completely with the OED presentation on the four key issues: early engagement, strong field presence, need to adapt processes and instruments to post-conflict situations, and importance of aid coordination.

I will confine my remarks to four points:

First, each conflict case is different. They differ in terms of the underlying causes, the depth of the destruction, and the duration; therefore, the responses have to be tailored to local circumstances. The circumstances in Bosnia-Herzegovina do not apply to Rwanda and vice versa. So, my first point is that, although there are generic lessons, there are country-specific issues that need to be addressed in each case.

Let me take one example. Rwanda in 1994 was one of the fastest genocides in human history: in three months, one million people were killed, including very highly skilled people—doctors, nurses and teachers—and because a particular community was targeted. In a situation like Rwanda, therefore, one cannot assume that there are skilled people to implement donor programs. But, many donor projects, including the Bank's, made unrealistic assumptions about the existence of local capacity. Bank staff were concerned that there were no accountants to monitor project units and that audits were not completed on time. But, Rwanda had no skilled accountants.

One lesson that I have learned from this experience is that one needs to understand the situation on the ground and design interventions accordingly. But, the Bank has a tendency to design a good project—a high-tech project—that may make sense in a more steady state economy, but that in a post-conflict country simply leads to frustration on both sides. There are currently two Bank projects in Rwanda that are performing unsatisfactorily, because unrealistic assumptions about local capacity were embedded in their design.

*   Honorable Minister of Finance and Planning, Rwanda.

125

Second, in Rwanda we are having great difficulties in mobilizing resources for higher education. Higher education is not popular nowadays. But, my impression from the Development Committee meeting yesterday was that infrastructure is being rediscovered. Higher education also needs to be rediscovered, because after the Rwandan genocide, as noted earlier, there is a need to train doctors and teachers to create a minimum capacity for the state to function.

Third, there is a need for close collaboration with other donors and especially the International Monetary Fund (IMF). In a post-conflict situation, the best way to support a country is through flexible lending mechanisms, particularly budget support. It is the best way to ensure quickly that the systems begins to function again. In terms of the debt situation and other macroeconomic considerations, the Bank and the IMF need to work very closely together. In Rwanda and other situations, the Bank has been willing to provide budget support and, hence, the resources needed to support the process of post-conflict building, but the IMF is cautious because of, for example, debt sustainability issues. Debt sustainability is important, but the Bank should not cede its responsibility to arrive at its own macroeconomic understanding of the situation. The Bank should not hand over its responsibility on macroeconomic issues to the IMF, as the Bank may be prevented from moving forward on the issues that it considers important in a country. This has definitely been the case in Rwanda.

Following up on this point, it is important to note that post-conflict is not a night and day situation. A country does not pass from conflict to nonconflict seamlessly; there is a continuum. In Rwanda, in 1994 the economy declined by 64 percent and inflation was in the high double digits. Now, the macro situation has stabilized. When one comes to Rwanda, unless one is informed that there was a conflict, one might not know there was such devastation until one sees half a million orphans and half a million child-headed homes. This implies that, although we have come from active conflict, the conflict still affects our society in important ways.

Rwanda's and Bosnia-Herzegovina's needs are still enormous. Rwanda's revenue base is very small, and, therefore, external support will be very important for some time. But it has to be an external support that is ambitious and realistic.

The Bank cannot do everything. It needs to mobilize other donors. The Bank and the IMF need to collaborate closely, so they can become leaders in the effort to mobilize other donors. Today, however, we are being forced to make a choice between aid from this donor or that donor. This is not productive. If the donor community is going to help rebuild countries from conflict, as is the case in many parts of Africa, closer collaboration among donors needs to be achieved so that these choices do not need to be made. We need to create an aid coordination framework on a long-term basis to plan and implement aid resources to rebuild societies that are emerging from conflict.

Fourth, the role of the state is important. Many economists—including myself—are rightly suspicious of the state. We think that the private sector can do a better job than the state. But, in a post-conflict situation, not only is the state weakened, but also the private sector. The state, hopefully, a democratic state, needs to be rebuilt, and that takes time. But—and this is important—the private sector also has to be rebuilt. Nevertheless, programs are formulated that set specific conditionalities for loan disbursements and timetables for privatization. So a privatization program is quickly put in place. The consequence is a bad transaction, but the conditionality is met and the money is received. But after the transaction is completed, one finds the objective of the transaction—economic efficiency—has not been achieved. In some cases, the enterprise needs to be placed back into the hands of the state. So, especially in a post-conflict situation, speed should not take precedence over the quality of the transaction.

In a post-conflict situation, one needs to assess carefully what the state can do, what the private sector can do, and what they can do jointly and in what period things can be accomplished.

Comments on Post-Conflict Country Lessons from Bosnia-Herzegovina

Minister Ljerka Marić*

I would like to discuss our case study, "Bosnia on the Road to Sustainability." This case study illustrates the substantial progress that we have made, as well as the challenges we continue to face.

First, I would like to give a brief overview on Bosnia-Herzegovina's economic progress since the end of the war. After the war, eight years ago, Bosnia-Herzegovina was a destroyed country: gross domestic product per capita fell from US$2,500 before the war to around US$400 after the war, the damage to physical infrastructure was enormous, and about 250,000 people lost their lives.

Despite this devastation, Bosnia-Herzegovina has made rapid progress in reconstruction and post-conflict recovery, and it has made a good start on the transition process; growth averages around 4 to 5 percent per year. Compared with the rest of the region, Bosnia-Herzegovina is growing at a faster rate. Inflation is low, and a small fiscal surplus was achieved in 2004. Also, reforms have led to higher foreign investment. The benefits of economic growth are also becoming more visible, as unemployment, which remains high, has declined in the past two years. In addition, to the challenge of unemployment, the current account deficit still remains large; the level of foreign aid is high, and the incidence of poverty is still a concern.

In conclusion, Bosnia-Herzegovina is on a steady path to self-sustainability. Although the extraordinary growth rates of the past were supported by a high level of donor assistance, private sector activity has begun to sustain growth in the past few years, as donor support has declined significantly.

Bosnia-Herzegovina has recently approved its medium-term development strategy, better known as the poverty reduction strategy paper (PRSP), which is being successfully implemented. The PRSP contains policies that will support a growth rate of 5 to 5.5 percent in the medium term. This growth will lead us to partial creditworthiness in international markets by the end of 2007. In addition, the implementation of

---

* Honorable Minister, Government Ministry of Finance and Treasury, Bosnia and Herzegovina.

the PRSP will move Bosnia-Herzegovina closer to European Union integration, and we hope to sign a stabilization and association agreement with the European Union this year.

This year, the Operations Evaluation Department (OED) of the World Bank published its evaluation report on the Bosnia-Herzegovina program. The World Bank has played the largest role in the recovery of Bosnia-Herzegovina. I would like to use this opportunity to thank the World Bank Board of Directors and management, with special thanks to Ms. Christine Wallich, Mr. Christiaan Poortman, and Ms. Orsalia Kalantzopoulos, our country directors.

The authorities fully endorse the findings of the OED report that in Bosnia-Herzegovina the World Bank was at its best. During the reconstruction period, Bosnia-Herzegovina received about US$5.1 billion in international assistance and the World Bank contributed US$1 billion in International Development Association (IDA) credits, about US$47 per capita. An additional US$700 million was secured through cofinancing of World Bank projects. Five donor conferences have been organized.

The assistance of the World Bank was effective for several reasons: *(a)* early involvement and the willingness of the Bank to adjust its procedures to allow this early involvement, *(b)* early, effective technical assistance to assess damage and the associated financing requirements, *(c)* procurement procedures streamlined to enable the rapid disbursement of funds (60 percent of World Bank funds were disbursed in the first four years of reconstruction), and *(d)* the Bank's assistance in donor mobilization and aid coordination.

There were, however, some criticisms of the Bank's engagement. First, even though Bosnia-Herzegovina was one of the biggest beneficiaries of IDA credits, this is a misleading statistic, because the initial IDA package was designed to offset the large pre-war International Bank for Reconstruction and Development (IBRD) borrowing that Bosnia-Herzegovina had to accept, which included around US$280 million of interest accrued during the war. For instance, Bosnia-Herzegovina settled about US$350 from IBRD pre-war debt, and until now, net inflows of IDA are only around US$430 million, which implies that Bosnia-Herzegovina received fewer IDA credits per capita than the average for post-conflict countries.

Second, a large amount of IDA credits, about 10 percent of total funds, were directed toward technical assistance, which was excessive. At the request of the World Bank, project implementation units were established for implementing projects. This mechanism hindered the development of government ownership, and it was expensive, because the costs were financed out of the projects.

Third, in many cases, conditionalities were set at unrealistic levels, leading to long implementation periods and an outflow of resources through commitment fees.

Fourth, the early projects that were focused on infrastructure and projects to support structural reforms were delayed. So, today, a lack of progress on structural reform is the biggest impediment to Bosnia-Herzegovina's recovery. In our view, more attention should have been paid earlier in World Bank programs to structural reforms.

Fifth, the World Bank had a poor record in supporting enterprise privatization. Although the privatization of the banking sector was a success story, the Bank did not take a leadership role in enterprise privatization and let others, including bilateral donors, get involved.

Sixth, as I noted, the World Bank played an important role in donor coordination. But, it did not manage to get the International Monetary Fund on board in terms of burden sharing. The IMF never extended any concessional lending to Bosnia-Herzegovina.

In conclusion, Bosnia-Herzegovina does represent the most successful case of post-conflict recovery. Today, it is a transition economy. The World Bank has played a crucial role in our reconstruction. Bosnia-Herzegovina, however, is not yet creditworthy, and the World Bank has decided to allocate only US$100 million of IDA lending for the next three-year period. This implies in the next two years an outflow of US$62 million to the World Bank, which is not favorable for a country that has not yet achieved creditworthiness. There is an obvious danger that our mutual efforts will be damaged by this lack of support to countries, such as Bosnia-Herzegovina, that are close to creditworthiness, but do not receive an adequate level of concessional funding.

I hope the lessons learned from our experience will help other countries in similar situations in the future.

Comments on Lessons from Post-Conflict Countries

Margaret Thomas *

What is a post-conflict country?

Although notions of a linear progression from a preconflict to post-conflict society are conceptually attractive, they mask the real complexity of peace-conflict dynamics, which are:
- Multidimensional
- Multilayered
- With zones of peace and zones of instability and reversals common.

It is better to talk of conflict-affected countries and recognize that they remain vulnerable to conflict (ongoing or latent), occurring at many different levels within society and subject to periodic recurrence.

Key principles for working in conflict-affected societies (as outlined in the AusAID Post-Conflict Development Policy):
- A comprehensive **understanding of peace-conflict dynamics**, that is, improved analysis of the structural and proximate causes of conflict, the stakeholders, their agendas, and so on.
  - This allows definition of short-term "peace dividends," as well as long-term strategies to address grievances that underpin outbreaks of conflict.
- **Flexible and responsive mechanisms** to take advantage of "windows of opportunity" to support capacities for peace.
  - This involves acceptance of a higher degree of risk than normal by development practitioners.
- **Coordination and partnerships**, with other actors attempting to bring a semblance of stability to society, particularly with conflict-affected communities themselves.
  - Peace cannot be imposed; it must be promoted and owned by those in conflict.
  - AusAID has particularly welcomed the opportunity to be involved in the World Bank joint needs assessment for the proposed Mindanao Trust Fund.[1]

---

* Assistant Director General, Pacific Branch, Australian Agency for International Development (AusAID).

- But, remember that **aid is not the panacea for conflict**.
  - Aid can catalyze peace processes and provide immediate and short-term "peace dividends," but conflict is essentially a political crisis that must be resolved through negotiation.
  - Aid can create the **"space"** for negotiation and mediation.
- Support for societies emerging from conflict should not be limited to providing solutions to the **grievances** that drove conflict in the first place—lack of access to services, poor employment opportunities, and so on—but must also incorporate elements to **promote attitudinal changes and behavioral modifications**.
  - It is the latter two objectives that distinguish peace-building approaches from more traditional developmental approaches.
- In the short term, peace-building approaches may require principles of **equity** to be subverted to principles of **equality**, that is, provide assistance on an arithmetical basis to ensure that everybody gets a "slice of the pie," rather than on a strictly needs basis.
  - Of course, with time and as the situation stabilizes, the relative weighting given to peace and development will shift.
- In the long term, however, it is important to engage with those who have been affected by conflict to define the sort of society that will emerge from conflict.
  - To this end, AusAID has begun to engage in **conflict vulnerability analyses**[2] as part of our strategy development process to inform our decisions better about likely peace-conflict impacts of our activities and options for our programs to support preventive and/or local capacities for peace.
- Ownership and capacity building are key criteria for any program that is intended to include peace building, conflict prevention, or violence reduction objectives.
  - Inclusive consultative processes are important for building ownership and culturally appropriate capacities.
  - Within the World Bank, a properly constituted poverty reduction strategy paper process offers a potential vehicle for achieving this by engaging communities in dialogue on a common theme that cuts across conflict cleavages, that is, poverty (Darvill 2002).

Solomon Islands Case Study

A Post-Conflict Setting

- The Solomon Islands is currently moving from a situation of recurrent violent conflict and conflict-prone conditions to transition and recovery.
- Referred to in the Solomon Islands as "the tensions," the period 1998–2003 was not only characterized by violent conflict among different groups in the capital Honiara, it included the forced resignation of a prime minister under threat of armed force and terrorization of villagers.
- The impact of the tensions was significant, including on basic government financial management and functioning and led to corruption, collapse of key private sector institutions that were a major source of national income, disengagement of some donors and the international financial institutions, as well as ongoing concern about the security situation.

Peace and Conflict Development Analysis

- A peace and conflict development analysis undertaken by the United Nations Development Program (UNDP) with Australian Government financial assistance identified the following guidelines and principles for programming:
    - Need for understanding of the causes of conflict and sensitivity to multiple intersecting conflicts
    - Need to reshape and redirect economic policies to promote increased equality
    - Capacity building, participation, and ownership as the core principles for all programming
    - Support for strengthening of the state.

This includes donors integrating peace-building aims within current governance support efforts in the Solomon Islands on issues of accountability, promoting the demand for good governance.

- Australia has sought to integrate post-conflict assistance into aid programming since the tensions, which has included the following:

- Budget support to ensure continuation of basic health service supplies and delivery through a Health Sector Trust Account
- Establishment of the Community Peace and Restoration Fund to promote village-level peace-building initiatives, including reintegration of former militants through high-impact projects that rebuild community-level infrastructure that had been destroyed
- Support for indigenous civil society organizations promoting the peace process.

The Regional Assistance Mission to the Solomon Islands

- The Regional Assistance Mission to the Solomon Islands (RAMSI) evolved at the request of Prime Minister Kemakeza with continued deterioration in the situation in the Solomon Islands.
- Under the framework of the Pacific Islands Forum's Biketawa Declaration, the Region agreed to provide comprehensive assistance to restore stability and security and promote economic recovery.
  - RAMSI commenced on July 24, 2003. A fundamental achievement has been a highly successful collection of weapons; nearly 4,000 weapons were collected in the first 100 days.
- Sensitivity to the post-conflict situation is a key principle in the strengthened assistance provided as a part of RAMSI.
  - The Australian Government has developed and implemented a program of strengthened assistance, initially focused on budget stabilization and support to the law and justice sector and now broadening to focus on the machinery of government and support to accountability institutions.
- In the first year of RAMSI through this strengthened assistance program, the following has been accomplished:
  - Stability in Solomon Islands has dramatically increased through critical support for policing and the law and justice sector.
  - Government discipline and expenditure control has been reestablished.
  - Government revenues have increased by 20 percent higher than budget forecasts.
  - Assistance to strengthen the functions of Parliament, the Electoral Commission, the Public Service Division, and Cabinet has commenced.

World Bank Engagement

- As noted in the work undertaken by the World Bank on lessons learned from post-conflict reconstruction, RAMSI was aware that it is difficult for the World Bank to engage when a program has been suspended, loan repayments are in arrears, and, as a result, there is currently no Bank presence in the country.
  - RAMSI was also aware that for economic recovery, reengagement of donors and the international financial institutions was essential for the Solomon Islands.
- To support this process, the Australian Government made an agreement that it would do the following:
  - Meet loan repayment commitments on behalf of the Solomon Islands Government (SIG)
  - Support (through the RAMSI program on budget stabilization) development of a SIG debt management strategy to facilitate SIG repayments, which are now underway.
- In terms of adapting services and products to post-conflict situations, the World Bank has adopted important guiding principles in assistance at this sensitive time in the Solomon Islands.
  - Along with the Asian Development Bank, committing to not providing any new loans until the SIG government financial situation is stronger
  - Not having an overly ambitious program.
- The flexible and responsive use of targeted technical assistance and sources of grant financing by the World Bank has been valuable from a donor coordination perspective; collaborations are underway with Australia, the European Union, and New Zealand.

We are aware that World Bank engagement has been time intensive for the Bank to identify and administer, but it is a strategic method of engagement in the Solomon Islands at present that shows sensitivity to the difficulties of the post-conflict environment.

Notes

1. Humanitarian/Peace-Conflict Adviser (Steve Darvill, AUSAid) took part in the joint needs assessment debrief and strategy formulation session in Manila, September 20–21, 2004. He also took part in consultations on phase IV of the parallel UNDP initiative, Mindanao Multidonor Peace and Development Program in Davao, September 22–24, 2004. Note also AusAID's input into the UNDP Solomon Islands in an unpublished report entitled "Peace, Conflict, and Development Analysis" (PCDA) (February 2004) and proposed joint conflict analysis with DFID and UNDP in Burma.
2. These conflict vulnerability studies cover Nauru, Papua New Guinea, Philippines, Burma, Sri Lanka, Solomon Islands, Middle East (Palestinian Territories), and East Timor (forthcoming).

References

Darvill, Steve. 2002. "The Appropriate Stage to Start the PRSP Process: An Australian Perspective." *Issues Note*. Internationale Weiterbildung und Entwicklung gGmbH (INWENT). Available at: http://www.inwent.org/ef-texte/conflict/darvill.htm.

Floor Discussion on Post-Conflict Country Lessons

A number of participants asked questions of the panel. One participant asked the ministers of the recipient countries how they perceived the role of conditionality in helping or hindering the process of post-conflict resolution. The second participant commented that from the middle to the end of the 1990s, the donors, including the World Bank, were trying to do too much, and there was insufficient prioritization of the issues. This was more than a sequencing problem. Governments in post-conflict countries are limited in what they can do, particularly initially. There is a need to do a better job in identifying priorities and what can be done at the beginning verses later. A third participant asked what, if any, lessons can be learned from reconstruction in Rwanda that might be applicable to the future of the Sudan.

A fourth participant made a comment based on experience in Mozambique, which is also a post-conflict country. Mozambique jumped very quickly from an emergency situation after the war into a more traditional program of policy design. But, now 12 years after the conflict ended, there are some continuing critical issues caused by the war. Physical infrastructure issues are isolating some areas and raising resentment again. There is also the issue of demobilized soldiers who have not been integrated in large numbers; they are getting old, yet their problems remain unresolved. Furthermore, some companies' were severely affected, yet they carry debt with the banks; now, they are ineligible for new credits, and nobody is interested in helping them write off their debt. This is an example of an issue that arises when a country jumps too quickly from a post-conflict situation to a more normal one. Another participant asked about the Operations Evaluation Department's (OED's) assessment of the Bank's involvement in demining and asked Ms. Thomas, if she would elaborate on her statement that strategies need to allow everyone to get a piece of the pie instead of addressing things on a needs basis.

A final participant, noting that the OED study mentions that early engagement is important, asked about the tension between an early engagement and the volume of assistance that is required in a post-conflict country and when it was appropriate to compare resource allocation for post-conflict countries with that of other countries. She stated that one of the characteristics mentioned was the destruction of infrastructure. Presumably, large gains can be realized from rehabilitating infrastructure in a post-conflict situation. But the Bank allocates resources based on the policy and institutional environment. So, there is a tension between having good policies and institutions in place, which could take 10 to 15 years, and the early substantive engagement necessary to get growth restarted and poverty reduced.

Minister Kaberuka discussed the issue of sequencing and selectivity, noting that the issue of sequencing is much more important than the issue of selectivity. The minister stated that one example of the tradeoffs between conditionality and sequencing had already been mentioned—demobilization. In most post-conflict situations, there are two combatant forces that need to come together for national reconciliation, which, in turn, implies at least initially a large army. Both the Bank and the International Monetary Fund (IMF) typically raise concerns about defense expenditures crowding out education and health expenditures. But, the importance of sequencing comes in when one is balancing the need to integrate combatants to secure the future stability of the country; however, it is also important to send children to school. In the long run, he stated that a country is more likely to succeed in sending children to school if it succeeds in bringing the former combatants together; therefore, for a short period, it may be better to allow defense expenditures to go up before beginning the program of demobilization and reintegration. But, if one begins with the objective of reducing defense expenditures to increase health and education expenditures, one runs the risk of damaging the reconciliation process.

On the question of Sudan, the minister stated that Rwanda does not yet have sufficient post-conflict experience to provide lessons to other countries, such as Sudan. The conflict in the Sudan is too recent for Rwanda to be able to distill lessons from its experience. At this point, all Rwanda has done is to help Sudan by joining the efforts of the African Union to contribute forces to assist in Darfur.

Ms. Thomas responded on the issue of giving "some of the pie" to many groups as a mechanism to ensure post-conflict reconciliation. She noted that in the immediate post-conflict situation when a fragile peace is just being established, there is a need to support the process and not undermine or exacerbate it. You are dealing with fractured societies where most people are conflict affected. As a consequence, it is important to focus on quick wins that deliver practical improvements to people's lives and demonstrate the benefits of peace, such as reestablishing first-aid posts, providing housing materials, rebuilding schools, and reestablishing rural roads. In the first instance, one should take a blanket approach to these issues. With time, one can gradually factor in a more detailed needs assessment. But in that immediate post-conflict period, it is important that aid is seen as evenhanded and addressing the needs of the entire community.

On the issue of an early and possibly large engagement upfront, Ms. Thomas responded that it was a matter of judgment on a country-by-country basis. The engagement needs to be sufficient to establish the foundations on which reconstruction and development can proceed. In Australia's experience, this has sometimes led to policing interventions backed by the military, which is an early, large, and potentially over-whelming intervention. But it is designed to ensure a fundamental, no-ticeable return to the rule of law, which is often essential for any devel-opment and reconstruction to proceed. It is important also to be specific about what gets tackled first and the sequencing of events, ensuring adequate ownership of the process in the affected country. We need to be reasonably limited in what we identify as early areas for action; with time the agenda will broaden.

Mr. O'Brien also responded on the issue of early engagement, noting that the OED report draws out strong contrasts.* In the case of Bosnia-Herzegovina, the Bank was very bold in becoming engaged, even be-fore the end of the conflict, although not physically in the country, and then moving quickly to put ample resources on the ground: people hired locally to work for the Bank and Bank staff sent from headquarters. This made all the difference in the Bank's ability to mobilize resources and assist the government in rapidly implementing a large and success-ful program. In other countries—Eritrea and, perhaps, Cambodia—the Bank engaged much more slowly on the ground. As a consequence, after a few years the slow pace of commitment of staff and resources on the ground did lead to a slower pace of reconstruction and transfor-mation. This slow response became an important factor, because these countries had not dealt with the Bank or other donors. Eritrea was a classic case. The government of Eritrea was a group of people who had been fighting for 30 years, and they had never dealt with the Bank. They knew nothing of Bank procedures for procurement and disbursement. And it became clear after a short period that just sending them some procurement manuals and disbursement guidelines was not enough for

---

*   F. Steve O'Brien is a consultant with the Operations Evaluation Department, World Bank Group.

them to be able to cope with Bank procedures. This created, in fact, a certain amount of ill will, which the Bank had to work very hard to overcome. So there are many reasons why early engagement is extremely important, even though it involves taking risks and every country does not have the same security situation. On the other hand, Bosnia-Herzegovina is one case in which the Bank certainly got it right.

On demining, Mr. O'Brien noted that in Bosnia-Herzegovina all the early reconstruction projects were rated satisfactory, with the exception of the demining project. The demining project was rated unsatisfactory, and the conclusion was that this was an area that the Bank should simply not have gotten into, because the Bank lacked both experience and expertise in this area and other agencies had practical experience and expertise and were much better equipped to take this on.

Mr. Poortman responded that the demining project was successful in terms of what it achieved.* The question on the project related to supervision of contracts; in that regard, the Bank has limited capacity. But demining remains an important issue in Bosnia-Herzegovina, and far too little has been done in terms of demining. It is still a real constraint that is daily experienced by people trying to work their fields or put up an electricity grid. This is also a major issue in all the post-conflict countries in which he had been involved and a major uncompleted agenda item, for which funding is inadequate; the international community is turning its face away from the issue, because it is expensive.

---

* Christiaan Poortman, Regional Vice President for Middle East and North Africa, World Bank Group. Mr. Poortman participated as chair for the "Lessons of the Post-Conflict Countries Session."

Part 6

Poverty Reduction Strategies

The Poverty Reduction Strategy Initiative: An Independent Evaluation of the World Bank's Support through 2003[†]

Victoria Elliott[*]

The World Bank and the International Monetary Fund (IMF) launched the Poverty Reduction Strategy (PRS) initiative in 1999 to improve the planning, implementation, and monitoring of public actions geared to reducing poverty. The initiative quickly became such a large part of the Bank's work and its relationship with low-income countries that the Operations Evaluation Department (OED) decided to undertake an independent evaluation of it in early 2003, when 23 countries had already completed a first poverty reduction strategy paper (PRSP) and another 20 had embarked on the process.

[†] This paper, authored by Shonar Lala, has been adapted from a presentation by Victoria Elliott at the OED Conference on "Effectiveness of Policies and Reforms." See World Bank (2004) for the full report of the evaluation. Bill Battaile and Shonar Lala were the lead evaluators on this evaluation.

[*] Manager, Corporate Evaluation and Methods, Operations Evaluation Department, World Bank Group.

Scope and Methodology

Although, in 2004 it is still too early to expect to evaluate PRSPs' impact on poverty, the review did assess progress under the new initiative and how effectively the World Bank has supported it. The initiative has two key features: five underlying principles (box 1) and several process requirements that require preparation of PRSPs and their endorsement by the boards of the Bretton Woods institutions for countries to gain access to resources.[1]

Box 1: Underlying Principles of the PRSP Initiative

- Country driven, involving broadly based participation
- Comprehensive in recognizing the multidimensional nature of poverty
- Results oriented and focused on outcomes that benefit the poor
- Partnership oriented, involving coordinated participation of development partners
- Based on a long-term perspective for poverty reduction.

The evaluation drew largely on ten country case studies for which OED conducted field work: Albania, Cambodia, Ethiopia, Guinea, Mauritania, Mozambique, Nicaragua, Tajikistan, Tanzania, and Vietnam.[2] OED conducted four of the case studies in collaboration with the IMF's Independent Evaluation Office, which was then doing a parallel evaluation.[3] Besides the case studies, OED conducted two workshops, an entry workshop in Washington D.C. to obtain feedback on the evaluation's approach and a stakeholder workshop in Addis Ababa, Ethiopia, to receive comments on the preliminary findings. In addition, the evaluation relied on surveys of World Bank staff, surveys of stakeholders in the ten case study countries, and two thematic studies, one on public expenditure management and the other on capacity enhancement. OED also conducted cross-country analyses from a broader sample of documents that had been produced for the initiative, including PRSPs, annual progress reports and joint staff assessments.

Progress So Far

The evaluation found that the PRS initiative has made good progress in four main areas.

First, it is a clear improvement over the policy framework papers, the instrument that it was intended to replace, as it is much more clearly the government's own document, even though the Bank and the IMF are still heavily involved.[4]

Second, the PRS process has improved the poverty diagnosis and poverty focus of national development strategies, as the process invites and encourages attention to the many dimensions of income and non-income poverty. It asks the country authorities to gather their sectoral programs under the common umbrella of poverty reduction. The focus on poverty diagnostics has highlighted how inadequate the data on poverty are in most of these countries. In some of the countries—Tanzania is a good example—the PRS process has spurred action to improve the database on poverty.

Third, the Bretton Woods institutions, as well as other donors, actively promoted broadly based participation in the initiative's design. As a result, governments conducted extensive consultations during the process, which has allowed a broader group of stakeholders to be involved in the domestic dialogue on development in most of the case study countries.

Fourth, the PRSP has provided a constructive framework for donors' dialogues with government. This is especially true in the countries where government leadership and aid management processes were already strong, for example, in Vietnam, where the PRS initiative provided focus to a group of like-minded donors that meet regularly to exchange information and coordinate activities. The PRS process has not had the same positive effect in the countries that had weak or donor-dominated aid relationships.

OED found, overall, that the PRS initiative is certainly relevant and the World Bank should continue to support it. But the initiative has not reached its full potential. The next section outlines some of the dimensions in which the evaluation found that the initiative is falling short.

Initiative's Design Inhibits Country Ownership

One of the main principles of the PRS is that the process should be country driven. At the same time, countries have been required to complete a PRSP and annual progress reports to maintain their access to concessional lending. Inherent tension exists between the principle of country ownership and country obligations to complete these reports.

As a result, in implementing the strategies, countries have understandably focused on completing the documents that give them access to resources. In particular, they tend to generate standardized strategies in the earlier PRSPs, which was reinforced by the World Bank's and IMF's initially very ambitious timetables for completion of first-round PRSPs in heavily indebted poor countries (HIPC) and those countries under programs supported by an IMF Poverty Reduction and Growth Facility (PRGF).[5]

In principle, the PRSP process is supposed to be adapted to each country's unique country circumstances, with benchmarks and targets set by the country authorities. But the Bank and the IMF have not provided much guidance on just how this should be done. This has resulted in countries producing somewhat formulaic or standardized strategies.

Joint Staff Assessments Fail to Meet Their Objectives

One of the key features of the initiative is the joint staff assessment. To receive concessional assistance from the Bretton Woods institutions, a country's PRSP must be endorsed on the basis of a joint staff assessment prepared by Bank and IMF staff. The instrument is designed to play two roles: provide the Bank and IMF boards with an assessment of the soundness of the PRSP as a basis for concessional assistance and provide constructive feedback to the country on how the PRSP strategy can be improved.

OED found that the instrument has not achieved these goals. First of all, the analytical quality of the joint staff assessments is mixed. OED reviewed all 28 joint staff assessments completed at the time of the evaluation. The review found they were particularly weak in their treatment of private sector participation and partnership issues.[6]

Second, joint staff assessments did not pay enough attention to assessing the strengths and weaknesses of the country's own processes that are relevant for a sustainable PRS process. They generally assess how good specific sector policies were, but not the quality of the information or the process that the countries use to arrive at those policies. For example, most joint staff assessments discuss the quality and realism of indicators and targets in the PRSP, but treatment of the role and usefulness of the information for line ministries and other decisionmakers receives much less attention.

Third, stakeholders in the countries were not aware of the conclusions of the joint staff assessments. The joint staff assessments did include advice and recommendations to the country authorities, but OED discovered that only a few key officials in central ministries are aware of them, and in most countries the governments did not circulate the joint staff assessments to nongovernmental organizations or people outside the government.

Country Commitment Varies

Country ownership is a key principle of the PRS process, because effective development requires policies and priorities to originate from and be driven by the national stakeholders. All the governments involved declare political commitment to the PRSP, but our interviews revealed that within the government, ownership or commitment to the PRSP is strongest among those closest to its preparation, typically the central finance and planning ministries. Commitment and ownership fades in the sectoral ministries and also at regional and local levels of government.

Governments consulted widely while they were formulating the PRSP, and the Bank very effectively encouraged and even funded this kind of activity, for example, by funding participation advisors or putting civil society contact officers in its local offices. But the evaluation found that the consultations did not sufficiently involve the private sector, parliaments, or labor organizations. This somewhat lopsided character of the participation is reflected in the content of the strategies themselves. When it came to actually implementing the PRSP after it was first formulated, participatory activities dropped off considerably. Mechanisms for consultations were, in the majority of cases, not sustained. Many NGOs, for example, were disappointed that they had little or no influence on strategies.

Even though the Bank and the IMF promoted consultations during the process, the parties that OED surveyed did not seem to be very clear about the objectives of consultation. As a result of the lack of clear and shared objectives, different stakeholders wound up with very different views about the extent to which the process had been country driven or country owned.

Figure 1 shows survey results on the degree to which various stake-holder groups in ten countries thought the PRSP was country driven. The figure illustrates that government and donor representatives had a more favorable view of the degree of country ownership of the PRSP relative to local and international nongovernmental organizations.

FIGURE 1
Was the PRS Process Country Driven?

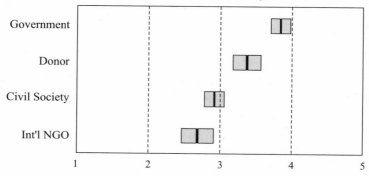

Note: The thick lines indicate the mean score from the survey of national stakehold-ers in the ten case study countries (from 1: "completely disagree" to 5: "completely agree") on a composite of four questions on whether the PRSP process was country driven. The box around the bands shows a 95 percent confidence interval.
Source: OED PRSP Study (World Bank 2004).

Donor Alignment Not Yet Evident

The PRS process was supposed to involve the coordinated participa-tion of development partners. As mentioned, it has bolstered aid man-agement processes where they were already strong. Mozambique and Tanzania are examples where the PRSP has helped donors to coordinate their budget support and streamline performance monitoring (box 2). But it has not been able to improve weak management processes. For instance, in Albania, the fragmented and large donor community per-ceived the PRSP as a Bank-driven process and was unwilling to align its own approaches to it.

Donors have generally provided well-coordinated assistance to gov-ernments to formulate the PRSPs, for instance, in Ethiopia, where the donors agreed on a common input to the national PRSP consultations.

But so far, not much evidence exists that donor assistance has actually aligned with the PRSP programs. Neither other donors nor the Bank itself has defined specifically how and whether the content of their assistance programs should change to reflect the country's PRSP. This is consistent with OED's finding that the PRSPs are very broad in scope and often lack prioritization, which makes it very challenging to demonstrate how an assistance program could become aligned with a PRSP.

Box 2: PRSP Helps Donors Coordinate Budget Support and Streamline Performance Monitoring

In Tanzania, the Poverty Reduction Budget Support Group coordinates members' conditionality using a single monitoring instrument, the performance assessment framework. The performance assessment framework uses Tanzania's PRSP as its guiding framework, and monitoring is synchronized with PRSP progress reports. With its first Poverty Reduction Support Credit, the World Bank joined the group and now uses the performance assessment framework for its conditionality. In Mozambique, the eleven donors that provide budget support are also developing a performance assessment framework, which is intended to align better with the PRSP and harmonize donor conditions (including alignment with the IMF's Poverty Reduction and Growth Facility and with a World Bank Poverty Reduction Support Credit in the pipeline). In Vietnam, a number of donors are delivering a significant share of their aid budgets through the World Bank Poverty Reduction Support Credit.

Strategies Do Not Feature Poverty Impact and Growth

OED also reviewed some aspects of the content of PRS strategies and had three major findings:

First, too little is known about the linkages between policies and programs, on the one hand, and poverty-related outcomes, on the other. So far, the PRSP process has not helped to bridge this knowledge gap. Most PRSPs do not make explicit the interconnections among the sources of growth, social impact of macroeconomic policies, and various macroeconomic, structural, and sectoral linkages. Of course, by themselves, the first round of PRSPs could not be expected to fill all these long-standing gaps, but the PRS process could have been used more effectively to identify the key analytical gaps and to develop a research agenda to address them.

Second, PRSPs have not really considered the full range of policy actions required for growth and poverty reduction. PRSPs in the case study countries focus largely on leveraging public expenditures to reduce poverty and have not fully explored other kinds of policies or actions for enhancing growth and poverty reduction, such as tax and revenue policies, exchange rate management, role of the private sector, trade, and privatization.

Third, even within the domain of public expenditures, PRSPs typically focus on budget allocations for the social sectors—education, health, and social protection—and tend to treat very lightly the productive sectors, such as infrastructure, agriculture, and rural development. This bias toward a focus on social sector spending derives, among other influences, from the origins of the PRSP in the HIPC Initiative, which emphasizes allocating "savings" from debt relief to the social sectors and tracking budget actions in education and health in HIPC countries; this imbalance continues to prevail.[7]

The evaluation assessed how well the Bank has helped to bridge some of these analytical gaps. The Bank did do about one-third more economic and sector work in the countries preparing PRSPs than it had in the preceding four years.[8] But most of this extra work took the form of required standardized assessments that are related to the Bank's own requirements, rather than to customized or country-specific economic

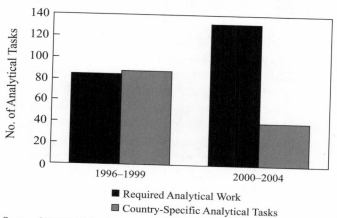

FIGURE 2
The Bank's Country-Specific Analytical Work Declined

■ Required Analytical Work
■ Country-Specific Analytical Tasks

Source: OED PRSP Study (World Bank 2004).

and sector work, which actually declined in the PRSP countries once the PRSP was introduced (figure 2).[9] This finding is validated by survey respondents, who gave the lowest ratings on the timeliness and relevance of the Bank's analytical inputs.

First, on policies, both PRSP countries and non-PRSP countries have seen improved policy and institutional frameworks, as measured by the Bank's Country Policy and Institutional Assessment (CPIA) index between 1999 and 2003 (figure 3).[10] But PRSP countries started off with better policies than the non-PRSP countries, which is consistent with them having been chosen or volunteered themselves as PRSP countries. So far, they are not improving any faster than the non-PRSP countries. This poses a big challenge for the initiative going forward, because the countries who have yet to complete a PRSP are the ones with on average a lower CPIA score. This implies that it is going to be even more difficult to see improvements in these countries.

FIGURE 3
PRSP Countries Began with Better Policies

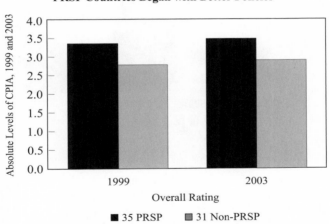

Source: OED PRSP Study (World Bank 2004).

A second area in which OED looked for impact was aid flows, because national stakeholders in PRSP countries expect that formulating PRSPs will attract more development aid. Donors' aid programs take a long time to adjust, so OED analyzed changes in aid flows between 2000 and 2002 in the eight countries with the longest PRSP implementation times.[11] Figure 4 illustrates that aid to those eight countries has perceptibly increased in the three-year period studied. But those countries were already receiving more aid than the 35 low-income countries with PRSPs or the 31 countries without PRSPs; thus, the eight most mature PRSP countries were already getting more aid and have continued to increase their aid flows, but no evidence exists, based on a short period so far, that aid to these PRSP countries has been increasing more than aid to the other low-income countries.

FIGURE 4
Aid to PRSP and Non-PRSP Countries Increasing

Average Net ODA Flows Per Country (2000–2002)

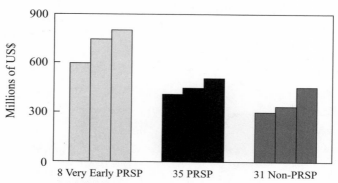

Source: OED PRSP Study (World Bank 2004).

Third, has the PRSP initiative had any impact at all on poverty so far? OED looked at the 12 mature PRSP countries that had already issued at least one annual progress report as of May 2004, but was unable to find enough data to answer that question even for these 12 countries (table 1).[12] Only a few indicators gave us enough data for enough countries to show improvement or lack of improvement. This illustrates the urgency of improving the database on tracking and demonstrating results on poverty reduction, as captured by the Millennium Development Goals or other indices. It will be rather difficult for both the donors and the recipient countries to maintain momentum or enthusiasm for the PRSP unless it is possible to demonstrate some results.

TABLE 1
Progress on MDGs in 12 PRSP Countries

Goal 1: Eradicate extreme hunger and poverty	Not Enough Data
Goal 2: Achieve universal primary education	Improved
Goal 3: Promote gender equality and empower	Not Enough Data
Goal 4: Reduce Child Mortality	No Improvement
Goal 5: Improve maternal health	Not Enough Data
Goal 6: Combat HIV/AIDS, malaria and other	Not Enough Data
Goal 7: Ensure environmental sustainability	Improved
Goal 8: Develop a global partnership for development	Not Enough Data

Source: OED PRSP Study (World Bank 2004).

Recommendations for World Bank Management

OED has four main recommendations for Bank management that result from the evaluation:

- First, the Bank should emphasize improvement of country processes for implementing public actions geared toward poverty reduction, rather than completion of documents. The Bank should actively promote tailoring of domestic processes to country conditions, for instance, ensuring that the timing of progress reporting derives from local processes and decisionmaking.

- Second, the Bank should develop a review procedure for PRSPs that is more supportive of country ownership and more effectively linked to decisions about the Bank's country programs. The Bank should provide feedback to the country on its PRSP in a form that is candid, transparent, and rigorous and strengthens partnership by involving other stakeholders. The Bank should do this either through a major redesign or discontinuation of the joint staff assessment instrument and process.

- Third, the Bank and other partners should do more to help countries identify the actions that are going to have the most poverty "payoff" to bridge the analytical gaps in PRSPs. Analysis should address areas such as sources of growth, quality of nonsocial sector strategies, and integration of the macroeconomic framework and structural and social reforms.

- Fourth, OED recommends that the Bank, in concert with other donors, should facilitate the use of the PRSP as a partnership framework and clarify expectations on how external partners, including the
  Bank, should support their PRSPs. To do this, the Bank should help
  countries improve the prioritization and costing of PRSP programs.

Notes

1. To obtain irrevocable debt relief under the Heavily Indebted Poor Countries
    (HIPC) Initiative, countries are required to produce an initial PRSP and imple-
    ment it successfully for a year, as reflected in an annual progress report. Recog-
    nizing the considerable time required to formulate a full PRSP and the need for
    HIPC countries to receive debt relief in the short term, debt relief is permitted
    to begin when a country completes an interim PRSP. To obtain concessional re-
    sources from the World Bank and the IMF, low-income countries are required to
    complete PRSPs or signal progress toward a full PRSP through an interim PRSP
    or a PRSP preparation status report. The boards of the World Bank and the IMF
    must endorse each of the required documents—interim PRSPs, PRSPs, annual
    progress reports, and PRSP preparation status reports—on the basis of a joint
    staff assessment prepared by Bank and IMF staff.
2. The countries were selected to cover a variety of country situations (geographic
    balance, coverage of non-HIPC countries, and initial conditions) and stages of
    PRSP implementation. The full country case studies and a summary volume are
    available on the evaluation website at: http://www.worldbank.org/oed/prsp/case_
    studies.html.
3. The Independent Evaluation Office's parallel evaluation focused on the IMF's
    support to the PRS initiative (see IMF 2004). Joint case studies were done for
    Mozambique, Nicaragua, Tajikistan, and Tanzania. These assess both World
    Bank and IMF support. OED conducted the case studies for Albania, Cambodia,
    Ethiopia, and Mauritania, and the Independent Evaluation Office conducted the
    case studies for Guinea and Vietnam.
4. A policy framework paper was a tripartite agreement among the government,
    Bank, and IMF, summarizing a country's medium-term economic framework and
    covering main reform areas. The process of writing policy framework papers was
    widely recognized as largely Washington driven, with initial drafts written locally
    in a minority of cases, but even then, they were often redone by IMF and World
    Bank staff.
5. Stakeholders in four out of ten countries (Cambodia, Mozambique, Nicaragua,
    and Tanzania) reported that they experienced pressure to complete PRSPs in time
    to meet World Bank and IMF deadlines, including those determined by the IMF's
    Poverty Reduction and Growth Facility cycle.
6. OED rated 11 issues and found that joint staff assessments in the aggregate
    treated five at a satisfactory level. Assessment of endogenous and exogenous
    risks and structural and sectoral policies were the best handled topics. The quality
    of joint staff assessments improved only slightly over the period studied.
7. Other influences are strong donor preferences for these sectors, also manifested
    in the relative dominance of social sector targets in the Millennium Development
    Goals; more likely "quick wins" in these sectors because of more mature pov-

erty-linked strategies; and paucity of analytical work in defining broadly based or pro-poor growth strategies and understanding their poverty impact.

8.   For analyzing data across countries, OED established a sample of 66 IDA-eligible countries (excluding small island economies, inactive countries, and India). For purposes of comparing countries with completed PRSPs with other low-income countries, these 66 countries were divided into two groups: 35 countries that had completed a PRSP by the end of 2003 and 31 that had not. In the 35 countries that completed PRSPs by that time, the Bank did roughly three more analytical reports per country between July 1999 and the end of 2003, compared with other International Development Association (IDA)–eligible countries, which did about one less report per country in the same period.

9.   Required analytical work includes five main products, and completion of all five is required at least every five years. The five products are country economic memoranda and development policy reviews, poverty assessments, public expenditure reviews, country financial accountability assessments, and country procurement assessment reports.

10. The CPIA includes 20 equally weighted dimensions in the overall rating for policies encompassing economic management, structural adjustment, social inclusion/equity, and public sector management and institutions. The finding on improvements in low-income country CPIA ratings accords with indicators of various dimensions of policy and institutional performance compiled outside the World Bank.

11. The eight countries are Uganda, Burkina Faso, Tanzania, Mauritania, Bolivia, Nicaragua, Mozambique, and Honduras.

12. The 12 countries are Uganda, Burkina Faso, Tanzania, Mauritania, Nicaragua, Mozambique, Honduras, Niger, Albania, Vietnam, Malawi, and Ethiopia.

References

World Bank. 2004. *The Poverty Reduction Strategy Initiative: An Independent Evaluation of the World Bank's Support through 2003.* Operations Evaluation Department, Washington, D.C. Available at: http://www.worldbank.org/oed/prsp/.

International Monetary Fund (IMF). 2004. *Report on the Evaluation of Poverty Reduction Strategy Papers (PRSPs) and the Poverty Reduction and Growth Facility (PRGF).* Washington, D.C. Available at: http://www.imf.org/External/NP/ieo/2004/prspprgf/eng/index.htm.

Comments on the Poverty Reduction
Strategy Initiatives

*Pedro Couto**

Having read OED's poverty reduction strategy (PRSP) study and followed the presentation, I was pleasantly surprised. Having been one of the persons consulted during the evaluation, I think that the report has done a good job to acknowledge what we wanted to put forward, explaining in general what happened. But that said and having the opportunity to comment, there are a few points I would like to make.

I like seeing the study's point that countries sometimes give too much attention to preparation of PRSPs when the most important issue is to have the process in place. This is very important, but I think we have to be a bit more radical.

It is more than process. It is not a question of labels. We have to go beyond labels. Nor is it a question of trying to solve the problem of poverty by itself. If we look at poverty as something we can solve by itself—something isolated or a fashion issue—we will in the end fail.

In reality, the problem to be addressed is the need for an effective process by which to analyze the situation, design policies, implement them, assess them, reassess them, redesign and implement, and so on—continuously. This is the only way you will obtain coherent and significant social and economic policies to take your country in a good direction. In my opinion, achieving such policies is the main issue.

As Mozambique has very high rates of absolute poverty, under the current circumstances in our country, poverty reduction is definitely very important. As such, it is the main objective of adopted policies. But I hope that soon or in time, we will have other targets, other important objectives to pursue. So in this sense, it is not a question of it being the "time" to look at poverty, likely followed by a "time" to do something else; we have to have an integrated social and economic policy framework.

We have just abandoned what we used to call the policy framework paper (PFP). I do not know why. It seems we have been sensitive to

---

* Director, Economic Studies Cabinet, Ministry of Planning and Finance, Mozambique.

the question of labels. It was, perhaps, not taking on board the issue of poverty and other structural issues. But it is not a question of calling it a poverty reduction strategy paper (PRSP) or PFP or something else. It is really a question of the process, as is stated in the evaluation document. Moreover, the processes have to be continuously adjusted, implemented, and revised, moving in a certain direction to pursue selected and relevant goals.

In this sense, if you look at the process as characterized, the question to be asked is: what is the problem? By now, the rates of poverty are very high in Mozambique. Average absolute poverty incidences continue at rates higher than 50 percent. In these circumstances, the objective is to eradicate or reduce poverty significantly, but how?

For us, it is by promoting social and economic development. You have to set action in place. You have to create an environment that will lead to poverty reduction, but through a process in which social and economic development results.

If you look at the problem in this way, you find that we are at the center of the issues to be addressed. We are actually trying to pursue the need for creating, consolidating, and expanding a solid, sustainable, and competitive economy that is integrated with normal trade relations into the world market. This is the main problem. Success in undertaking action, from this stance, will promote sustainable poverty reduction, without setbacks. We have to establish processes that do not depend forever on aid.

Serious issues are connected with these options, however. First, priority has to be given to creation of "human infrastructure"; hence, the so-called social sectors (whose prioritization has been mentioned in the evaluation report as associated with a certain bias) are critical. For Mozambique, there is no bias on their emphasized selection. These sectors are crucial, because the situation is so bad that innovation is the key word in our countries. We have to be continuously innovating, adjusting, and moving.

You cannot do it if you are ignorant—if you lack the knowledge to adjust, innovate, and integrate with the world. Otherwise, you will be lost. To create wealth, you currently have to master knowledge; you cannot do it based on ignorance.

A solid, dynamic, and diversified economy is something that depends very much on innovation and technological development; this is why the issues of human capital and human development are key.

But there is also the need for physical infrastructure that together with human capital or capacity becomes an important trigger for private sector development—the creation of wealth in the country, employment, and so on.

In addition, there is institutional infrastructure. There are some institutional issues we cannot avoid, specifically, the openness of the economy. There is a reasonable level of openness of the economy that we have to pursue. We cannot continue to protect the economy as we have done in the past. This was a mistake. Adequate macroeconomic management, however, cannot be overlooked; we have to adjust from huge macroeconomic imbalances.

That said, it is easy to understand why we ended up selecting those fundamental areas of action, including issues addressing human capacity, creation of basic infrastructure for economic activity and private sector development, as well as institutional issues. Having clarity about the options, what is the problem then? What are the challenges?

The most serious problem is connected with capacity. This is the basis of ownership. The only way to achieve adequate programs is to respect ownership. But for ownership, we need domestic capacity, which cannot be replaced with technical assistance. Technical assistance is needed, but limited in the short term. In the long term, we need domestic capacity to rely on what we are doing. It is not a question of being chauvinistic, but being realistic. This is a problem of confidence and fidelity. When you are dealing with certain issues, you often hire consultants. There can also be problems when we discuss important issues and recommend that the conclusions are included in the report. The response surprisingly is sometimes: "you are really right, but the person paying me will not like to see that in the report." The need exists, therefore, for our own technical staff also to assess the issues and design and implement adequate options.

Ownership and capacity are very important, starting with the capacity of the state itself. In a large country, such as Mozambique or Angola, this issue is very serious because capacity resides with the central government. But, this becomes even more significant when countries require decentralization; thus, capacity building is a serious issue that has to be addressed.

The issue of capacity (from the central to local institutions) refers to the capacity for analyzing, formulating, detailing, implementing, assessing, and also managing strategies, policies, programs, plans, and projects. The capacity of managing issues for implementation is critical, because you can have a very nice, quite detailed policy document, but if the daily or monthly management does not happen, it will never be implemented.

Recognizing the importance of capacity, how do you build it? For Mozambique, there is the issue of training. This is probably different for Ghana, Nigeria, or Kenya. The human resource portfolio in Mozambique is gloomy; even after 25 years of independence, we continue to have a very limited number of trained individuals. So we need to provide training programs. But after training, at least in the public sector, the issue of retention of personnel becomes critical. In terms of reasonable salaries, the state cannot compete, for instance with UNDP or other international agencies "in town." The public sector also cannot compete with the demand for skilled personnel exerted from abroad. So the issue of capacity is quite important.

In addition, I would like to address one of the most important issues—resources. You can have good plans, good projects, and some capacity, but then you have to implement them. For this, you need resources: human, but also financial and other resources.

I have to admit that in Mozambique, we do not have enough resources to move ahead. Most of our programs are unfunded. Although some funding exists, there is room for improvement in the effectiveness and efficiency in the use of existing resources and for raising the ability to collect domestic resources

There are also, however, restrictions. With a very high incidence of absolute poverty, we cannot increase the collection of domestic resources forever; hence, we have to rely on foreign and concessional resources in the medium to long run. Yet, these do not flow in a stable, significant, or predictable manner, which puts us in a very difficult situation, because expectations have been raised. The people believe that, if they are consulted, they will be involved in all of this—that things will improve and results will show. But this has not been happening, also due to the shortage of resources.

Why have significant flows of resources not been recorded? The only response I find is probably that, up until now, the issue of aid has been seen as charity, which is very wrong. We have to move toward a situation in which the developed countries are interested in engaging in true partnerships with Africa or African countries, recognizing that aid is an investment toward normalizing the situation and promoting future trade with those same countries.

We have to change the situation in our countries structurally to have normal relations with other developed parts of the world. Only then will the picture change. It is not a question of looking at our faces or at the children and giving some money in the meantime. Genuine partnership is needed, based on an understanding that the future will require an African continent with more developed countries that are able to engage in normal trade relations. Otherwise, we will continue to be lost in discussion and postpone what we need and want to do, deceiving ourselves and so on. I do not think that will be good.

Comments on the Poverty Reduction Strategy Initiatives

Eveline Herfkens *

The Operations Evaluation Department (OED) evaluation of the poverty reduction strategy papers (PRSP) is a good report, and I hope that Bank management takes its recommendations seriously into account. I am not sure whether this is in fact happening, but perhaps the debates by the Board can help. There was some good news, especially considering that this instrument is only five years old (which is not too long in an organization such as this).

On the whole, there is relatively more participation and information. Considering how the Bank used to be when I was a Board member here in the early 1990s, these developments are quite revolutionary. More than a decade ago, if you would talk with Bank staff about participation, the reaction would be along the lines of: "We should not only talk to the finance minister, but maybe also with the health or education ministers." This is the extent to which the Bank was participatory.

On ownership, I recall the first generation of the policy framework papers (PFPs). In the Baltic PFPs, there was the same typo on the same page in reports of different Baltic countries. The Latvia PFP had one page where suddenly the country referred to was Lithuania. This kind of cut-and-paste job shows how little national priorities drove the process at that time.

On poverty, country dialogues in many parts of the world did not even mention the word "poverty." Donors did not talk with each other, and the Bank only engaged with donors in the context of consultative group meetings when they needed to inflate numbers after consultations to be able to say to recipient governments: "look at what we did for you." Also here, fortunately, there has been some progress.

The key question I would like to address is to what extent have poverty reduction strategies (PRSs) been helpful in achieving the Millennium Development Goals (MDGs). Of course the PRSs pre-date the MDGs, but that is not an excuse, because the Millennium Declaration was the codification of international consensus at the highest political

* Executive Director, United Nations Millennium Development Goals Campaign.

level. The Bank was in fact one of the first advocates of these goals, so we expect the Bank to implement them at all levels of their work.

You do not have to mention the goals explicitly, as long as you are focusing on the substance of them—poverty, HIV/AIDS, and so on. But it is surprising how few of the PRSPs are actually based on these goals.

There are five major reasons, in my view, why the PRSs were created and I would like to focus my presentation on these areas. The need for *(a)* poverty reduction, *(b)* ownership, *(c)* partnership, *(d)* participation, and *(e)* long-term framework.

Poverty reduction. To what extent is poverty reduction the focus of the PRSs, and to what degree are they focused on the MDGs? Here, I agree entirely with the report that they are too much about social expenditure; however, you cannot lift people out of poverty just by improving education and health: there is another debate not accounted for here. The first goal is to reduce the number of poor people. This is by far the most important; it is about incomes, jobs, economic growth—about growth being equitable, labor intensive, and pro-poor. There is also the importance of trade.

On these issues, the PRSPs are still extremely weak. The Bank publicly stated, as early as in the 1990 World Development Report, that we need the type of growth that reduces poverty—labor intensive and pro-poor. I remember the Board asking what that would entail. Fourteen years later, still very little research on these issues has been undertaken, and this is very disappointing.

What is also disappointing is how little rural development is covered in PRSs. Two-thirds of the world's poor live in rural areas. How can rural development be overlooked in any discussion on poverty reduction? Another omission not mentioned in the evaluation report, is that most of the poor are women, and few PRSs consider what actually matters for women.

I am disappointed how little—and this is what the report also says—the poverty and social impact assessments (PSIAs) have been developed on macro policies, macro programs, and so on. Eight years ago the PSIAs were very much a donor-driven, trust fund–financed initiative, but it was supposed to be mainstreamed into the Bank's core work. They were supposed to become the cornerstone of the PRSs, including social impact assessments of macro policies. Again, this has not happened. The issues of where the sources of growth are; what kind of growth reduces poverty; what kind of policies are needed to empower poor people and give them access to opportunities, assets, markets, and credit; what barriers women face if they want to inherit, own, control, or use assets are still not part and parcel of the process. On this, the OED PRSP study is too mild. It is time for the Bank to help its clients with better research and analysis on these issues.

Ownership. Although this has improved, the approach is still too much "one size fits all." Here, I think the OED PRSP study makes a very important point: The Washington signoff process does not help. How can you ever get real ownership if countries feel they have to draft PRSs in a certain way to get Board approval to get the money? This undercuts ownership.

Why cannot the Board just focus on the joint staff assessments? If they have to be discussed by the donor community, let the consultative group discuss the PRSPs. In that context, the same rich countries are at least represented as are on the Board, but in their capacity as donors, rather than through the voice of finance ministers or central banks. Unless you actually stop requiring Board approval, the benefit of the doubt will never be in favor of ownership and external critics will always say that it is not possible. Board approval also forces timelines that by themselves undermine the links to domestic processes, and process—the document—will always be favored over content or real-world processes.

Furthermore, by being more specific in linking the objectives set in the PRSs to the MDGs, more ownership can be created, as many of these countries are currently holding public debates on the goals. Linking the PRSPs specifically to the MDGs will bring the process more into the public arena and create local ownership that extends beyond government ministries. This will also help in setting MDGs that are more tailored to national priorities, because this is exactly what is now happening with the MDGs. Global goals are useless unless they are discussed at home, tailor made, and localized.

Partnership. The Bank could make better use of the PRSs to identify the financing gap and lobby donors for more money. On the issue of partnership, the Bank is still not as strong as it should be in naming and shaming rich countries for their lack of progress in delivering on their promises, that is, the MDG number 8. The upcoming "Global Monitoring Report" for the next Development Committee Spring Meeting should name and shame individual rich countries.[1] It has never been a problem for the Bank to name individual developing countries, so it should start doing it with rich countries. The PRSs are not really being used to also remind the international community of their other obligations to their commitment on goal 8, the global partnership for development. These commitments go beyond aid to also include trade policies.

When the Board agreed to have country assistance strategies discussed, the deal was that these strategies would include a strong chapter dealing with, in "Bank speak," the "external environment." To what extent, for example, are trade policies of rich countries hampering the country's development? I would want to see more of that included in the PRSs.

I acknowledge that the Sri Lankan PRSP does mention the concern related to phasing out of the textile quotas. But this is an exception; PRSPs should be much more explicit, for example, on potential labor-intensive growth through food processing (e.g., the sugar industry in Mozambique), hampered by tariff escalation and lack of market access. For PRSs to be vehicles for global partnership, they should cover these issues, for example, how Mozambique is paying for the present European sugar regime. This is a lost opportunity.

Participation. In this area, there has definitely been improvement. But consultation focuses very much on traditional civil society. There are two important groups of elected representatives that are not sufficiently engaged: labor unions and parliamentarians. This is a grave mistake.

Labor unions can be helpful in the process by focusing the agenda more on MDG number 1—issues of jobs and income, the need for labor-intensive growth, and questioning to what degree macro policies are actually hindering growth. They can help to focus the debates on equity and distributional impact of policies.

The lack of parliamentary input is an even more serious omission, especially given the attention the Bank has recently given to the issue of governance. How can we talk about governance without understanding that, in democracies, it is parliaments that hold the purse and set the laws of the land?

Let me quote a study undertaken by the German Technical Cooperation (GTZ) on parliamentary involvement in PRSPs in Sub-Saharan

Africa: " . . . the role of parliaments was marginal. This contradicts democratic principles and in some cases even breaches constitutional rights. In addition, the potential offered by parliamentary involvement is not being harnessed. Practice in current PRS processes is thus not only undermining the long-term institutional development of parliamentary democracy in Africa, but also wastes opportunities for effective poverty reduction."

I believe you can get much more ownership if you involve parliamentarians. They define the local domestic debate and local domestic political agenda. This can also help to ensure that poverty reduction strategies are more focused on concrete goals such as the MDGs, as parliaments worldwide are starting to engage in debates on these goals.

Long-term framework. The goals are set for 2015, and poverty reduction strategies have a three-year focus. I read the President's note to the Development Committee and thought he phrased this dilemma very well: it is about marrying the aspirations for the future with the resources and capacity constraints of the present.

Poverty reduction strategies clearly failed to make that bridge to these long-term aspirations, which would have implied identifying today, not a few years from now, what is needed to achieve these goals. Two years ago, I quite successfully lobbied the Development Committee membership—not successfully with the management—to make a statement in the communiqué that the PRSPs should analyze the gap between the resources and policies needed to achieve the goals, on the one hand, and the actual available resources and policies on the other hand. This includes both domestic and external resources, and domestic and external (e.g., trade) policies. It is a missed opportunity that this has never actually been achieved, because you have to invest today in capacity building, delivery mechanisms, revenue boosting, and timely scale-up to achieve these goals. Yet, many PRSPs are not sufficiently costed, and this is a serious failure.

Now, I know that my colleague, Jeff Sachs of the Millennium Project, is very much engaged with the international financial institutions on this issue. If even Mozambique—a country that did everything the international community ever asked them to do and is fairly generously treated compared with others—still does not feel it has sufficient external support to make it happen, you have a clear case that large scale up in the ambitiousness of PRSPs is needed to achieve the goals.

It is not just about what these poor countries should be doing, but about much greater focus on rich countries' trade and aid policies. The Bank should be much tougher in bullying donors on their quantity of aid, but also push them to deliver more effective, high-quality aid and implement the harmonization agenda. First, however, the Bank has to harmonize itself to have the credibility actually to do that.

Notes

1. The Development Committee is a forum of the World Bank and the International Monetary Fund that facilitates intergovernmental consensus building on development issues. Known formally as the Joint Ministerial Committee of the Boards of Governors of the Bank and the Fund on the Transfer of Real Resources to Developing Countries, the committee was established in 1974. The committee's mandate is to advise the Boards of Governors of the Bank and the IMF on critical development issues and the financial resources required to promote economic development in developing countries. Over the years, the committee has interpreted this mandate to include trade and global environmental issues in addition to traditional development matters.

Comments on the Poverty Reduction Strategy Initiatives

Ana Quirós Víquez*

When we talk about poverty reduction strategies, I like to remind myself what I mean by poverty. I understand the lack of opportunity for well-being and development, and not just how much I get or how much I can spend, which is usually how poverty is measured.

The poverty reduction strategy paper (PRSP) evaluation has been an important and positive step forward. From reading the OED PRSP evaluation, you could see the tensions it had caused within the institutions. Bank management and Board discussions provide a good picture of all these tensions.

What we have heard in our countries, those that have been evaluated, also shows some of these tensions. Some people say that they were deceived by the results of this evaluation because they were not strong enough or critical enough. My government, however, says that they were too strong, too critical, that they did not address the good issues of PRSP in Nicaragua.

In my opinion, it would be too generous to say that the gender perspective is taken mildly. The Bank has made a commitment through the strategy to mainstream gender, to include gender as a main issue in their policies and in the PRSPs as one of the issues. But we do not see that commitment to mainstreaming in the evaluation.

If something is not going to be evaluated, you will not pay attention to it. If gender is not going to be evaluated, why should the governments pay any attention? Why would the Bank representatives pay any attention to gender?

Even by looking at the Millennium Development Goals (MDGs), we can see that they are all related to gender issues; yet, if we do not address gender, we will not get anywhere in terms of the MDGs. So I would like to see a stronger commitment to mainstreaming gender in both the strategies and evaluations. We have to take that seriously.

---

*   General Director, Centre of Information and Advisory Services on Health, Nicaragua.

I agree with most of the conclusions of the evaluation, but when I read the responses from management about, for example, country ownership, I wonder how country ownership is understood. Sometimes country ownership is the excuse not to address some of the issues. It is occasionally an excuse to disengage from some of the main worries that we have in civil society. But at the same time, they are not renouncing their commitment to put a hand in on other issues—I will give you an example.

One of the cross-cutting issues for the Nicaraguan PRSP was decentralization. Just recently, the International Monetary Fund had its mission to Nicaragua. Following the mission, the recommendations to the government were that the commitment to increase the money transfers to the local governments would off-balance the goals of the Poverty Reduction and Growth Facility in Nicaragua; therefore, the transfers should not be increased from the current levels. So where do they draw the line for country driven? The poverty reduction strategy was decided on by the country—local governments, national government, and Parliament—to provide more money to local governments. But then the International Monetary Fund says that you should not do that—that it would put you offtrack, thus, forgetting that these are country-owned or country-driven strategies.

In the case of participation, it is true that there is more participation, but primarily through consultation, not through real participation. Most of the time, it stops at the designing process. The evaluation process is rarely participatory, and we would like to see that more strongly declared.

I think the poverty and social impact analysis, should be more focused and done more frequently. Certainly, it would be a good help in evaluating the gender approach and gender perspective in these policies. It would also provide data that are more reliable.

The chart about the MDGs was impressive in that most countries do not have enough information or data to see if they have improved or not. One of the things we were told at the beginning of the PRSP discussions was that it would come with a better data system, because it was also a commitment to more transparency.

If you do not have the data, how can you talk about transparency? How can you talk about letting people have more information? For the second-generation PRSPs, we would like to see more commitment in terms of transparency and real participation throughout the process, not just in the design.

I am also in agreement with Pedro Couto; we need more consistent aid in the long term and not just done punctually. Otherwise, any plan would be insufficient, incoherent, and incapable of achieving any of the goals.

Comments on the Poverty Reduction Strategy Session

Session Chair: Danny Leipziger*

One common theme that seems to come across in all three presentations—and maybe either the panelists or the audience would like to bring these up in the floor discussion—is the question of ownership; I think the Operations Evaluation Department (OED) poverty reduction strategy paper (PRSP) study mentions it as well. It seems to be something that people find has not yet reached the level that they would like from this process.

I agree that we are not talking about the documents so much as the process. So one challenge to the participants as well as the panelists is: what can you do on ownership, realizing that you are actually committing governments to certain courses of action? On the other hand, a lot of actors in society need to participate, if it is going to be an effective poverty reduction strategy.

The second issue, in a variety of ways, is the time under which we are operating; this was raised in a number of different contexts. Eveline Herfkens mentioned that the PRSPs have a three-year and the Millennium Development Goals (MDGs) have a 15-year horizon or longer. Both Victoria Elliott and Ana Quirós said they were surprised they did not see more results in the assessment of the PRSPs from 1999 to 2003. Although it is a whole series of them, some may only have come on stream in 2001, for all we know.

In any event, there is an expectation that you are going to get results that are monitorable and measurable. And I think the issue—as Pedro Couto alluded to it—is that this is a process, whether you call it PRSP or something else that governments go through. The question is how do you judge whether or not you are making progress? I think there was some disappointment that there has not been more progress made.

---

*   Vice President and Head of Network, Poverty Reduction and Economic Management Network, World Bank Group.

Floor Discussion on Poverty Reduction Strategies

AUDIENCE PARTICIPANT: Earlier in the conference, the minister of finance from Bangladesh told us there was a choice between democracy and liberal democracy that allowed for participation to take place on the one hand and a more directed process through authoritarian government on the other.

It seems to me that one of the other elements of this discussion raised this morning was the issue that the Bank does not, by definition, get involved in political affairs. And, yet, if donors want to help civil society to develop, of necessity, that implies an intervention into the political process of the country.

In that sense, a dilemma exists, because if you want a recipient country to promote participation as a necessity for societal ownership of a program, such as the poverty reduction programs, something needs to be done about that the gross underdevelopment of civil society in most poor countries.

The second point that has not been touched is how do you factor in the issue of corruption in diminishing the effectiveness of poverty reduction strategies, because by definition, the poor are powerless. How do you factor in the decisions to fund, not to fund, to move forward, or to stop?

MS. ELLIOTT: I want to respond to the question on how the PRSP takes account of corrupt practices. The Bank, as you know, does have a mechanism for assessing each country's level of governance and degree of reliability and openness. In that system, which is called the Country Policy and Institutional Assessment, governance does have a big impact on lending allocations.

Interestingly, there is so far not much linkage between the PRSP process and the mechanisms that determine lending allocations on the basis of these assessments. So, that is an illustration of the PRSP being slightly outside some of the mainstream decision-making tools the Bank uses.

MS. HERFKENS: Let me say a few words on participation and whether the Bank can be involved in politics. This sounds like a debate from a decade ago here in the Bank, and I never understood it while I was here in the 1990s. But since I have been working in other capacities, at the United Nations in New York and as an ambassador in Geneva, I find this is a concern raised only in this institution.

At the United Nations, where these same countries are represented, albeit by another ministry at perhaps a higher level, agreement exists that governments have to be held accountable and civil society has a role to play. As an ambassador in Geneva at the International Labor Organization, the labor or social affairs ministries of the same countries that make a fuss here about the Bank not being political find a tripartite dialogue in the country very important—not only in the way that the Bank sees the private sector, the employers, but also with labor unions.

In terms of consulting parliaments, every country in the world has a parliament, even if the power of these parliaments differs. What is the point of having it in the first place, if you do not have a debate with them on the policy? I just do not understand.

I knew how sensitive a question this used to be here, but I was amazed at how this was really a problem that only came up on 19th Street in Washington and does not seem to be a problem if you meet these same countries at often higher levels in Geneva or New York.

On corruption, it can only be addressed if people themselves hold their governments accountable and demand that public expenditures become transparent and public, so that people can debate and see where the money goes. We know that governments are only accountable to their own people, not to international institutions. If you want to fight poverty and you care about poverty, you need to be open to civil society and you need an influential parliament.

MR. COUTO: I would like to make a few comments about participation. First, the issue of participation and consultative process is important, but we have to be careful. Ms. Herfkens has raised the issue of parliamentarians and elected bodies, and she is right. There is sometimes a tendency for confusion. We have to respect the elected bodies and the institutionalized government according to the constitution; so participation occurs mostly through consultation. There is no point of coming along later (especially if something went wrong) and stating that the eventual failure was caused by the adoption of a wrong proposition advanced through consultations. There is consultation, but then the relevant bodies are required to make decisions either accepting or rejecting whether a certain point should be included in the program document. Otherwise, there would be serious confusion.

Second, and this is a personal view, poverty problems are very serious; hence, we have to avoid the danger that consultation becomes a matter for "professionals." For the poorest people, there is sometimes too much consultation; there have to be tradeoffs. For instance, you cannot expect a poor peasant to spend two, three, or four days discussing documents; this has to be avoided. But, at the same time, the poor should not be replaced with "professional" participants, who can spend one or two months "being consulted." This is not a useful alternative.

MS. QUIRÓS VÍQUEZ: I fully agree that we elect our governments, but we do not give them a blank check on everything. So the participation process is needed, and it has to be strengthened, not just for the professionals in consultation, but for the people—people who are going to be affected by those policies.

Just recently, we had a sectoral plan designed in Nicaragua. Eighty-five percent of the participants in the consultations were people from the government. So what kind of participation are we talking about? We want the people participating. It is true, we need the people from the government to have a say in what is going to be designed. But that is not good enough, especially in policies that are going to be influencing or determining what is going to happen in my city, in my neighborhood, with my health, and with the education of my children.

This is one of the issues and that is one of the reasons why there is a completely different perspective if you are in a government or in a civil society organization. We certainly want more discussion. We want them to take into account more of what we are saying.

We just had a good example of this. Not too long ago—after five years of discussing the privatization of the pension system—the Bank says to the Nicaraguan government they should not continue in this direction. We had been saying this privatization should stop for more than five years now; it had already cost the country more than US$70 million, which could have been avoided if our view had been taken into account five years earlier. That is why we want to be part of this. That is why we want to be heard, and not just heard, but taken into account.

AUDIENCE PARTICIPANT: I agree with the panel members that both the PRSPs and the MDGs are a step forward in terms of establishing some sort of results framework for the international organizations and for the governments. But, as one of the members of a previous panel noted, what they have basically done is moved from the five-year plans they had under the centrally planned model, rejiggering them and calling them poverty reduction strategies.

In a sense, both the OED report and some of the discussants have mentioned that there is a disconnect between long-term goals, especially poverty reduction, and specific projects and programs that are in place. There is not a logical connection or a logical model to explain how the activities and outputs will lead to those long-term outcomes.

I would agree with Ms. Herfkens that there is the need for much more country-specific analytical work to establish the main determinants of poverty and then develop the policies and programs to address those specific determinants in each country. And as OED and the discussants have mentioned, many of them have nothing to do with social expenditures, but rather with job creation, rural development, and private sector development. So there is this disconnect, and I do not see clearly how to establish that.

MS. HERFKENS: I made my point about the long-term framework earlier. But, I am really concerned about it. This is a wasted opportunity. Unless PRSPs look today at what is needed in 2015 and what we have to do now in terms of training numbers of teachers and nurses—what kind of investment is needed now to boost our revenues, what kind of changes need to be made now in our trade policies to allow more labor-intensive growth—we are never going to meet these goals. PRSPs are fairly useless if they are only looking at the short term—limiting the scope to present budgets and how to move 1 percent within present budgets. This is not impressive.

MR. LEIPZIGER: I will skip my turn, except to say that I think the issue on which we can probably get a pretty quick consensus is the issue of length of the framework in which we are operating. I think that is a real issue we should think about.

MR. COUTO: About poverty analysis and poverty determinants: yes, we did our job. We did not just take what had come from central planning. No, poverty analysis has been undertaken for a long time—since 1988 or 1989. Poverty issues started to be studied slowly, then you had the household survey, and so on. It has been used, and other programs are being designed.
Determinants of poverty have also been investigated, and some of the policies that you will find in the strategy document have been drawn from those. For example, a very high correlation exists between education and the level of poverty and so on. It is probably not perfect, but it has been done like that.

AUDIENCE PARTICIPANT: I am interested in the fact, from the presentation, that most governments seem to "completely agree" that the PRSP process was country driven. This would seem to belie the criticism that we hear in many quarters that the PRSPs are written by staff from an international financial institution (IFI) to meet their concerns, rather than the concerns of the countries themselves. It would also seem to suggest that the countries themselves have greater ownership in the content of those documents than do the IFIs, the World Bank, or the IMF.

I am wondering, however, what does this mean to say "governments"? Does this mean the finance ministry or does it also include program ministries that would administer the programs? I am also interested to see that civil society in the countries disagree so substantially with the views of their governments. Does this mean that they are disappointed that their views were not accepted, or does it mean that they are simply uninformed as to the contents of the PRSP documents?

MS. ELLIOTT: On the perceptions of country ownership, we certainly did not find any evidence or even an accusation that these papers were being written by IFI staff. Our finding on government ownership was that there is a fair degree of ownership within the country governments, but it is a narrowly held group of people within the government who really understand what the PRSP is supposed to be doing and the function it is supposed to provide. It has not really permeated to all the levels of the bureaucracy.

The government officials we surveyed were the people involved in the PRSP, therefore, they naturally perceive it to be much more country driven than people who participated from outside government.

MR. COUTO: The idea has been raised that the PRSP on Mozambique was written by Bank staff. I do not know what happened in other countries, but in Mozambique, that is not true. The document was domestically written. I was not just told this; I was part of the team writing the strategy.

We had written this document drawing from work completed previously. In the evaluation document, it mentions that there was a reaction in Mozambique against the idea of designing a poverty reduction strategy. I was one of those who reacted against it originally, because I thought it was a repetition of the past. But then I recognized that the Bank was genuinely open to accepting what we could put forward; thus, we wanted to recap what we had already done in the line ministries for education, health, and infrastructure. This work, in some cases done more than eight years ago, was brought into the strategy.

The Bank reacted negatively to some issues our drafts. Some of their criticism was accepted and incorporated into the document; some was rejected. In the end, the Bank accepted the document as it was, with its weaknesses and good points.

MS. QUIRÓS VÍQUEZ: In the case of Nicaragua, it was slightly different. The PRSP was written in English first by people who were borrowed from either the International Monetary Fund or the World Bank, and months later we got the PRSP through the Bank in Spanish, not through our government.

Part 7

Improving the International
Context for Reform

Seven Deadly Sins: Reflections on Donor Failings[†]

Nancy Birdsall[*]

The donor community may look back on the 1990s as a watershed. In that decade, some developing countries took off in growth terms, apparently benefiting from and effectively exploiting the increasing integration of the global market. But others—in sub-Saharan Africa, Latin America, and much of Central Asia—seemed stuck. Many of the countries where growth faltered had been major recipients of development assistance during several decades and under the tutelage of the donors had implemented structural reforms and thousands of projects. In doing so, some had accumulated substantial debt to multilateral and bilateral creditors to the point that the donors were engaged in a major effort to write down those debts. For many of the world's poorest countries, the record of development and development assistance seemed dismal.

As a community, donors responded in the past decade with new efforts to assess their own policies and practices. The end of the Cold War made it possible to imagine ensuring that foreign aid could more

---

[†] This presentation was part of a larger paper originally prepared for the Bangladesh Economic Association Conference on Emerging Global Economic Order and Developing Countries, June 28–July 1, 2004, Dhaka, Bangladesh (see Birdsall 2004).

[*] President, Center for Global Development.

directly address fundamental development problems. As a result, there have been not only new calls to increase the volume of development assistance, but rather new resolutions to reform the process by which assistance is designed and delivered.

In this presentation, I focus on the "sins" of donors as a community in the hope it will enrich the ongoing discussion of reform of what might be called the "business" of development assistance. I deal with the shortcomings of the donor countries as donors, that is, as providers of development assistance, leaving aside in this presentation their shortcomings in such other areas as trade, security, and international migration that also affect the developing countries (what the donors have come to call the need for "policy coherence").[1] In referring to donors and the donor community, I refer both to bilateral donors and the World Bank, the International Monetary Fund (IMF), and other international institutions that provide credit at below-market rates to developing countries and whose policies and practices are heavily influenced by the rich countries.

The sins I discuss are, in the order in which I address them:
1. Impatience (with institution building)
2. Pride (failure to exit)
3. Ignorance (failure to evaluate)
4. Sloth (pretending participation is sufficient for ownership)
5. Envy (collusion and coordination failure)
6. Greed (stingy and unreliable financing)
7. Foolishness (underfunding of regional public goods).

A brief concluding section summarizes possible "fixes" for the sins of the donors.

1. Impatience with institution building

Impatience for "results" has led to programs and projects in which monitoring focuses on visible short-run inputs (such as purchase of goods and issuing of contracts) and sometimes intermediate outcomes (such as an increase in government spending on social programs).

Impatience to disburse money and see something happen precludes attention to the fundamental institutional problems, such as political patronage influencing teacher placement in the case of education programs or vested interests preventing banking sector or judicial sector reforms.[2]

Persistence of project implementation units (PIUs). In their impatience to implement "their" projects, donors continue to constitute special units outside of the recipient country governments as a mechanism to bypass the bureaucratic, salary, and other constraints of recipient governments.

Impatience for policy change leads donors and official creditors to abstract from the political constraints that reformers face in their own governments, sometimes undermining the efforts of reformers, rather than supporting them. Willful naiveté about political reality may help explain why many structural adjustment programs supported by the IMF and the World Bank and endorsed by the larger donor community have failed to generate growth.

I have a related reflection on donor impatience and the Millennium Development Goals (MDGs). On the positive side, the MDGs allow for and invite a relatively long planning horizon. The forthcoming report of the Millennium Project is likely to put a healthy emphasis on a ten-year planning horizon and on current investments in institutional capacity to absorb the future infusions of resources without which the goals cannot be met in the poorest countries.[3] On the negative side, countries that by historical standards are succeeding beyond measure, such as Burkina Faso, Mali, and Uganda[4] (chart 1A), are currently characterized as "offtrack" on such measures as education and infant mortality in U.N. reports (e.g., UNDP 2003), which uses a simple linear measure of trends), and unless they can accelerate progress even more dramatically will not meet certain of the goals by 2015. For example, Burkina Faso is "offtrack" from meeting the goal of universal primary schooling by 2015. The net primary enrollment rate was just 35 percent in 2000, and by one estimate (extrapolating from historical experience of more than 100 countries, which takes the form of a logistics curve [Clemens 2004]) will reach "only" 59 percent by 2015. Compared with the historical performance of today's rich countries, however, that rate of progress would be impressive. It would roughly match South Korea's progress between about 1945 and 1955, but far outpace the progress of the United States, whose rate, starting at Burkina Faso's current enrollment rate of 42 percent, took 30 years to increase to 57 percent (chart 1B).

Given our limited understanding of how to create and sustain the institutional setting that must complement additional donor transfers to achieve the strategic goals in those countries, the MDGs create the risk that the donor community will succumb (even more) to the distortions that impatience creates. The MDGs should not become a lightning rod around which countries that have been unusually successful (compared with historical trends and given their income and institutional capacity) are in 2015 characterized as "failures." Better that the MDGs become a lightning rod for ending donor impatience, so that additional donor transfers to the poorest countries can be more explicitly attuned to institution building.

2. Pride (failure to exit)

The impatience of donors is ironically accompanied by an inability and unwillingness to exit from programs and countries where their aid is not helping. By "exit" in this context, I mean discontinuing new large grants and loans, not withdrawing from continuing engagement through dialogue, technical advice, and even small transfers for training and technical assistance. (Impatience and inability to exit are not inconsistent. Impatience to spend money, even badly, is unfortunately fully consistent with an inability to stop big spending, while remaining engaged.)

Pride (and bureaucratic politics, including coordination failures among donors, discussed below) have generally precluded exit as a way to minimize waste. Even the design of the Millennium Challenge Account indirectly reflects the difficulty of exit; it limits the risk of failure by restricting large transfers to recipient countries where there is minimal risk of failure. In recipient countries in the gray zone, where there is a reasonable, but not high expectation of adequate performance, the donors once committed tend to let misguided optimism (and an enlightened commitment to "do something" for the reform-minded minister of agriculture or health or finance struggling in a weak or corrupt system) trump good judgment.

3. Ignorance (failure to evaluate)

Official and private agencies that develop and manage development assistance programs hesitate, with some justification, to advertise the limits of their craft. In the donor countries that finance assistance, suspicion that much such assistance is wasted runs high, and exposure of a program's current shortcomings could reduce its future funding.[5] Even if only a cover for lack of generosity, such suspicions are politically important. It is easier to limit than to expand foreign aid budgets, and in the interests of the latter, those who see and work with the urgent needs of people in poor countries have no obvious incentive to invest in long-term evaluation of what they do.

Moreover, rigorous evaluation of the impact of an intervention is costly. It is likely to seem a distraction for donor officials wanting to be sure programs get implemented and to add to the burdens of the limited number of experienced local staff. For many development assistance programs, there is also the attribution problem. Without baseline information and a controlled experiment, it is difficult to attribute program success or failure to the programs themselves, as opposed to the environment in which they operate and the unpredictable shocks— positive and negative—that influence their effectiveness. Those who develop and manage assistance programs are cursed by their own intimate knowledge of this particular complication and are understandably wary of subjecting their work to the crude political criticism and limits on new resources for aid programs that transparent evaluation might trigger.[6]

The multilateral banks do fund internal ex post assessments of the projects and programs they finance (as in the Independent Evaluation Office and Operations Evaluation Department studies of the IMF and World Bank[7]). But they face tremendous attribution problems, and their results and implications are rarely immediately internalized in new decisions, especially if they challenge conventional wisdom or raise awkward questions regarding donors' strategies.[8] Examples include the heavily indebted poor country program of debt relief, in which even the second "enhanced" funding has (predictably, given the optimism of the original projections) not been adequate to ensure debt sustainability of the recipient countries[9]; the continuing failure of the poverty reduction strategy paper (PRSP) approach to deliver donor coordination and country ownership[10]; and the structural adjustment programs of the IMF, the World Bank, and other donors.

Although the donors have financed billions of dollars worth of projects, few of these projects include the ingredients for a systematic evaluation. This lack of emphasis on good evaluation has been and continues to be immensely costly. In the absence of timely, credible, and independent evaluation, many aid dollars have been misdirected.

4. Sloth (pretending "participation" is sufficient for "ownership")

It took too long, but experience and empirical analysis led to the recognition in the 1990s that the conditionality typically included in World Bank and IMF loans (and often implicitly or explicitly followed by other official creditors and donors) was not effective, except where it was in effect irrelevant.[11]

But that discovery led to a new kind of simplification (in practice if not in conception), namely that "participation" of citizens through civil society groups is sufficient for securing "ownership." The misguided imposition of policy conditions morphed into the misguided imposition of "participation."

In principle, the logic of widespread participation in setting a reform agenda makes sense. The theory is that reforms that are not politically feasible will not endure, even if they are implemented (itself unlikely). The expectation of economic actors that reforms will not endure in turn undermines the credibility of promised reforms and thus their potentially positive effects on investment and growth. (Encouraging participation also was seen as a healthy if modest step in building democratic institutions where they do not exist.)

But the prevailing approach to participation, as demanded by donors, has been narrow and apolitical. It would be wrong to condemn the idea of greater participation in itself. But it would be equally wrong to delude oneself that participation creates or indicates political and social ownership of major reforms.

5. Envy (collusion and coordination failure)

In contrast to the early days of development assistance, when, for example, the United States was the dominant donor (the only donor in the case of the Marshall Plan), recipient countries now cope with dozens of official creditors, bilateral donors, the United Nations, and other public agencies and international nongovernmental organizations. All of these in turn operate in dozens of countries—more than 100 in the case of Germany, the Netherlands, the United States, France, Japan, and the United Kingdom (chart 5A). In each country, donors also typically operate in many sectors with many projects. Managing their "own" projects increases donor visibility, and doing so in many countries maximizes donor countries' ability to leverage the diplomatic support of small countries for their position (and sometimes their candidates for high posts) in the United Nations and other international settings. In 2000–02, the United States disbursed about US$100 million of aid in Tanzania, financing 50 different projects at an average of just US$2 million apiece (chart 5B). With a total of more than 1,300 projects in that period and an estimated 1,000 donor meetings a year and 2,400 reports to donors every quarter, Tanzania several years ago announced a four-month holiday during which it would not accept donor visits.[12]

The donors are neither competing nor collaborating. They are in effect colluding, something that is easy to do for suppliers in the absence of a competitive market.[13] The proliferation of colluding donors (i.e., the tendency of donors to operate in many countries and in many sectors within countries) creates what is now called donor fragmentation, the flip side of donor proliferation; the measure of fragmentation is rising with the number of donors and the smaller their aid shares. The cost to recipients of these behaviors goes well beyond the reduction in the monetary value of donor transfers because of the high transactions costs recipients face (with many different missions, reporting requirements, procurement rules, and so on). With many donors competing with each other for visibility and quick success, donors end up treating the limited public sector capacity (and the limited recurrent budget) of recipient countries as a common-pool resource (Brautigam and Knack 2000), undermining that resource rather than building it up.

6. Greed (stingy and unreliable financing)

Stinginess is also apparent in the tendency for donors to portray actual transfers as higher than they are. Of an estimated US$20 billion reported by bilateral donors as disbursements to the low-income countries in 2002, after subtracting about US$7 billion for emergency aid and technical cooperation funds (spent mostly on donor contractors), and almost US$3 billion in repayments of loans and interest, only 50 percent or US$10 billion actually went to the low-income countries for direct support.[14] Donors are stingy even in relation to their own publicly agreed commitments. Only Denmark, Norway, Sweden, and the Netherlands have met the 0.7 percent of gross domestic product to which all committed at Monterrey, Mexico, (confirming even earlier commitments) in 2002.[15] Other European countries, including the United

Kingdom, have increased their aid budgets since Monterrey, as has the United States, but from levels still far below the 0.7 promise.

Donor financing is also unreliable from the point of view of those managing the economies of low-income countries. It is volatile, unpredictable, and, in the more aid-dependent countries, procyclical—declining at times when countries need the external infusion most, for example, because of a commodity prices shock and increasing procyclically when a country's own tax revenues are growing.[16]

7. Foolishness (underfunding of regional public goods)

Donors direct almost all of their resources to individual recipient countries, as opposed to regional groupings and global public goods.[17] Financing for global public goods has grown in the past decade, primarily in response to the pressures of environmental groups in the rich countries. In the case of global goods, rich countries have an evident self-interest, although, of course, much of the spending benefits developing countries as well. Regional public goods, however, have not yet received much attention. Of the approximately US$60 billion in development aid disbursed in 2002, a rough guess would be that at most US$1 to US$2 billion was spent on multicountry programs and projects in the developing world, such as harmonization of stock markets in Africa, development of a shared electricity grid in Central America, or multicountry roads and watersheds in Asia (chart 7A).[18]

A Summary of Donor Fixes

(a) Impatience (with institution building). This is the most central and fundamental challenge. A first step would be for the donor community to acknowledge its overall past failure and undertake a collective assessment of how to address that failure in close and constant consultation with wise people from the developing countries. If it cannot be done collectively (for example at the Development Assistance Committee [DAC] of the Organisation for Economic Cooperation and Development [OECD]), leadership will have to taken by a single large bilateral donor such as the United States or the United Kingdom.[19]

(b) Pride (failure to exit). New long-term, more accordion-like instruments are needed that make exit (defined as stopping the flow of large transfers, not as abandoning engagement through dialogue and

advisory services) the default. Exit should be established as the norm, not as punishment or judgment, but as a natural response to signs that investments being financed will not yield adequate returns.

(c) Ignorance (failure to evaluate). A minimum number of major donors could make a collective agreement to self-finance a fully independent evaluation entity, which would in turn contract third-party evaluations of selected donor-financed projects and programs and of donor behaviors and modalities.

(d) Sloth (pretending participation is sufficient for ownership). Donors need to end their apolitical approach to ownership and engage instead in assessment of the interests of politically powerful stakeholders, the record of existing governments on difficult reforms, and governments' vulnerability to an ouster if they take certain steps. This is particularly critical in the case of pro-poor reforms, because they usually undermine powerful interests and have weak domestic constituencies. It may ultimately be the case that only when developing country recipients have more voice (and votes) in the major institutions will they assume real "ownership" of pro-poor economic and political reforms that altruistic donors wish to support.

(e) Envy (collusion and coordination failures). Minor fixes could include agreement of the bilateral donor governments to increase the portion of their total assistance spending that goes to multilateral institutions and programs (even this is not so easy to imagine happening), agreement to the concept of lead donors in highly aid-dependent countries, and financing through DAC of grants to developing country policy groups to report on in-country performance of the individual donors. Similar to impatience, however, this challenge is fundamental and may not yield to minor fixes. The major fix would be establishment of a true common pool of donor funds.

(f). Greed (stingy and unreliable financing). Instruments that build in less volatile and more predictable financing are needed, as well as larger aid budgets. New ideas are on the table, in part impelled by the commitments rich countries made in the context of the MDGs. But they are more visible with respect to the amount of aid than with respect to its predictability; the latter requires more radical rethinking of current instruments and practices.

(g) Foolishness (underfunding of regional public goods). Financing of regional goods, especially in Africa, needs a champion, probably the British or the French, who would push for a revamping of the singular

country focus that now prevails. Grant funds at the multilateral banks would create internal incentives for supporting regional investments; they could be supported in part by transfers of net income from the hard windows of the banks, if the middle-income countries whose borrowing costs were affected were given more control over use of those "regional" resources.

My purpose has not been to condemn the donor "sins" (because in this area shame and blame are not likely to work anyway), but to put them on the table for discussion. Some "sins," such as the tying of aid to a donor's own services and goods, are already on the reform agenda of the official community and I have not discussed them here. Instead I have tried to focus on shortcomings of the "business of aid," on which new research has or could shed light and which have not yet been adequately or explicitly incorporated into the donor community's reform agenda. These shortcomings of the business matter tremendously, especially in the context that the focus on achieving the MDGs by 2015 has brought. That is because research shows that they reduce considerably the effective value of the aid that is transferred and in the most aid-dependent countries may even mean that the "business of aid" actually undermines those countries' long-term development prospects.

CHART 1A
The Transition in net primary enrollment: all countries 1960–2000

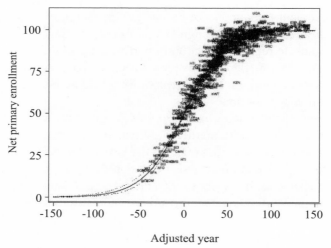

Adjusted year

Notes: "Adjusted years" are the elapsed time since 50 percent enrollment. Data points show country-years, spaced quinquennially.
Source: Clemens (2004).

CHART 1B
Burkina Faso—Unlikely to Meet the School Enrollment MDGs but
Performing Strongly By Historical Standards

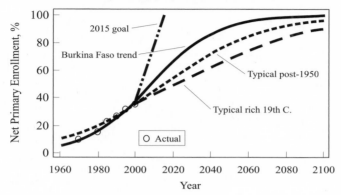

Source: Clemens, Kenny and Moss (2004).

CHART 5A
Index of Donor Proliferation, 1999–2001 Average
(A Higher Score Indicates Higher Donor Proliferation)

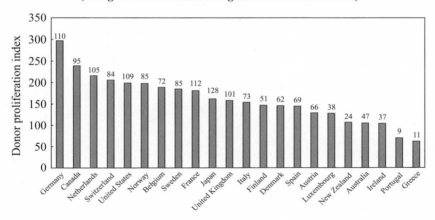

* The figures above the bars indicate the number of countries that received aid from each donor.

Note: The donor proliferation index is the inverse of a Theil index, multiplied by 100 to avoid decimals. There is more donor proliferation (aid dispersion) when a donor's aid is allocated to a larger share of the total number of potential aid recipients, and when each aid recipient gets a relatively equal share of the donor's total aid.

Source: Acharya, de Lima and Moore (2004) .

CHART 5B

Tanzania: Average Aid Spending Per Project By Donor, 2000–2002 Average (Thousands of US$)

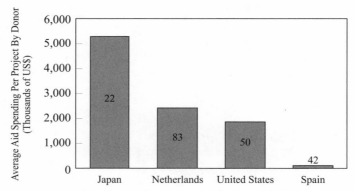

* Numbers in columns indicate the number of projects each donor has in Tanzania.

Source: Center for Global Development and Foreign Policy (2004).

CHART 7A
Donor Commitments to Regional Programs and Projects for Selected Multilateral and Bilateral Donors in 2002

	Regional Public Goods Commitments by Each Donor (millions of US$)	Regional Public Goods Commitments as Share of Total ODA Commitments by Each Donor (percent)
World Bank[6]	n/a	n/a
African Development Bank	30	1.2
Inter-American Development Bank[5]	20	0.4
Asian Development Bank[4]	45	0.7
European Bank for Reconstruction and Development[7]	99	2.7
UNDP[1]	55	2.1
WHO[2]	138	7.1
United States[3]	303	2.4
United Kingdom[3]	98	2.6
Total	788	2.1

Notes: To the extent possible, commitments shown are for programs and projects that were managed by a regional organization such as the West African Monetary Union or the Central American Development Bank, regardless of the source. Commitments are from sources where they are probably shown in nominal terms.

1. The UNDP figure is for 2001. The UNDP also granted an additional US$9.5 million for interregional and global projects that year and US$16 million total for intercountry programs in 2000.

2. The WHO figure is for 1998–99. The same amount was spent in 1996–97.

3. These figures are probably inflated, because they are figures for all "unspecified funds" going to a region and are likely to include funds that in fact went to individual countries.

4. The Asian Development Bank's regional commitments reflect one project only, the Trade Finance Facilitation Program.

5. The Inter-American Development Bank (IDB) also reports regional disbursements in addition to regional commitments. In 2002 regional disbursements were US$67 million. In the past, IDB has also made concessional loans to the Central American Bank for Economic Integration and to other subregional development banks.

6. The annual reports of the Inter-American Development Bank (table IV. "Yearly and Cumulative Loans and Guarantees"), The African Development Bank (Annex II-7 "Bank Group Loan and Grant Approvals by Country"), the European Bank for Reconstruction and Development (projects signed in 2002 section), and the Asian Development Bank (public and private sector loan approvals by country) all include a line item showing annual commitments to regional programs and projects. The World Bank Annual Report does not seem to provide a comparable line item.

7. This is the capital of six private equity or debt funds established to invest in or lend to private firms across two or more countries; whether these funds should be counted as multicountry programs as defined in this essay is not entirely clear.

Source: Birdsall (forthcoming).

Notes

1. On these broader issues, see Birdsall and Clemens (2003) and Center for Global Development (2003), as well as Cline (2004) and other materials, available at: http://www.cgdev.org.
2. For all its value, even the recent emphasis of the World Bank and its partners on expenditure monitoring in the context of poverty reduction strategy paper programs does not in itself go to the heart of the problem.
3. The draft synthesis report is available at http://www.unmillenniumproject.org/html/about.shtm.
4. See Clemens (2004) on education and Clemens, Kenny, and Moss (2004) on education, infant mortality, and other goals.
5. It is true that such suspicions seem less powerful in Western Europe than in the United States, Australia, and Canada. (Of 21 rich countries, the latter three rank 19th, 13th, and 10th in the size of their public foreign aid budget as a portion of their economy in 2002.) Various theories have been suggested to explain the persistent differences across donor countries in the amounts of public foreign aid. One is that where tolerance for income inequality varies across countries and such inequality is higher, it is associated with the view that people get what they deserve and if they are poor in faraway places, perhaps that is all they deserve. The other is that the form of government in the United States, in which it is possible to have an opposition party controlling the legislative branch, is particularly unfriendly to foreign aid (see Lancaster forthcoming). Goldstein and Moss (2003) show that in the United States the most auspicious arrangement for a higher appropriation of foreign aid has been a Republican in the White House and the Republican party in control of the Senate and the House of Representatives.
6. The official agencies do sponsor internal ex post assessment of the interventions they finance. The World Bank has, for example, its Operations Evaluations Department, as do the other multilateral banks and bilateral aid agencies. The International Monetary Fund recently established an Independent Evaluation Office (IEO), although it took more than 50 years before it felt the need to do so, finally responding to the pressure of civil society groups highly critical of its adjustment loans and then its approach during the Asian financial crisis. These offices do a creditable job (the first studies of the IEO are impressive); however, their studies are subject to the review and comment not only of staff in the institutions, but of the countries whose programs are often the subject of the evaluations. There is a natural process of minimizing the harshness of language, awareness of which rebounds back to those undertaking these "evaluations." More to the point, it is difficult for these internally sponsored evaluations to deal with some fundamental problems: lack of a baseline against which to judge an intervention and, of course, lack of a counterfactual.
7. See footnote 6 above.
8. For an example, see Birdsall, Vaishnav, and Malik (forthcoming), on the World Bank's decade of lending for poverty reduction in Pakistan.
9. Birdsall and Williamson (2002); Birdsall and Vaishnav (2004).
10. World Bank (2004a). The OED report does not use the term "failure," but the evidence it presents can be so interpreted.
11. For example, see Collier and others (1997) and Gunning (2000).
12. Birdsall and Deese (2004) use this example to introduce an essay on the current U.S. foreign aid program, which is largely unilateral in conception and implementation.

13. Thus Easterly (2002) labels the system a cartel of good intentions. "Once a collusive agreement (among donors) is in place, bureaucracies will not cheat on the agreement by supplying a larger quantity of foreign aid services at a lower price" (p. 10). Collusion also allows sharing the blame of failures, which dictates minimal effort at evaluation.
14. United Nations Millennium Project (2005).
15. In Pearson (1969), 1 percent of GDP was agreed to as the objective. That goal was eventually dropped as unrealistic.
16. Bulir and Hamann (2001).
17. This section is taken mostly from Birdsall (forthcoming), which includes sources and citations for the points made here.
18. Some private foundations such as Gates and Rockefeller put large portions of their total grant making into global programs that sometimes operate at the "regional" level, but even in these cases, the focus is global.
19. The World Bank could be asked to do technical work; much is already set out in World Bank (2004b). It is a matter of turning analysis into ideas for new instruments, procedures, and practices.

References

Acharya, Arnab, Ana Fuzzo de Lima, and Mick Moore. 2004. "The Proliferators: Transactions Costs and the Value of Aid." *IDS Working Paper*. Institute of Development Studies, Sussex, U.K.

Birdsall, Nancy. 2004. *Seven Deadly Sins: Reflections on Donor Failings*. Working Paper no. 50. Center for Global Development, Washington, D.C. Available at: http://www.cgdev.org/Publications/?PubID=183.

———. (forthcoming) "Underfunded Regionalism in the Developing World." In Kaul and others (eds.) *The New Public Finance: Responding to Global Challenges*. Oxford University Press: New York.

Birdsall, Nancy, and Brian Deese. 2004. "Hard Currency Unilateralism Doesn't Work for Foreign Aid Either." *Washington Monthly* (March).

Birdsall, Nancy, and John Williamson. 2002. *Delivering on Debt Relief: From IMF Gold to a New Aid Architecture*. Center for Global Development, Washington, D.C.

Birdsall, Nancy, and Michael Clemens. 2003. "From Promise to Performance: How Rich Countries Can Help Poor Countries Help Themselves." *CGD Brief* 2(1). Center for Global Development, Washington, D.C.

Birdsall, Nancy, and Milan Vaishnav. 2004. "Getting to Home Plate: Why *Smarter* Debt Relief Matters for the Millennium Development Goals." Prepared for the Helsinki Process on Globalisation and Democracy, March 26–28. Available at: http://www.cgdev.org/docs/Debt%20Relief%20and%20the%20MDGs.pdf.

Birdsall, Nancy, Milan Vaishnav, and Adeel Malik. Forthcoming. "Poverty and the Social Sectors: the World Bank in Pakistan." Report for the Operations Evaluations Department, World Bank, Washington, D.C.

Brautigam, Deborah A., and Stephen Knack. 2004. "Aid Dependence, Institutions, and Governance in Sub-Saharan Africa." *Economic Development and Cultural Change* 52(2): 255–85.

Bulír, Aleš, and A. Javier Hamann. 2001. *How Volatile and Predictable Are Aid Flows, and What Are the Policy Implications?* IMF Working Paper No. 01/167. International Monetary Fund, Washington, D.C. Available at: http://www.imf.org/external/pubs/ft/wp/2001/wp01167.pdf.

Center for Global Development. 2003. "Ranking the Rich." *Foreign Policy* (May/ June).

————. 2004. "Ranking the Rich 2004." *Foreign Policy* (May/June).

Clemens, Michael. 2004. *The Long Walk to School: International Education Goals in Historical Perspective.* CGD Working Paper No. 39. Center for Global Development, Washington, D.C.

Clemens, Michael, Charles J. Kenny, and Todd Moss. 2004. *The Trouble with the MDGs: Confronting Expectations of Aid and Development Success.* CGD Working Paper No. 40. Center for Global Development, Washington, D.C.

Cline, William. 2004. *Trade Policy and Global Poverty.* Center for Global Development, Washington, D.C.

Collier, Paul, Patrick Guillaumont, Sylviane Guillaumont, and Jan Willem Gunning. 1997. "Redesigning Conditionality." *World Development* 25(9): 1399–407.

Easterly, William. 2002. *The Cartel of Good Intentions: Bureaucracy Versus Markets in Foreign Aid.* CGD Working Paper No. 4. Center for Global Development, Washington, D.C.

Goldstein, Markus P., and Todd J. Moss. 2003. *The Surprise Party: An Analysis of U.S. ODA Flows to Africa.* CGD Working Paper No. 30. Center for Global Development, Washington, D.C.

Gunning, Jan Willem. 2000. "The Reform of Aid: Conditionality, Selectivity, and Ownership." Paper presented at Aid and Development Conference, Stockholm, Sweden, January 21–22. Available at: http://www.sida.se/Sida/articles/3600-3699/3676/pap-gun.pdf.

Lancaster, Carol. (forthcoming). "Fifty Years of Foreign Aid." Center for Global Development, Washington, D.C.

Pearson, Lester B. 1969. *Partners in Development: Report of the Commission on International Development.* New York: Praeger.

United Nations Development Program (UNDP). 2003. *Human Development Report 2003: Millennium Development Goals: A Compact among Nations to End Human Poverty.* New York: Oxford University Press.

United Nations Millennium Project. 2005. *Investing in Development: A Practical Plan to Achieve the Millennium Development Goals.* United Nations Development Programme, New York, N.Y.

World Bank. 2004a. *The Poverty Reduction Strategy Initiative: An Independent Evaluation of the World Bank's Support through 2003.* Operations Evaluation Department, Washington, D.C.

World Bank. 2004b. *World Development Report 2004: Making Services Work for the Poor.* New York: Oxford University Press.

Effectiveness of Policies and Reforms

Kemal Derviş*

I am going to take the opportunity to look at the Bank from my own perspective, from my own experience, both for many years right here, but in the recent past in Turkey as minister of economy and now as someone looking at it from a parliamentary perspective.

First, for the money spent on foreign aid, adjustment lending, or even on project lending to be effective—for development to work—an effective macro strategy is needed. Serious mistakes in macro strategy can be dramatic and create a tremendous amount of damage, as evidenced in the past decades. If the macro strategy is wrong, despite the little bit of help that can be rendered at the project or sector levels, most of the financing is going to go to waste. And worse, unless the financing is in the form of pure grants, it is going to create larger debt for the country.

The most dramatic example of this has been Argentina. Here, the implementation and continuation of a mistaken macro strategy and macro policy caused extreme damage to the Argentine economy. The creation of a fixed exchange rate currency board compared with the dollar was fundamentally wrong in design. The dollar accounted for only 30 percent of the current account transactions of Argentina. The Euro zone accounted for close to another 30 percent. And Brazil, with its flexible exchange rate system, accounted also for close to 30 percent of Argentinean transactions. When Brazil devalued, there was thus a tremendous impact on Argentina. To have maintained this system for a short period to exit from hyperinflation, would have been one thing, but its continuation is what created the damage.

Another recent example is a small country that has zero inflation, 40 percent unemployment, as well as other problems. For some reason, they had adopted a fixed exchange rate regime as an anti-inflation device, despite actual inflation being zero. Again, this is a case in which incorrect macro strategies cause enormous damage.

---

* Member of the Turkish Parliament and Former Minister of Economic Affairs, Turkey.

The importance of these macro strategies must be kept in mind, especially regarding the interaction among the International Monetary Fund (IMF), World Bank, nongovernmental organizations, and the academic community. On many occasions—and maybe I am biased because of my history at the Bank—the World Bank was actually right on the macro issues vis-à-vis others, particularly the IMF at times.

This creates a dilemma, because at the end of the day, it is the IMF that calls the shots on macroeconomics, and it should. Yet, so much of the Bank's own work—staff input, financing, and so on—depends on the macro framework that the Bank has to keep a certain ability to give a second opinion on the macro side. The Bank cannot give up its macroeconomic work and macroeconomic judgment, because too much is at stake. It needs to be able to provide input, while, of course, acknowledging that the IMF is the lead institution in this arena.

Macroeconomics is a necessary, but not sufficient condition for success. Once the macro framework is in place and the macroeconomic mistakes avoided, the real work can begin on the structural issues, social policies, institution building, and all other necessary issues. This is a vast amount of work, and not something that can be designed quickly. Nor will success follow immediately. It requires tremendous involvement, not only with government agencies, but with civil society, institutions, unions, and all stakeholders. It is this long-term work that is the essence of the Bank's work.

From the Turkish perspective—that of the recipient—the ability to access the Bank's knowledge in a quick and convenient way was invaluable. It is true, that in today's world, thanks to the Internet, you can access Bank knowledge without necessarily having to go through the Bank. Yet the Bank can be a great facilitator—a great filter. It can accelerate the process and can quickly bring people—women or men who have actual hands-on experience—to the table to share their experiences and knowledge. This is a tremendous input.

There is also a great need for financing. Not everything can be done by the private sector. Much of the activity remains in the domain of the public sector for parts of infrastructure, education, social sectors, and health. From both the global and country perspectives, there is high demand for the Bank's core work on institutions, poverty, social policies, infrastructure, education, and health, especially in the very poor countries and the emerging markets.

But then comes the great paradox. There is great need and demand for services, and the Bank has these assets, the capacities, and the knowledge; however, if you measure the actual financial flows from the Bank, it is minimal—something like US$6 or US$7 billion for the International Bank for Reconstruction and Development this year. This is nothing. Then, in terms of IDA, funding is constrained by donor money; thus, a contradiction exists between the tremendous need for both the work and financing, and a World Bank that in a sense is becoming smaller and smaller.

So what are the reasons explaining this paradox? First, the problem is in the many fiscal frameworks that do not sufficiently distinguish between current expenditures and capital formation. The primary deficit or surplus is fixed in aggregate terms, but in the dialogue with the IMF, little distinction is made between this and current expenditures, which neither create net worth in the public sector nor meet future needs in terms of fiscal sustainability. For example, there is a difference in giving an across-the-board increase in salaries to civil servants, compared with creating new public assets in the education, health, and infrastructure sectors that will actually improve the net worth of the public sector.

Inadequate investment is being made in fiscal frameworks, and this underinvestment on the public side is what harms both growth and debt sustainability in the long term. This also constrains the role of the Bank, because it works through the public investment program.

Second, the Bank, unfortunately, is largely unable to deal directly with municipal authorities, because of the need for a central government guarantee. Yet, decentralization, which is required and necessary, increasingly shifts many of the central government functions to local governments and local authorities.

Perhaps the time has come to revisit this issue in the World Bank. For were the Bank able to work more directly with the local and municipal authorities, including in terms of financing, efforts would be very welcome and lines of business apt to increase tremendously. It would enable the Bank to become a more prominent partner to the municipal authorities in their own programs. Of course, this would require a high-level decision, however, perhaps a consideration allowing a certain percentage of World Bank lending to go to municipal authorities without the central government guarantee would be enough to start the process.

Third, the debate on loans compared with grants to poor countries continues. There is obviously the question if it is a good thing in itself to only provide grants—no loans, not even concessional loans—to these countries. But does this mean that future resources will be cut? How are you going to finance? Is it a politician's tactic to look good in the short term, while endangering the long-term resource transfer to the poorest countries?

The aspect to emphasize here is that there is an extreme binary approach. Grants are given to poor countries until they achieve a certain income level, which is still extremely low. When this level is reached and the country graduates to "middle-income" status, all of a sudden they have to move to commercial lending terms. This change in lending terms occurs despite the fact that there can still be many poor people in the country.

I would argue that there is a strong case for a more graduated approach that would allow the World Bank to transfer some resources at a cost marginally below commercial rates to these lower middle-income or even middle-income countries, such as Brazil or Turkey, where poverty rates are still high. What are needed are financial facilities that blend near-commercial resources, including some conditionality with some amount of grant resources to reach the middle-income countries, particularly the poor in these countries.

By incorporating these elements—a greater emphasis in the macro framework on public investment, ability to work with municipal authorities more directly and allowing some percentage of resources to be transferred without central government guarantees, and movement away from the extreme position of IDA grants or commercial loans—an enabling environment could be created in which the World Bank could expand to address better the needs and demands existing in both poor and middle-income countries.

There was a time, when the Bank had headroom problems financially. Now, the opposite is true, there is a huge amount of headroom, even using the most conservative financial approach. Yet, somehow there is an inability to transfer resources.

But we live in a very strange world in which the richest country is actually importing a huge amount of capital from Asia and even from Latin America. Brazil, for example, is running a large surplus on its current account and as such has become capital exporter to the United States, which will import something close to US$600 billion of capital from around the world this year. This turns the whole economics framework on its head when you think that capital should actually be flowing to the poorer countries.

Yet, even if all these things are in place, there is still the point of legitimacy. The Bretton Woods institutions, both the IMF and the Bank, unfortunately suffer from a strong sense of illegitimacy in many developing countries. They are perceived as neither impartial nor politically neutral. On the contrary, they are assumed to be managed almost exclusively by the G-7.

Although this perception maybe somewhat exaggerated, nonetheless, the perception that these institutions are foreign challenges the legitimacy under which they must operate. This was extremely frustrating in Turkey when trying to discuss the substance of an IMF or Bank economic program. The very fact that it was supported by these institutions made it impossible to have an impartial discussion; the immediate reaction would be ". . . well you know, this is supported by Washington, Tokyo, Berlin," or whatever.

As an example, the Turkish government, working with the World Bank, had promised that the inefficient agricultural support price policy would be replaced by direct income support. Turkish researchers, specialists in the ministries, as well as World Bank specialists had designed a new system—a better system. As the program was being implemented, however, the government changed and then war in Iraq erupted, and the national budget was in jeopardy of not fulfilling its targets.

As is the case in these situations, people from the Turkish finance ministry and treasury and the IMF teams sat together looking for monies that could be cut to make budget. A big chunk of this money, despite resistance, came from an agricultural direct income support project. The World Bank country director at the time, Ajay Chhibber, loudly protested that this was a violation of the program and the promise made to the poor farmers. Nevertheless, the next day in the press, the following speculation was published: "The World Bank, because it is headed by an American, wants to derail the IMF program so as to make Turkey more vulnerable to U.S. pressure and force Turkey to join the United States in the Iraq war." Of course, this was totally ridiculous, but it is a fantastic example of how the debate, instead of focusing on the actual policy, which thankfully was later reinstated, gets hijacked because of the perception of who runs the Bank.

Yet, can you blame people for believing that things work in this conspiratorial way? After all, the big speculation now is on what will happen in a year, when President Bush appoints the next World Bank President. This does not help create international legitimacy for these institutions.

For these reasons, a high priority for the international community needs to be the focus on reforming the legitimacy of these institutions so that their good work and great capacity can be deployed fully. The lack of legitimacy—the perception that these institutions are at the service of only one superpower or group of countries—undermines the work that can be done.

The move toward ownership is very appropriate; however, here again, legitimacy plays a role. If the international community is going to deploy large amounts of resources in support of poor countries—within a poverty reduction strategy paper framework or in support of emerging market economies—big packages may be necessary at times to prevent larger crises. You cannot, however, ask the international community to have these packages or these resources without conditionality. Call it an agreement on good policies if you do not like the word "conditionality." But there will not be a large amount of resources flowing in terms of foreign aid or emerging market support programs without conditionality.

Yet, the only way we can live with this conditionality—well-structured and intelligent as it may be—is if there is greater legitimacy on the part of the international donors. This establishment of legitimacy allows both sides to sit together and agree on packages without the public scrutiny that these packages have been imposed by an illegitimate or foreign organization.

One last example, there was a survey that asked Turkish citizens what they thought of the IMF, World Bank, United Nations, and European Union. The positive ratings for the IMF were a meager 12 percent. The Bank did slightly better with around 18 percent. The United Nations was around 35 percent, despite the fact that at that time the Cyprus issue was a problem and there was the Annan plan, which you would have expected to upset the nationalist side of Turkey. The European Union, which provides almost no money to Turkey and continually criticizes the country for all kinds of things, received a 50 percent approval rating. This is a very vivid example of legitimacy at work.

The European Union, because it is a group of countries that have come together voluntarily and a group that Turkey wants to join, is considered a legitimate supranational framework. Despite criticism, despite lack of financial assistance, despite the grief, 50 percent of the population still had positive views of the European Union. Unfortunately, the Bretton Woods institutions do not have that. Here, despite the degree of autonomy of the organizations and the professional credibility of the staff, legitimacy is still a major problem. This is a problem not only for the staff, it is a problem for the reformers in the countries who want to work with the institutions on reform. Because of the governance problem, the institutions are having difficulties being perceived and accepted as legitimate partners in this process.

Index

A

Adjustment lending
  effectiveness of, 33, 53
  policy reform and, 28–29, 53
Advisory and analytical work (AAA), 65, 121
Afghanistan, transitional support strategies for, 115–116
Ahmed, Masood, 30, 39
Aid Coordination, 119–121
  donor collaboration, 120, 127
  effectiveness of, xxvi, 25
Anderson, Robert J. (Andy), 39
Angola, transitional support strategies for, 115–116
Annual Review of Development Effectiveness (2003) (ARDE), ix, 4, 15
  benefits of, 25, 31, 33–34, 36
  comments on, 25–37
  conclusions of, 5, 15–24, 47, 64–65
  implications of, 35, 68
  World Bank support for policy reform and, 15–24
Argentina, macroeconomic policy in, 197
Australia, assistance to Solomon Islands from, 133–135

B

Bangladesh, poverty-reduction strategy and, 8–9
Belarus, European Bank for Reconstruction and Development and, 62–63
Bosnia-Herzegovina
  coordination of aid in, 120
  economic progress in, 128–129
  post-conflict reconstruction in, 109, 110, 112–114, 116–119, 126, 129–130, 140
Brazil
  as capital exporter to United States, 200
  development strategies for, 79–80, 101–103
  economic and sectoral work in, 51
  effects of devaluation in, 197
  relations between World Bank and, 100–101

Bretton Woods institutions. *See also* International Monetary Fund (IMF); World Bank
    economic reform and, 4–6
    perception of, 201–203
    poverty reduction strategy initiative and, 144, 145
Budget management reform, 61–62
Bulgaria
    economic and sectoral work in, 51–52
    reform commitment in, 54
Burkina Faso, 183, 191
Burundi, transitional support strategies for, 115–116

C

CAEs. *See* Country assistance evaluations (CAEs)
Cambodia
    post-conflict reconstruction in, 113, 118, 139
    technical assistance in, 119
Canuto, Otaviano, 40
Capacity building
    emphasis on, 5, 7–8
    importance of, 51, 158–159
    in post-conflict settings, 118
    training for, 159
Chhibber, Ajay, 105, 201
China, development strategies for, 76–79
Civil service reforms, 50
Collier, Paul, 62
Conditionality
    concerns regarding, 60, 70
    country ownership and, 34
    ex ante, 31
    ex post, 30–31
    function of, 6, 30, 34–36, 64, 69
    policy reform and, 26, 29, 33, 202
    political, 62
    post-conflict resolution and, 137, 138
    private sector project, 61
    transition, 61
Conditionality Revisited conference (World Bank), 35, 36
Conference on Effectiveness of Policies and Reforms
        (Operations Evaluation Development)
    issues raised by, xi–xii
    purpose of, ix–x
Consensus building, xxi–xii
Country assistance evaluations (CAEs)
    for Brazil, 79, 80
    for China, 77, 79
    description of, 45–46, 56, 76
    findings of, ix, 46–49
    lessons from, 49–55
    outcome ratings and, 47, 48

in post-conflict settings, 118
for Tunisia, 81–82
Country Assistance Evaluation Retrospective (CAE retrospective), 45, 68
Country assistance strategy (CAS)
for post-conflict situations, 117–118
timing of, 47
for Tunisia, 97–98
Country Policy and Institutional Assessment (CPIA) indicator
application of, xxiii, 17, 19, 21–23, 27–28, 47, 151
growth outcomes and, 28
as representation of composite policies, 27–28
Country Risk Service Rating (Economist Intelligence Unit), 16
Couto, Pedro, 169, 170, 172–173, 175, 176–177

D
Demobilization and Reintegration Program, 117
Democracies, 10–12, 68–69
Democratic Republic of Congo, transitional support strategies for, 115–116
Denmark, 187
Derviş Kemal, 106
Developing countries
growth in, xvii–xviii
policy reform in, 15–24
Development Support Credit (World Bank), 9
Development Under Adversity: The Palestinian Economy in Transition
(Diwan and Shaban), 121
Donor failings
collusion and coordination failure, 184–185
failure to evaluate, 184–185
failure to exit, 184
fixes for, 188–190
impatience with institution building, 182–184
overview of, 181–182
participation, 186
stingy and unreliable financing, 187–188
underfunding regional public goods, 188

E
Economic and sectoral work (ESW)
capacity building for, 5
dissemination of, 68, 69
funding for, 83
need for ongoing, 67–68
policy reform outcomes and, 23, 24
timeliness of, 51–52
World Bank and, 55, 83–84
Economic growth
link between institutions and, xviii–xx
relationship between economic policies and, 33–34
relationship between economic policy and, xiii, 18–19, 64

El Salvador Peace Accords (1992), 120
Elliott, Victoria, 170, 171, 176
Environmental programs, 102
Eritrea
    post-conflict reconstruction in, 110, 115, 119, 139
    technical assistance in, 119
    transitional support strategies for, 115–116
Ethiopia, poverty reduction strategy initiative and, 148
European Bank for Reconstruction and Development (EBRD)
    function of, 60
    political conditionality and, 62–63
    private sector project conditionality and, 61
European Union (EU), xii, xiv, 202–203

F
Financial Sector Reform Loans, 52

G
Gaza. See West Bank and Gaza
Gender, poverty reduction strategy initiative and, 167
Georgia, World Trade Organization accession in, 62
German Technical Cooperation (GTZ), 164–165

H
Haiti
    coordination of aid in, 121
    post-conflict reconstruction in, 115, 117, 118
Heavily indebted poor countries (HIPC), 146, 150
    HIPC initiative, 150
Herfkens, Eveline, 170, 172, 175
Holst Fund, 120
Husain, Ishrat, 67, 70

I
Income growth, xxviii–xxix
Index of Economic Freedom (Heritage Foundation), 16
Institutional development, xxvii–xxix, 50, 118, 182–184
Inter-American Development Bank, 115, 193
International Bank for Reconstruction and Development (IBRD). *See also World Bank*
    funding, 87–95, 104, 129, 199
International Country Risk Guide (ICRG)
    composite index, 16
    governance rating, xviii
    overall country risk rating, 16
    political risk indicators, xix
International Development Association (IDA)
    Bosnia-Herzegovina and, 129, 130
    China and, 78
    country assistance evaluations and, 47

funding issues and, 199, 200
IBRD contributions, 90
performance-based allocation and, 8, 16
selectivity, 34
International Finance Corporation, 102
International financial institutions (IFIs)
    policy influence of, 33, 34, 175–176
    programmatic budget support and, 61
International Monetary Fund (IMF)
    conditionality and, 60
    macroeconomic policies and, 198
    Nicaragua and, 168
    perception of, 201, 202
    post-conflict countries and, 126, 138
    poverty reduction strategy initiative and, 143, 146, 147
    Poverty Reduction Growth Facility (PRGF), 9, 146, 168
    role of, 36
    stabilization program with, 119–120
    Tunisia and, 97

J
Jordan, economic and sectoral work in, 52

K
Kaberuka, Donald, 138
Kalantzopoulos, Orsalia, 129
Kazakhstan, economic and sectoral work in, 51
Kenya
    implementation failures in, 55
    policy slippage in, 54
Keynes, J. M., 4
Killick, Tony, 30, 38, 40
Klaus, Vaclav, 83
Krueger, Anne O., 3
Kyrgyz Republic, World Trade Organization accession in, 62

L
Latin America (LAC). *See also specific countries*
    as capital exporter to United States, 200
    capital flow cycles in, 67
    pension reform in, 68
Latvia, 161
Lebanon
    civil war in, 109
    post-conflict reconstruction in, 113, 114
Leipziger, Danny, 175
Linn, Johannes F., 100, 103–106
Lithuania, 161
Low-income countries under stress (LICUS), xii, xxv, 70
    aid reliability, 188

M

Macroeconomic policy
   effects of, xv–xvii, 197–198
   World Bank programs and, 67
Mali, 183
Middle-income countries (MICs)
   development challenges facing, 67, 87–88
   development strategies for, 75–85
   explanation of, 75
   lessons from programs for, 104–106
   role of World Bank lending in, 76, 82–85, 87–94
Millennium Development Goals (MDGs), 25, 161–164, 167, 168, 170, 183–184, 189, 190
Moldova, World Trade Organization accession in, 62
Mongolia, private sector development in, 51
Mozambique
   capacity building in, 159
   as post-conflict country, 137
   poverty reduction strategy initiative and, 148, 156–159, 165
   sugar industry in, 164

N

National Board of Revenue, 9–10
The Netherlands, 187
Nicaragua, poverty reduction strategy initiative in, 167–169
Nongovernmental organizations (NGOs)
   partnerships with, 10, 120, 147
   Poverty Reduction Strategies initiative and, 10, 120, 147
Norway, 187

O

O'Brien, F. Steve, 139–140
Operations Evaluation Department (OED)
   Annual Review of Development Effectiveness (ARDE). *See Annual Review of Development Effectiveness*
   Bosnia-Herzegovina and, 129
   country assistance evaluations, 45–56
   establishment of, ix
   function of, 24, 25, 64
   low-income countries under stress and, 70
   middle-income country development strategies and, 75–85
   post-conflict report, 110–112, 114, 115, 117, 120, 137
   Poverty Reduction Strategy Evaluation (PRSP study). *See Poverty Reduction Strategy Evaluation* (OED)
Operations Policy and Country Services (OPCS) Network, 70
Organisation for Economic Cooperation and Development (OECD), 85, 188
Oslo Accord (1993), 112
Ownership
   capacity and, xxviii
   conditionality and, 34
   country assistance evaluations and commitment to, 46, 49–50, 83

encouragement of, xxiii–xxiv, 64
participation and, 184, 189
poverty reduction strategy initiative and, 145–148, 163, 168

P

Pakistan, policy reform and economic growth in, 64
Pension reform, 68
Performance-based allocation, 8
Persuasion, of policy reformers and stakeholders, 30–32
Peru
    Financial Sector Reform Loan in, 52
    policy slippage in, 54
    privatization and civil service reforms in, 50
Policy decision determinants, 33
Policy framework papers (PFPs), 156–159, 161
Policy reforms
    adjustment pending linked to, 28–29
    classification of, xiv–xv
    complementarity of, 50–51
    conditions for, 20–21
    consensus building for, xxi–xxii
    democracy and, 10–12, 68–69
    effectiveness of World Bank support for, xxii–xxiv, 26–41
    for fragile and conflict-ridden states, xxiv–xxvi
    future outlook for, xxvi–xxix
    key policy issues for, xv–xxi
    politics and, 4
    process of, 64–65
    reasons and timing for, xii–xv
Poortman, Christiaan, 129, 140
Post-conflict countries
    conditionality and, 137, 138
    description of, 131–132
    Solomon Islands case study and, 133–135
Post-Conflict Fund (World Bank), 110
Post-conflict reconstruction
    aid coordination and partnerships with donors during, 119–121
    in Bosnia-Herzegovina, 128–130
    early engagement in, 112–114, 137–140
    field presence in, 114–115
    lessons learned from, 111–121, 137–140
    in Rwanda, 125–127
    statistics regarding, 109–110, 122
    World Bank services and products adapted to, 115–119
Post-Conflict Unit (World Bank), 110
Poverty
    in Bangladesh, 8–9
    in Brazil, 79–80
    growth rates and, 19, 20
    in Mozambique, 156, 157, 159
Poverty and social impact assessments (PSIAs), 162

Poverty Reduction Growth Facility (IMF), 9, 146, 168
Poverty Reduction Strategy Evaluation (OED), ix, 5, 143–144, 156, 161, 163, 167, 170
   comments on, 156–170
   findings from, 145–152
   Recommendations, 153–154
Poverty reduction strategy papers (PRSPs)
   Bosnia-Herzegovina and, 128–129
   effectiveness and, 61, 62
   function of, xxiii, 143
   Mozambique and, 156–160
   Nicaraugua and, 167–169
   problems related to, 5, 185
   Tanzania and, 149
Poverty reduction strategy (PRS) initiative
   comments on, 156–170
   country ownership and, 147–148, 163, 168
   design of, 145–146
   donor alignment and, 148–149
   establishment of, 143
   evaluation of, 144, 145
   floor discussion on, 171–177
   joint staff assessment and, 146–147
   long-term framework for, 165–166
   Millennium Development Goals and, 161–165, 167, 168, 170
   poverty impact and growth and, 149–159
   principles of, 144
   recommendations related to, 153–154
Premature lending, 34
Private sector, 61
Private sector development (PSD)
   country assistance evaluations and, 48, 49
   elements of, 51
Privatization
   in Kazakhstan, 51
   in Peru, 50
   problems related to, xx
Project implementation units (PIUs), 183
Project management units (PMUs), 114–115, 119
Public sector management (PSM), 48, 49

Q
Quirós Víquez, Ana, 170, 173–174, 177

R
Rahman, M. Saifur, 68
Ramachandran, S., 104, 105
Regional Assistance Mission to the Solomon Islands (RAMSI), 134, 135
Risk analysis, 53–54

Rural development
    country assistance evaluations and, 48, 49
    poverty reduction strategy initiative and, 162
Rwanda
    coordination of aid in, 121
    genocide in, 109, 112, 125
    post-conflict reconstruction in, 115–117, 125–127

S

Sachs, Jeff, 165
Socialist Federal Republic of Yugoslavia, 113
Solomon Islands, 133–135
Somalia, collapse of government in, 113
South Korea, 183
Sri Lanka, 164
Subnational governments, 91
Sudan, 137, 138
Sweden, 187

T

Tanzania
    financing of projects in, 187, 192
    poverty reduction strategy initiative and, 145, 148, 149
Technical assistance, 52, 119
Technical assistance funds, 62
Transition economies, 50, 121
Thomas, Margaret, 137–139
Tunisia
    development strategies for, 81–85, 97–99
    economic policies in, 96–97
    women in, 96
Turkey, 201, 202
Turkmenistan, 63

U

Uganda, 183
United Kingdom, 187–188
United Nations Development Programme (UNDP), 115, 133, 159
    Human Development Report (UNDP), 9, 183
United Nations (UN)
    partnerships with, 120, 121
    peacekeeping operations of, 110
    perception of, 202
    Rwanda and, 112
U.S. Agency for International Development, 115
Uzbekistan, European Bank for Reconstruction and Development and, 63

V

Vietnam
  economic and sectoral work in, 51
  poverty reduction strategy initiative and, 145

W

Wallich, Christine, 129
Washington Consensus, xi, xxvii
West Bank and Gaza
  coordination of aid in, 120–121
  post-conflict reconstruction in, 112, 114, 116–119
  technical assistance in, 119
World Bank
  Brazil and, 79–80, 100–103
  China and, 76–79
  conditionality and, 60
  cost of doing business with, 84–85
  for economic and sector work, 83–84
  effectiveness of policies and reforms of, 197–203
  as funding source, 82–83
  as learner and conduit, 85
  macroeconomic policy and, 197–198
  middle-income countries and, 76, 82–85, 87–94
    (*See also* Middle-income countries (MICs))
  perception of, 201, 202
  post-conflict reconstruction and, 109–130 (*See also* Post-conflict reconstruction)
  Post-Conflict Unit, 110
  poverty reduction strategy initiative and, 143–145
    (*See also* Poverty reduction strategy (PRS) initiative)
  reform role of, 3–5
  support for policy reforms and, xxii–xxiv, 15–24, 26–41
  Tunisia and, 81–85, 96–99
World Trade Organization (WTO), 62, 193

Z

Zimbabwe
  implementation failures in, 55
  indigenous ownership in, 50